Understanding

Digital
PHOTOGRAPHY

Joseph A. Ippolito

Understanding

Digital
PHOTOGRAPHY

Joseph A. Ippolito

THOMSON
DELMAR LEARNING

Australia Canada Mexico Singapore Spain United Kingdom United States

Understanding Digital Photography
Joseph A. Ippolito

Business Unit Director:
Alar Elken

Executive Editor:
Sandy Clark

Acquisitions Editor:
James Gish

Editorial Assistant:
Jaimie Wetzel

Executive Marketing Manager:
Maura Theriault

Channel Manager:
Fair Huntoon

Marketing Coordinator:
Sarena Douglas

Executive Production Manager:
Mary Ellen Black

Production Manager:
Larry Main

Production Editor:
Tom Stover

Cover and Book Designer:
Liz Kingslien
Cover image: Joseph A. Ippolito

Library of Congress
Cataloging-in-Publication Data

Ippolito, Joseph A.
  Understanding digital photography / Joseph A. Ippolito.
      p. cm.
Includes index.
  ISBN 0-7668-2079-3
  1. Photography--Digital techniques.
I. Title.
  TR267 .I67 2002
  778.3--dc21

                          2002009377

NOTICE TO THE READER

Publisher does not warrant or guarantee any of the products described herein or perform any independent analysis in connection with any of the product information contained herein. Publisher does not assume, and expressly disclaims, any obligation to obtain and include information other than that provided to it by the manufacturer.

The reader is expressly warned to consider and adopt all safety precautions that might be indicated by the activities herein and to avoid all potential hazards. By following the instructions contained herein, the reader willingly assumes all risks in connection with such instructions.

The Publisher makes no representation or warranties of any kind, including but not limited to, the warranties of fitness for particular purpose or merchantability, nor are any such representations implied with respect to the material set forth herein, and the publisher takes no responsibility with respect to such material. The publisher shall not be liable for any special, consequential, or exemplary damages resulting, in whole or part, from the readers' use of, or reliance upon, this material.

TABLE OF CONTENTS

PREFACE

Intended Audience

Understanding Digital Photography is a book that addresses digital photography from a photographer's perspective, written by a photographer for photographers. The field of digital photography is approached in a way that relates these new technologies to their traditional photographic predecessors. In this way, new photographers can make better-informed decisions about the craft of photography, while more experienced photographers have the benefit of relating new technologies to the media and craft they already know.

Approach

The development of digital photography has changed forever the way we look at photographs. The truthfulness of a photographic image is no longer presumed. This is due to the new tools of photography—the digital camera and the digital darkroom—with which we have gained advanced imaging techniques. Historically, mastery of the photographic craft took many years. Now, digital photographic tools have given many more people access to the darkroom magic that was known only by the photographic elite of the past.

While the discipline of photography is changing rapidly, this book addresses those changes regarding the broader field of photographic technologies in relation to these new digital trends.

Many of the books you will find on digital photography take either an engineer's/photo-science approach or a solely conceptual/aesthetic approach. The main problems with this are that on the one hand you need to be an engineer to understand the subject matter, and on the other hand you don't gain any *practical* skills. While both approaches are valid for certain situations, the approach taken here can be more directly applied to your photography. Thus, *Understanding Digital Photography* offers a new, more pragmatic approach to digital photography, which is presented in a well-illustrated style throughout the book.

Beginning with the basics, the first area of this book explores the new digital darkroom environment: the computer. Although it may seem to be a technical start, an understanding of the tools to be used is significant in gaining an appreciation for the possibilities and limitations of working in the digital realm of photographic imaging. From here, the other half of the digital photography equation—digital cameras—is explored. Beyond the purely digital realm, we acknowledge that film does still exist and that many people choose to shoot film. Therefore, two chapters of this book are dedicated to introducing traditional images into the digital darkroom, and then managing these images. Of course, we also deal with introductory through advanced topics related to image editing in the digital darkroom, as well. Further, in order to allow you to gain mastery of the digital medium, a chapter has been dedicated to color management and workflow. To address the business aspects of digital photography, we have included a chapter on using service bureaus to outsource your digital production work, and finally a chapter on copyright and intellectual property rights to assist you in protecting your creative works.

Features

Overall, this book features a range of related subject matter that will aid you in gaining a fuller, more practical understanding of digital photography. Some of the key features of this book are:

- Offers chapter objectives and main points for each area of discussion
- Presents review questions and thoughts for further discussion with each chapter
- Provides a thorough review of digital darkroom technologies
- Addresses both Mac and Windows cross-platform issues
- Surveys basic image editing techniques and offers a focused view of advanced image-editing techniques
- Explores useful production techniques such as batch processing and creating customized tools
- Illustrates the process of designing a personalized color management system
- Offers a survey of output devices and media ranging from film to inkjet prints, through dye sublimation prints and output for offset printing devices
- Describes intellectual property rights in a way that relates to the photographer's needs and illustrates how to use technologies to protect your images
- Provides an overall discussion that can either be used in the sequence of chapters presented, or as individual modules for topical studies

About the Author

During the more than sixteen years that I have been teaching photography, I have had the good fortune to deal with all types of learners. I have literally taught rocket scientists and surfers in the same class when teaching at the community college level. What I have found is that the binding experience we all have is a passion to create photographic images. This is true of creating traditional and digital photographs. The main difference is, of course, that we need to prepare ourselves in more areas to be competent visual communicators when we include all of these new digital technologies into our studies of photography. In this respect, I have pursued numerous degrees in photography and photographic education. Beginning with an industrial photographic foundation at the associates' level, I went on to study commercial and advertising photography at Rochester Institute of Technology. While working in the graphic design industry, I was able to expand my photographic abilities, as well as my graphic design sensibilities. From there, I went on to work in the aerospace industry as an industrial photographer and a coordinator of interactive digital multimedia. Years later, as I was teaching at the university level, I decided to further my education, to explore new ways of approaching digital media. In addition to attaining a Master of Fine Arts degree to explore philosophical, conceptual, and aesthetic issues, I also attained Master of Science and Ph.D. degrees to explore the more academic issues surrounding these new technological media.

Having had the opportunity to be both an artist/photographer and an academic, I have been fortunate to gain a perspective that is quite different from many others, allowing me to walk on both sides of the street, so to speak. I have been lucky enough to be invited to give numerous international lectures regarding digital photography in places such as Beijing, China; Sydney, Australia; and London, England. I have also enjoyed having my creative and academic works published and distributed internationally. These experiences have led to a way of looking at digital photography that is steeped in tradition, and is informed from a variety of perspectives from the aesthetic to the technical.

Understanding Digital Photography is *your* place to begin your adventures in digital photography. I hope you will find this book to be a useful tool in your pursuit of photography.

Acknowledgements

I would like to thank my wife, Judith Muñoz Ippolito, for her support, patience, and sacrifice throughout my development of this book. I would also like to thank Tom Schin, Jim Gish, Jennifer Thompson, and Tom Stover for their support and efforts to help me make this book become a reality.

In addition, I would like to thank the following reviewers for their insightful comments and suggestions throughout the development of this book:

Robert Crites, Art Institute of Philadelphia, Philadelphia, PA
Denis Defibaugh, Rochester Institute of Technology, Rochester, NY
Christopher James, Art Institute of Boston, Boston, MA
Glenn Rand, Art Academy of Cincinnati, Cincinnati, OH

CHAPTER 1

Computers: Understanding the Digital Darkroom

Objectives:

This chapter will introduce you to the digital darkroom environment: the computer. From a technical perspective, the computer is described in a way that will enable you to understand the inner workings of this new digital darkroom environment. Upon completion of this chapter, you should have a better understanding of:

- How to identify key components that make the digital darkroom/computer function for your own digital darkroom needs
- How to determine your hardware and software needs to equip your digital darkroom
- How to make decisions about purchasing components and/or full digital darkroom systems

Introduction: The Digital Darkroom and the Role of the Digital Image

For anyone who has been involved with photography for a while, it may seem a bit odd to begin a book about photography with a chapter about computers. This, however, is a sign of the times. The world of photography has changed forever, and the sole technology responsible for this paradigmatic shift is that of the microchip.

For traditional photographers, the intrusion, if you will, of microtechnologies into the coveted realm of image-making has been both a blessing and a burden. Some believe that these new technologies have destroyed the integrity of the photographic image. Yet for others, computer technologies have created a renaissance of possibilities for the photographer—opening up opportunities to create some images that were literally impossible to achieve with traditional photographic materials and technologies.

As we head into this discussion, try to keep an open mind to the possibilities that these new technologies can offer to you as an image-maker. Further, regardless of the direction of the discussions in this book, remember that as new imaging media become more widespread and prevalent in our society, traditional media do not necessarily become obsolete. Rather, traditional media, such as historical photographic processes and silver-halide/film-based imaging take on new roles for the photographic image-maker.

Although in some ways the digital image is dramatically different, in the end the digital photographic image is simply a photograph recorded or stored on digital media instead of film. While this is an oversimplification, the details of significant ways that digital and traditional images are similar and differ are elaborated upon throughout this text. Most significantly, the main philosophical difference between the digital and traditional image lies in a technical distinction between the accessibility to skilled and unskilled manipulation techniques presented to the photographer in the traditional and digital darkrooms, respectively.

Why do I need a computer to make photographs?

Many people have asked this question. The answer is clear: you don't! However, if you want to work with digital images, in any sort of serious fashion, the answer is quite different. Quite simply, the computer has become the darkroom tool of choice for many photographers. This does not devalue traditional photographic media, however, because these media have a place as well. The consideration here is that this new photographic tool—the computer—is simply a new way of processing photographic images. Consider that even the most die-hard photographers don't generally create all of their images as calotypes or daguerreotypes—right? This being the case, these image-makers have accepted the fact that scientific technologies have afforded a

continuing stream of technological innovations that have made the photographer's job easier. Whether in the form of higher quality optics, better film emulsions, more advanced chemical formulations, or even the use of pre-sensitized paper, technology has always been closely allied with the creation of photographic images.

Therefore, one should consider the addition of computing technologies into photographic imaging in the same way as any other new photographic tool; just as a new lens, camera, enlarger, film, or developer had traditionally enhanced their tools, digital technologies are simply new photographic tools. Of course, these new "shooting" or "darkroom" tools have not only altered the way we make images, they have altered the way we think about photography and photographs more than any other innovation in the history of photography.

For these reasons and many others, consider the computer as just another tool, and software as just another technique that the photographer needs to learn to become an effective visual communicator.

NOTE that this chapter goes into a detailed description of computer hardware. It is believed that by presenting this information early on in our discussion, we will have a common understanding of the main image-processing tool you will be using: the computer. If, however, the discussion delves into more detail than you are interested in approaching up front, don't be dismayed. Simply go on to the more *photographically* oriented chapters. You can always return to this chapter later, as needed.

What is a computer platform, and what does this mean to the photographer?

In basic terms, a computer platform is the combination of a specific type of computer hardware (physical computing devices) with a specific type of general operating software (the set of instructions that determine what the computer will calculate in order to let a person (user) interface with the machine). In the computer industry, there are many different computer platforms available. For home and small business users, however, there are only a few dominant choices. A brief list of the most common computer platform areas is presented here (see sidebar).

Common Desktop Computing Platforms

IBM PC-compatible *hardware* with a version of Microsoft's **Windows** operating system (*software*)

Apple Macintosh *hardware* with a version of Apple's **MAC OS** operating system (*software*)

IBM PC-compatible hardware with a version of the UNIX/**LINUX** operating system (software). **Note:** Linux software runs on the Apple Macintosh as well, but is less prevalent in the marketplace.

Silicon Graphics (SGI) is a high-end graphics-processing computer. Generally used by high-volume service bureaus for advanced imaging applications and graphics work, such as animation.

For the photographer, this initial choice of hardware and software combination—or computer platform—will establish the environment for processing images—their new digital "dry" darkroom.

Hardware and Software Considerations

You will find that as you begin to discuss how to build your computer system, or *digital darkroom* as we like to refer to it, many will offer passionate arguments on why you should definitely NOT buy a Mac or NOT buy a Windows machine. It seems that photographers have always loved their technological gadgetry—to the exclusion of all other options. For example, ask someone who has been shooting photographs with a Nikon 35mm camera system for years if you should buy a Canon system. Almost certainly you will hear every reason why Nikon is superior to Canon—and no reason why Canon has features to offer that may be better suited to your needs than those offered by Nikon. Why? Photographers have always been a brand-loyal breed. Whether, for example, it is the debate over Kodak or Ilford photographic paper, or why Hunt or

Russell photographic chemistry is better, photographers tend to love what they know and trust, based upon their own experiences.

So, let's get back to our discussion of computer considerations. What this means for the digital photographer is that you should try to listen to the latest discussions concerning hardware and software choices, but be discriminating as to which information you heed. Basically, the Apple Macintosh OS and the various Microsoft Windows platforms offer nearly equal access to digital imaging, in terms of software and hardware support. It is an individualistic choice, with one caveat however. Note that for many in the art, design, and photographic imaging communities, the Apple Macintosh has traditionally been the computer platform of choice. However, in business and industry, Windows is the main computing platform. These days, most significant imaging software is cross-platform, or has a cross-platform counterpart. That is, software such as Adobe Photoshop™ is available for both the Mac and Windows platforms. Thus, you should also consider your need to be able to be compatible with your peers, service bureaus, and business partners. This may help you to determine which platform is more appropriate for your needs.

Computers and Photography: How to make them work together

To restate a point already discussed, it is suggested that the computer simply be considered as just another device to add to the photographer's tools. Think of it as using a new film developer or printing process. Having said that, there are essentially two main categories of technology you will need to become familiar with. First, there is the hardware that makes up the computer system—the physically tangible devices. Second, there is the software that instructs the computer on how and what to compute. Although there are many subtle issues to consider when determining hardware and software choices, these two broad categories encompass all of the devices and information processing options you will need to consider.

What Hardware is needed?

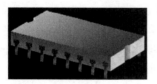

The first thing that is needed is a base computer. This will involve deciding which type of computer system and CPU (central processing unit) to purchase.

Here there are a number of considerations, such as:

- Is a portable or stationary computer needed?
- What speed is the microprocessor (CPU)?
- How much RAM does the computer have installed, and can it be upgraded?
- How much storage space is available, or can be added?
- What types of DVD, CD, or other reading/writing devices are included/available?
- What types of communications devices are included or available, so that the computer can be connected (or networked) with other computers?
- What kind of graphics display system is incorporated?
- What types of removable storage are available: Zip, floppy, ORB, Jaz, or other storage devices?
- What type of expansion is available: serial ports, parallel ports, USB and FireWire ports, internal expansions slots, 3.5" and 5.25" internal expansion bays, etc.?
- What is the display size, and how accurately can it be calibrated?

Many, if not all, of these requirements will change over time. Our discussion specifically addresses the main considerations for photographers.

The speed of the processor is significant because photographic images represent some of the largest files a computer will need to process. Next, the amount of RAM (random access memory) needs to be considered because this is where the large image files will be stored during processing; the larger your image files, the more RAM you need. This leads us to storage. If image files are large, a great deal of storage space will be required—enough to accommodate all of the images to be stored, as well as leaving a reasonable amount of free space.

What Software is needed?

Depending upon your intentions, there is a variety of software available for the digital photographer. The premier software choice has consistently been Adobe Photoshop since its inception.

This is a professional-level software package that handles almost all of the needs of a photographer, graphic artist, or fine artist. It is the de facto standard in the photographic and graphic arts industries. There are many other choices available, however.

In addition to the high-end image editing software packages, consumer-level software is available to address a number of imaging tasks.

If, for example, your intentions are to create digital photographs so you can e-mail them to your family members, there are many less sophisticated software packages that are more than adequate. For less traditional needs, software such as the iPIX and MGI Photovista allow photographers to "stitch" together multiple photographs to create panoramic views. MGI PhotoSuite also allows you to create montages from libraries of images. So as you can see, many choices are available to the photographer, to accomplish countless imaging goals. Yet, it is not the intention here to suggest that these are the only options for imaging software. Rather, the above examples are used purely for illustrative purposes. In the Appendix section of this book, many more examples of imaging software are presented.

In order to decide which software is necessary, your answers to the following questions can serve as a guide for choosing the software that will be required for your digital darkroom.

- How much can I afford to spend on software for this project, and future projects as well? This is significant because imaging software ranges in cost from $20 USD to over $1,000 USD, for the basic image processing application.
- How and where will I use these images? If you are only generating low-resolution images for the Web or screen display, your needs will be radically different than if you are handling 40"x 60" images to be reproduced as high-resolution commercially printed posters.
- What do I want to do to these images? If you only want to crop an image, and adjust brightness and contrast, your needs will be quite different than if you intend to create high-resolution "seamless" photographic montages or manipulations.

The main thing to remember is that the software, which is utilized for a given image-processing task, needs to be matched to the end goals of the photographer's project. Just as you would choose to shoot black-and-white film for some projects, and color for others, the software to be utilized in a project in many ways determines the quality and limitations of the end product: the image.

What Peripherals are Needed?

Here, you need to determine what you want to do with your digital darkroom in order to decide what add-ons or peripherals are needed. Basically, peripherals are devices that extend the capabilities of the computer. When determining what is needed to develop your digital darkroom, choices of peripheral types become significant. For example, if you want to convert traditional photographic prints into digital images, a flatbed scanner will be needed. However, if you have negatives and slides that you want to use in your digital darkroom, a film scanner will be needed.

Examples of Computer Peripherals

Flatbed Scanner

Expansion Card

Networking Device

There are numerous types of peripheral devices available to extend the capabilities of the base computer. Some of these are:

- DVD and CD players and recorders (burners)
- Video capture devices—to input standard video (NTSC/PAL), digital video, and still video signals for editing and other computer-based uses
- Scan converters—to output computer generated monitor signals to standard video devices (NTSC/PAL)
- Networking adapters
Inkjet printers, plotters
- Laser printers—color and black-and-white
- Photographic printers such as thermal dye sublimation
- Scanners such as; drum, flatbed, film, and handheld
- Film recorders—to change digital images back into film-based images

This is a short list of some of the peripheral devices available to enhance your digital darkroom. As you can see, there are near-limitless choices of devices to enable your computer to perform a wide variety of tasks. Generally, photographers will purchase peripherals on a need-to-use basis. Given the relatively short compatible lifespan of many computer-related products, you should consider purchasing only those technologies that are needed presently. More peripherals can always be added at a later time. Remember, these technologies become outdated much faster than traditional cameras or enlargers.

Sample Photographic Workflows

Traditional Workflow:

1. Photographer chooses film, and records the image.
2. Film is then chemically processed to reveal images on the negative.
3. The negative is projected onto light-sensitive paper.
4. The photographic paper is processed, and then washed and dried.

   Products: 1) a film negative 2) a photographic print

Digital Workflow:

1. Photographer chooses digital media, and records the image.
2. Digital image data is transferred into the computer.
3. From a software application, the image is printed onto various media through a computer printer or other peripheral.

   Products: 1) a digital image data file 2) a photographic print

Hybrid Workflow:

1. Photographer chooses film, and records the image.
2. Film is then chemically processed to reveal images on the negative/slide.
3. The negative/slide is scanned and stored on digital media.
4. From a software application, the image is printed onto various media through a computer printer or other peripheral.

   Products: 1) a film negative 2) a digital image data file stored on digital media such as a CD or DVD 3) a photographic print

Film or Digital Media:
How image needs affect computer choices

As with traditional photography, digital photography is a scientific process whereby the resultant image is derived from a series of cumulative choices. Therefore, the process of determining whether to create the first generation of an image—the film-based or digitally-based image—has remained relatively unchanged, from that which photographers have been utilizing for many years. What has changed is the impact on the rest of the workflow.

Determine Final Output Needs First

Just as with the choice of software, this is another case of looking ahead to the end of the project in order to determine what will be needed to begin. This working methodology is no different than what photographers have been familiar with traditionally. For example, if one is to photograph a building and the image is intended to be as "true" to the architectural form as possible, you would probably not use a 35mm camera to create the image. Rather, a large-format camera with full perspective control might be a more appropriate choice.

When presented with the choice of whether to utilize film or digital media, the end goal of the project must first be considered. That is, will the image be used for screen-resolution image display only, offset lithographic reproduction, or true photographic output? Next, and quite important, how big does the final image need to be in terms of its width and height? Only after these types of questions are answered can the initial choice of recording media (film or digital) be made.

Other considerations need to be addressed as well. The following list illustrates some of these concerns.

- Is time a factor? Does the image need to be utilized immediately, such as with news photography?
- Is the final form of the image to be digital or print based? Either way, how much image information is needed during the recording of the image?
- What range of visual information needs to be recorded? Realize that digital cameras capture a different gamut (tonal range) than film.

So, you might ask how does all of this affect the choices that need to be made in terms of computing hardware and software? Well, remembering that with digital imaging the ends determine the means, you need to know how much image information you will need in the end, in order to determine your computing needs. For example, if your only needs are to create images for Web pages, the images will generally be quite small. Therefore, a slower computer can be utilized with less RAM, a smaller hard drive, etc. However if your needs focus on creating images for print media or true photographic reproduction, your computing needs will be greater. Here, a faster processor, more RAM, and a larger hard drive will be needed—in relative terms.

How much computer is really needed?

Considering the discussion thus far, how much computer you need is really quite dependent upon your particular imaging needs. Just remember, photographic images represent some of the largest, and most complex, objects for a computer to process. Therefore in general, in order to use a computer for digital imaging, a higher-level (more advanced) computer will be required than the general consumer-level machine.

How Much Computer is Needed for the Digital Darkroom

Based on comparisons to general mainstream computing technologies, the following may help in determining what level of technological investment is required at a given time.

The CPU: Generally, the fastest CPU (central processing unit) available is needed for image processing; however, it is usually advisable to buy a CPU that is one or two models slower than the "latest" technology. The reason for this is that the price differential between the technology that has just become available and the technology that has just moved down a notch is usually quite dramatic. Remember, the latest CPU today is old technology in a couple months.

RAM: I don't think it is possible to have too much RAM (random-access memory) for photographic imaging. Your bank account may disagree, however. Therefore, the minimum amount of RAM required at a given time is usually two to three times the average of that which is supplied with most mainstream computers.

Storage: As with RAM, it is difficult to have too much storage. Just remember, the more storage you have, the more information you need to back up. The minimum amount of storage required at a given time is usually two to three times that supplied with most mainstream computers.

Up to here, you may have noticed that the discussion has been a bit general in terms of actually listing particular items of hardware and software. There is a reason for this. Because the computing and imaging industries are technologically advancing at such an accelerated rate, any list of specific CPU models, software, or peripherals might soon be out of date. What won't be out of date is a logical and methodical approach to determining your own needs at any given time.

Building Your Own Digital Darkroom

At this point, you can see that there are many choices for the photographer, both in terms of hardware and software. The discussion that follows will add clarity to some of these choices, in terms of creating your own computer system for digital image processing. First, however, note that the discussion is intended to explain the components that make up a computer system; it is not intended as an instruction guide for building a computer system. Because technology changes so rapidly, all of the information presented here should be verified before you attempt to take on the task of building a computer system from scratch. Finally, there are many well-engineered, preassembled solutions available for the digital photographer. It is *not* suggested that you build a system yourself. Rather, this discussion will aid you in understanding some of the complexities of a computer system's architecture. While this discussion will focus on the IBM-style PC computer architecture, Macintosh systems are similar, regarding this discussion of system components. Again, this discussion is only intended to examine the components that make up the internal workings of your digital darkroom.

To Build Your System from Components, or to Acquire a Preassembled System

The first consideration here is whether to build a computer system from components, or to buy a system that has been preassembled and preconfigured. What this means is, are you comfortable enough to take on the task of buying components such as a CPU, mainboard, video card, network card, RAM, hard drive, floppy/Zip/super/Jaz/ORB drive, CD/DVD drive/burner, sound card, etc.? Then, will you feel comfortable changing jumper settings on the mainboard (and other cards), cabling your EIDE, ATA, SCSI, FireWire, and USB devices—both internal and external? Also, do you feel comfortable changing system BIOS settings, and formatting and partitioning your hard drive(s)—and installing your operating system(s)? If the answer is no, then consider this discussion as an academic dialogue that will aid you in understanding more about your new digital darkroom tools. Additionally, if the answer to any of the above questions is no, it is recommended that you buy a system that has been preengineered and preassembled by a reputable computer manufacturer like Apple computers, IBM, Dell, or Gateway, to name a few.

Selecting the Right System or Components

The Case and Chassis

There are two basic varieties of structural frames, or boxes, that can serve as the basic enclosure for a computer system: a desktop case and a tower case—although other types are available as well. The illustration here shows a Macintosh case, even though this does not fit with the idea of assembling your own computer. As you can see, even preassembled computers such as the Macintosh allow for expansion and modification by the user.

When choosing a case, there are several considerations. First, what size mainboard is the case designed to accommodate? For example, mainboards have different form factors; that is, they range in size designations from micro AT, Baby AT, AT, LPX, NLX, ATX Mini-ATX, and Micro-ATX to others.

Therefore, you need to know which mainboard is to be utilized to determine the form factor of the case. Second, the type of power supply that is supplied with the case, or that the case will accommodate, needs to be considered in your design. This consideration is in regard to both the physical size of the power supply (will it fit in the case you want to use?) and the electrical specifications (i.e. 120/240 volts, 200 watts or 300 watts, 6 amps or 4 amps, 50 hz or 60 hz), and how many power leads are available, with what type connectors, etc. When selecting a case, consider which internal devices you will want to have included in the computer system that will become your digital darkroom. This will aid you in determining what size case and chassis are appropriate.

Once you have determined which case you want, you will need to acquire a mainboard.

Mainboard/Motherboard

The mainboard, also referred to as the motherboard, is the primary circuit board of a computer.

It usually contains, or allows the addition of, the BIOS, CPU, memory (RAM and cache), interfaces, and controllers, as well as expansion slots and ports. The collective gathering of the chips that are housed on the motherboard is referred to as the computer's **chipset.**

As discussed, the type of mainboard to be utilized will limit the selection of the main chassis or case.

Especially when choosing a mainboard for an image processing-type of computer system, there are several important factors to consider.

■What type of RAM expansion is available?
■What is the fastest processor supported?
■What type of secondary cache (also referred

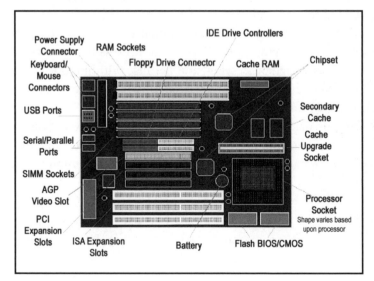

to as external or Level 2 cache) is on board, and can cache expansion be accommodated?

■ What type of BIOS is on board, and is it upgradeable—software (Flash) or hardware?

■ What ports and controllers are on board?

■ How many and what type of expansion slots are available?

■ What type of drive controllers are on board, and what standards do they support? (i.e. EIDE, Ultra DMA, SCSI, floppy drive, etc.)

Finally, one needs to consider the chipset that a particular mainboard utilizes. This is because the chipset controls the transfer of data between the mainboard's bus, the CPU and the cache, and RAM areas of memory.

CPU:

Commonly referred to as the processor, the CPU is the main computation center of the computer.

As an analogy, it is the brains of the computer. The CPU is the most significant component of the computer system. On desktop and workstation-type computers, the CPU is housed in a single chip called a microprocessor. The microprocessor is the main component of the computer system, and as such, it will do most of the image processing. Therefore, the faster the computer's processor, the quicker the image-processing operations will be performed.

RAM:

RAM, or random-access memory, is the main area of a computer's memory. This type of computer memory is enabled to read and write data.

When designing a computer system for digital image processing, it is virtually impossible to have too much RAM since RAM is the area where information is being stored during image processing, and because within the RAM all read and write operations are conducted as electronic signals—without moving parts, as with a hard drive. Additionally, for more rapid image handling, RAM is the most ideal area to store large image file data during processing. Essentially, RAM acts as an intermediary storage area between the computer's hard drive (or other storage media) and the CPU. Therefore, the more data housed in RAM, the faster the computer will process your image data.

Bus:

The computer's bus is a collection of wires and circuits over which data is moved between various parts of the computer. When one refers to the width of the bus, they are referring to how much data can be moved or transmitted at a given time. For example, a 32-bit bus can transmit 32 bits of data, whereas a 64-bit bus can transmit 64 bits of data. Furthermore, the speed at which this data is transferred is referred to as the clock speed of the data bus, and is measured in units such as megahertz or gigahertz. For digital imaging, the faster the bus speed, the quicker image information can be transferred. Hence, the more rapidly imaging applications can access and process digital images.

EIDE Bus:

The Enhanced IDE (Integrated Drive Electronics) mass storage device interface standard allows the mainboard and its components to communicate, and transfer data, to varied mass storage devices such as hard drives and CDs/DVDs. EIDE is sometimes described as Fast IDE, Fast ATA or ATA-2—essentially the same standard. Additionally, Ultra ATA also described as ATA-3 is yet another mode of the IDE standard, which transfers data at much higher rates than other EIDE modes. With respect to digital imaging, and especially when considering using software such as Adobe Photoshop which uses hard drives as scratch disks, the faster the mass storage device interface bus, the faster your imaging software can run. Additionally, with large images, the type of bus that is incorporated into the basic computer system will dramatically affect the amount of time required for opening and saving image files. To achieve even faster data transfer rates—and to further optimize their photographic workflow—many photographers choose to design their digital darkroom's computer system with a SCSI bus to communicate with their storage devices.

SCSI Bus:

The Small Computer System Interface is a mass storage device interface standard that allows the mainboard and its components to communicate, and transfer data, to varied mass storage devices—similar to the EIDE bus, although generally quicker. A parallel interface standard, the SCSI (pronounced "scuzzy") bus interfaces provide very fast data transmission rates. Note that even though SCSI is an ANSI standard, SCSI devices may not be compatible with each other. When choosing a SCSI bus for your digital darkroom, make sure the devices you plan to use support the same SCSI standard (see sidebar).

SCSI Standards and Transfer Rates

- **SCSI-1:** 8-bit bus—data transfer rates of 4 Mbps*
- **SCSI-2:** Same as SCSI-1—uses a 50-pin connector instead of a 25-pin connector. This is the basic SCSI device standard.
- **Wide SCSI:** 168 cable to 68 pins—supports 16-bit data transfers
- **Fast SCSI:** 8-bit bus—doubles the clock rate—data transfer rates of 10 Mbps
- **Fast Wide SCSI:** 16-bit bus—data transfer rates of 20 Mbps.
- **Ultra SCSI:** 8-bit bus—data transfer rates of 20 Mbps.
- **SCSI-3:** 16-bit bus—data transfer rates of 40 Mbps. This is also known as Ultra Wide SCSI.
- **Ultra2 Wide SCSI:** 16-bit and 32-bit bus—data transfer rates of 80 Mbps.
- **Ultra 160:** 32-bit and 64-bit bus—data transfer rates of 160 Mbps.

Mbps: Million bits per second

USB / IEEE 1394 Bus:

The Universal Serial Bus, is an external bus standard that allows up to 127 external peripheral devices to be connected to a computer, at a data transfer rate of 12 Mbps for USB 1 devices and 480 Mbps for USB 2, about 40 times as fast as its predecessor. This type of bus allows for hot-swapping devices. This means that devices such as digital cameras, scanners, printers, and such can be plugged in and unplugged without shutting the computer off or restarting.

FireWire as it is named by Apple Computer, otherwise known as IEEE 1394, is an external bus standard that allows for data transfer rates of 400 Mbps. IEEE 1394 allows up to 63 external peripheral devices to be connected to a computer. This type of bus also allows for hot-swapping devices. As with USB 1 and USB 2 bus devices, IEEE 1394 allows devices such as digital cameras, scanners, printers, and such to be plugged in and unplugged without shutting the computer off.

Storage Devices

The following devices are used in conjunction with your computer system to store data, such as digital image files, offline—that is, on media other than the computer's internal hard drive. You need to determine whether these technologies will be included as internal devices—meaning, built into the computer's chassis/case—before assembly begins as many of these devices are available in external IEEE 1394 or USB configurations, in addition to internal models.

Floppy Drive:

A floppy disk drive is an internal or external drive that allows removable media to be used for data transfer and storage. The floppy disk only holds a maximum of 1.44MB of data, and this type of drive has been phased out completely on newer Macintosh computers.

Zip Drive / SuperDisk:

Both Zip disk and SuperDisk drives can be either internal or external devices, which allow removable media to be read from and written to, for data storage and transfer.

The Zip disk has either a 100MB or 250MB storage capacity. While the SuperDisk has a storage capacity of 120MB, it also has the unique feature of being backward compatible, that is, it will also allow you to read and write to conventional 3.5-inch 1.44MB floppy disks as well. The main disadvantages of these storage technologies are that their read/write access speeds are very slow, when compared to hard drives or Jaz or ORB-type technologies. The main advantage they offer, however, is that most photographer's existing digital darkroom systems utilize these technologies.

Jaz Drive / ORB:

Similar to Zip and SuperDisks, both Jaz and ORB disk drives can be either internal or external drives, which allows removable media to be read and written. The Jaz disk has a 1GB or 2GB storage capacity, whereas the ORB disk has a storage capacity of 2.2GB. Both of these technologies have fast access rates for data transfer, and can be used as removable hard drives. The primary difference between these technologies is the cost of the removable media; 1GB Jaz cartridges cost around $100 USD, and 2GB Jaz cartridges around $125 USD, whereas 2.2GB ORB cartridges cost around $25 USD.

Hard Drive:

The hard disk drive is the main storage device for your computer system.

This is where data such as the computer's operating system, software applications such as Photoshop, and digital images and other data files are stored. Generally, hard disks can store a great deal of data for rapid read and write access. When choosing a hard drive, several factors should be considered (see sidebar).

Considerations for Hard Drive Selection

- What is the capacity of the hard drive, meaning, how much data can be stored?
- What type of interface is required for the device:SCSI, EIDE, IEEE 1394, USB?
- At what speed (rotations per minute) does the drive spin? Higher rpm's mean quicker access.
- What is the drive's formfactor—will it fit in a 5.25-inch, 3.5-inch, or 2.5-inch bay?

CD-ROM / CD-R, CD-RW and DVD-ROM / DVD-R, DVD-RW:

These devices allow you to accomplish many tasks, from playing audio CDs (Compact Discs) and DVDs (Digital Video Discs) to archiving data on CD or DVD discs. The type of disc technology you choose to incorporate into your base computer system will determine the format used for sharing large data files ranging from music to photographs to movies.

The basic CD-ROM (Compact Disc-Read Only Memory) drive allows a computer to play (read) audio and data compact discs. Two variations of this technology are the CD-R (CD-Recordable) and the CD-RW (CD-ReWritable) disk drives. These two devices allow writing to CDs as well as reading from them.

The CD-R disk drive enables the user to create or "master" a CD-ROM or audio CD. For digital photography, it is important to choose a CD-R drive that has multisession recording capabilities. This will enable you to keep adding photographs (or other data) to a CD-ROM over time. CD-R media can only be written to one time for any given location on the CD media.

The CD-RW drive allows for the writing, rewriting, and erasing of information to a special type of CD media known as a CD-RW. CD-RW media can be written to multiple times, and used just as one would use a floppy disk or a hard drive. The only drawback to this type of rewritable storage medium is the read-write time is quite slow, as compared to hard, Jaz, and ORB drives.

Emerging DVD Formats

- **DVD-RAM drive**—supports 2.6GB per disc side (uses a rewritable (erasable) disc)
- **DVD-RW drive**—supports 3 GB per side (uses a rewritable (erasable) disc)
- **DVD-ROM drive**—a read-only high-capacity data storage device (uses a prerecorded data disc)
- **DVD-Audio drive**—an audio-only storage device, similar to a CD audio drive (uses a prerecorded data disc)
- **DVD-Video drive**—a high-capacity data storage device, designed for viewing of full-length motion pictures (uses a prerecorded data disc)
- **DVD-R drive**—a write-once read-mostly storage device, similar to a CD-R (uses a rewritable (erasable) disc)

Standards

- **DVD-5**—4.7GB single-sided single-layered disc
- **DVD-9**—8.5GB single-sided double-layered disc
- **DVD-10**—9.4GB dual-sided single-layered disc
- **DVD-18**—17GB dual-sided dual-layered disc

The DVD (Digital Versatile Disc or Digital Video Disc) can store at least 4.7GB of data, and a maximum of 17GB of data in its various forms.

These drives are usually backward compatible, which means that they can also play CD-ROMs, video CDs, CD-I discs, and CD-R discs. When choosing a DVD device for your digital darkroom, be sure it supports a standard that will suit your needs. The DVD disc (media) is the same size as a standard 1.2mm thick, 120mm diameter CD.

As for writable DVDs, there are currently several formats. Although DVDs are widely used, no one standard has been officially adopted. Currently several DVD standards exist (see sidebar), but DVD-R seems to be the emerging standard.

Whether we are discussing CD or DVD technologies, there are two important factors to consider. First, *access speed* refers to how fast information can be transferred to or from a CD or DVD reader/recorder. Second, *write speed* refers to how fast a given recorder can write data to a CD or DVD disc. Both of these factors need to be considered when choosing an appropriate device for archiving data. The specific speeds are usually expressed as 72x/100x/64x,where the first number is the read speed of the device, the second number is the write speed to CD-R or DVD-R media, and the third number refers to the write speed to rewritable media such as CD-RW or DVD-RW. These numbers change rapidly with the development of new technologies, so the rule of thumb here is to purchase something that will read/write to and from popularly available media.

Video Card

The video card is a plug-in expansion card that enables the display capabilities of the computer. Most standard video cards plug into the AGP slot on the computer's mainboard. A port on the back of the card, which sticks out of the back of the case, is used to connect the monitor cable to the mainboard. The majority of modern video cards include memory, so as to not use the computer's RAM. Additionally, most video cards currently include their own math (graphics) coprocessor, known as a *graphics accelerator.*

Minimum Video RAM Requirements

Monitor Resolution	256 colors (8-bit)	65,000 colors (16-bit)	16.7 million colors (24-bit)
640 x 480	512K	1 MB	1 MB
800 x 600	512K	1 MB	2 MB
1,024 x 768	1 MB	2 MB	4 MB
1,152 x 1,024	2 MB	2 MB	4 MB
1,20 x 1,024	2 MB	4 MB	4 MB
1,600 x 1,200	2 MB	4 MB	6 MB

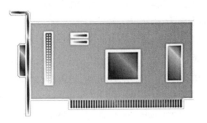

Video cards are also referred to as videoadapters, displayboards, videoboards, graphics cards, and graphics adapters. Note that some mainboards have an integrated onboard graphics adapter. This type of adapter shares the computer's RAM for video display tasks. If a computer has plenty of RAM, and the integrated video chip supports the color bit-depth and required refresh rate, this type of adapter can be utilized. For most serious graphic work, however, a dedicated video card with its own graphics processor and memory are usually required.

Audio Card

The audio card is a plug-in expansion card that enables the computer to play sounds in programs, and from media such as audio CDs. Most standard audio cards plug into a PCI (Peripheral Component Interconnect) slot on the computer's mainboard. A port on the back of the card, which is accessible from the back of the computer case, is used to connect the external devices such as a microphone or speakers to the mainboard. Most sound cards are Sound Blaster-compatible. These cards can process commands written for the Sound Blaster™ card, the de facto standard for Windows-based sound.

Analog to Digital Audio Conversion Methods

There are two fundamental methods to convert digital information into analog audio:

- **FM Synthesis** imitates various musical instruments based on built-in formulas.
- **Wavetable Synthesis** depends on recordings of real instruments to construct audio, and produces a higher-fidelity audio file.

Modem

A modem (modulator-demodulator) is a device that allows a computer to transmit data over telephone lines. The modem converts the data between analog (audio phone signals) and digital (computer) data. As technology advanced the modem has given way to technologies such as DSL (digital subscriber lines), cable modem, and other higher bandwidth communications devices.

High-Speed Network (Terminal) Adapter

As communications bandwidth requirements increase, so will the need for faster communications devices. High-speed terminal adapters allow a computer to connect to a network, such as the Internet, with a high rate of data transfer. What this means is that one can more rapidly upload and download information such as images, videos, and music, for example. Unlike a modem, terminal adapters do not convert signals from analog to digital information. Rather, they facilitate digital-to-digital communications between computers. Examples of terminal adapters are ISDN, Cable, DSL, and ADSL adapters. Choosing which device is appropriate is dependent upon what type of subscription service is available in a your area.

NIC

A network interface card also known as a NIC, is an expansion card which is inserted into one of the PCI slots on the mainboard, in order to allow the computer to be connected to a network. The most common NIC is a 100 Base-T network adapter, which allows a computer to be connected to a local network. This device is only needed if the computer is to be connected to other local computers.

A SPECIAL NOTE ABOUT THE MACINTOSH COMPUTER

It has not been the intention here to omit information relevant to the Macintosh computer; however, Apple has designed the Macintosh computer as a relatively *closed architecture* system. That is, many of the Mac's parts are proprietary, and you cannot "build" a Mac from off the shelf components. Much of the discussion above is applicable to the Macintosh, at least in theory. While you may not be able to choose a mainboard and a custom case for a Mac, you can add a hard drive, Zip, DVD drive, expansion cards, etc. Additionally, the theory behind the architecture of the computer is quite similar for Windows, Linux, and Macintosh computers.

Building a Digital Darkroom System: Process and Consideration

Now that we have discussed most of the computer's system components and their significance, our discussion will turn to the explanation of how all of these parts come together to make a computer system. This discussion will be brief and not fully explanatory; this is not intended to be a "build your own PC" course, but rather to give information regarding which components are significant for the digital darkroom, although it may seem like a computer science course at this point. The reasonably detailed discussion above is intended to explain the choices that need to be made in terms of setting up a computer to be used as a digital image-processing machine. Even if you are considering a preengineered and preassembled computer system, with the knowledge presented here, you can make informed choices about the way most any computer system needs to be configured for digital photography.

The actual process of building a system — that is, assembling the components — is not very difficult if the correct components are used. If you plan to assemble your own computer, you should consider the following steps.

NOTE that one should always be careful when installing *any* components into a computer. Computer equipment is very sensitive to static electricity; even a little static electricity can destroy a mainboard or other components.

Step I

First you will need to remove any access panels necessary in order to install all of the internal components. Generally the case comes completely assembled, with a power supply preinstalled. Simply remove the screws on the access panels, and remove the outer case from the chassis.

Step II

Now you need to install your internal drives, such as the hard drive, floppy drive, CD/DVD, Zip/SuperDisk/Jaz/ORB drives, and so forth.

Basically there are two different types of drives and three types of bays in a standard case. The two types of drives are:

1. Internal hard drives that do not need to be physically accessible to a user, and
2. Internal drives that do need to be accessible from the outside of the computer, such as floppy drives, CD/DVD drives, Zip/SuperDisk, and Jaz/ORB drives.

Other drive bays inside the case, where the various drives will reside, are generally either 5.25 inches wide, for devices like CD/DVD drives and larger footprint internal hard drives, or 3.5 inches wide for standard internal hard drives, or floppy, Zip, or SuperDisk-type drives.

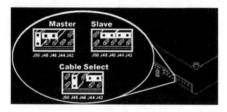

Note as you install the drives that it is important that you set the drive's jumpers first, as instructed by the hardware manufacturer.

These jumper settings designate whether a drive is a master or slave drive for the IDE bus, and which SCSI ID number the drive represents.

Step III

Next you will need to install the CPU and RAM onto your mainboard. Actually this can be done inside the case as well, but it is easier to do this step before you install the mainboard. Also, you will need to set a few jumpers on the mainboard; the guide that comes with the mainboard and/or the CPU will aid in determining where to set these jumpers.

Step IV

Next, the mainboard needs to be incorporated. This is simply a matter of installing the mainboard inside the case, and making sure all of the external access ports are aligned. Then the mainboard is screwed down to attachment posts in the computer case. Next, the power supply cable needs to be attached to the mainboard. Finally, all of the wires for the power switch, hard drive lead, speaker(s), reset switch, and any other case lights/switches need to be plugged into the mainboard, as instructed in the mainboard documentation.

Step V

Now, the accessory cards need to be added. Note that even if you purchase a preassembled computer, you may need to add expansion cards at some point.

This is quite simple. You need to determine what type of card is to be installed, and choose the right type of slot to insert the card into. The order in which the cards are installed doesn't really matter. Therefore, for our example, we will assume the following: the video card is an AGP card, the modem/terminal adapter is a PCI card, and the sound card is a PCI card. In this example, the video card will be installed in the only AGP slot, and the audio and modem/terminal adapter cards will be installed in any of the available PCI slots. This type of card installation is a common task, and you will probably need to add some type of expansion card to your digital darkroom computer system eventually.

Step VI

Connecting the cabling is the last step for assembling all of the internal hardware. First, all of the drives need to be supplied with power. The keyed-power leads from the power supply need to be plugged into the back of each of the drives. Next, all of the data cables for the internal devices need to be connected.

First, the floppy drive controller on the mainboard needs to be connected to the floppy disk drive. Then, the IDE controller on the mainboard needs to be connected to the back of the hard drive, and then the CD. If more internal devices are present, the second onboard IDE controller will be connected to those devices. Note that there are technical specifications that you need to know when connecting devices, for example, which drive is the primary/master, and which is the secondary/slave drive. Beyond setting the jumpers on the back of these devices, the order in which the cable is connected is significant; the IDE master drive begins at the end of the cable, and the slave drive is connected between the mainboard controller and the master drive connection.

Step VII

Lastly, all of the external components need to be plugged in: monitor, keyboard, mouse, Zip drives, etc. Now, turn on the power to your the new computer system. The first thing to do is set up the BIOS settings, which identifies what type of hardware you have installed. Next the operating system needs to be installed, and all of the devices configured to work with your new computer system. Finally, the software needs to be installed, such as Photoshop, and you are ready to begin using your new digital darkroom.

Again, remember that this discussion is not intended to be a user guide to building a computer. Rather, this discussion of the components and steps involved in building a computer is intended to enable you to appreciate the architecture of your new digital darkroom. Just as you might discuss the color temperature of a light source in an enlarger, or the chemical composition of a film developer, understanding your tools and materials is key to mastering the medium.

Although it is not actually necessary to understand any of the internal workings of a computer to pursue digital photography, this basic understanding will help you to achieve better control of the digital darkroom, or a better understanding when purchasing an appropriate preassembled Mac or PC computer.

How to cope with technological advances: Keeping your digital darkroom current

Finally, exactly how does one cope with all of the ongoing changes in technology? This is a very good question to which there is no one definitive answer. There are, however, a number of factors to consider in keeping your digital darkroom up to date. Below is a list of factors for.

First, however, some general problems with technological advancement need to be discussed. Consider that the current professional lifespan of computer-based technological products is approximately eighteen months (and getting shorter all the time). What this means is not that a computer purchased today won't continue to operate properly in eighteen months, but rather that new software and hardware that are available—and in the mainstream—won't necessarily be compatible with the older hardware and software. If a person works in isolation, and never needs to share their images with anyone else—or use any new features/innovations developed in subsequent versions of hardware and software—there would theoretically never be a need to upgrade their digital photographic or computer system. The main problem here is that the world we live in operates differently . If you want to take advantage of the latest printing technology, for example, you may need to save your images in a new image format, on a new type of storage media. This is where the dilemma is presented. In order to utilize the new image format, you may need a faster computer with more RAM and storage space to run the new version of the software. Now you are faced with the choice of becoming increasingly less compatible with the rest of the photographic and computing world, or upgrading (or replacing) your computer hardware and software. So how do you address staying compatible with this never-ending stream of technological innovations? The following sidebar offers several considerations that will help you in staying afloat in the stream of emerging technologies.

Staying Afloat: The Stream of Emerging Technologies

When purchasing computer hardware, the following issues should be considered to allow for future upgrades and expansion.

- Does the case allow for physical expansion needs?
- Is the motherboard upgradeable and to what speed?
- How much RAM can be added to the motherboard?
- What type of internal expansion is available for video, expansion cards, different types of bus systems?
- What type of external expansion is available for different types of bus?
- What operating systems will be compatible with the computer hardware?
- Does the motherboard/CPU support all of the features that your imaging software requires, such as dual processors, math coprocessor, etc.?
- If you replace your computer, what components would you be able to keep, and potentially utilize in the new computer system?

Computers and Photographic Images

Beyond the fact that computers have altered the way we create, process, and print images, they have had a more significant impact upon the meaning of images. Although people have manipulated images almost from the birth of photography, there has always been a presumption of the "truthfulness" of the photographic image. Since the widespread diffusion of computing technology for image processing, this presumption has been challenged in the minds of many in the general public. In part, the reason for this is that the computer allows even an amateur with relatively little experience to alter photographic images in a believable and well-crafted fashion. In the past, it would take a photographic craftsperson many years to develop the skill to manipulate images in credible ways—in terms of the photographic technique.

So what does this have to do with understanding computers and digital photography? Well, everything! Beyond the technology in the digital realm lie numerous layers of creative, technical, ethical, and legal issues. So, when approaching these technologies, be mindful that just because you can do something doesn't make it right. This has been one of the most significant areas of change with respect to photographic imaging. What it has meant for the general public is that there is now a general distrust of the "truthfulness" of the photographic image, even when presented in documentary forums such as the news media.

Conclusions

At the beginning of this chapter it was stated that the computer has been both a blessing and a burden for photographers. It is a blessing, in the sense that the photographer now has technological advances which allow for the creation of images that are the embodiment of almost anything imaginable. However, with this great power comes responsibility. A responsibility of making ethical decisions of how, why, and where this technology will be utilized—along with a contemplation for the potential impact of these decisions—and here lies the burden for contemporary image-makers.

With the advent of digital photography, photographic tools have forever changed both how we make and how we understand images.

Review Questions:

1 What is a computer platform? What are the two primary computing platforms that are used by digital photographers?

2 How does the choice of computer platform affect the digital photographer's workflow?

3 List three of the main components of a digital darkroom-type computer system:

a. _____

b. _____

c. _____

4 In the digital darkroom, is it better to have more or less computer RAM? Explain.

5 When designing a digital darkroom computer system, what are the two most significant pieces of hardware?

1 Why do photographers need to use computers?

2 Why is it important for the digital photographer to understand technical specifications of the components and internal workings of a computer?

3 Why would anyone decide to buy a preengineered and preassembled computer system, even if they know how to "build" their own computer system?

4 Does it matter if a computer system, to be utilized as a digital darkroom, is upgradeable?

CHAPTER 2

Digital Cameras and Image Capture

Objectives:

This chapter will introduce you to the digital camera and other digital image capture devices. The discussion will range from the technical to the pragmatic, regarding the selection of an appropriate digital camera and capture technologies.

Upon completion of this chapter, you should have a better understanding of:

- How to identify appropriate digital camera technologies
- What types of imaging sensors to look for in a digital camera
- How to make purchasing decisions regarding digital cameras and accessories
- How to differentiate between "consumer/ novice," "prosumer" (cross between professional and consumer), "professional," and "advanced professional" digital cameras and digital capture devices
- When to capture images on film, or on digital media
- How to determine the advantages and disadvantages of various digital camera technologies, and when to use digital cameras

Introduction to Digital Cameras and Digital Images

■ So, just what is this thing we call a digital camera?

■ Why should we consider shooting photographs with a digital camera instead of with a traditional film-based camera?

■ How are these decisions going to affect our photography?

In this chapter we will attempt to answer these and many other questions asked by contemporary photographers when choosing when to capture images as latent silver halide images (traditional film) or as pixels (in digital form).

The discipline of photography is presently at interesting crossroads in its evolution. Since its inception, photography has always been a process whereby images were captured on specially prepared materials such as daguerreotype plates, emulsion-coated glass plates, or films, as we know them today. Regardless of the media, photography has always been a discipline that required supplemental materials upon which images are recorded. With the advent of electronic imaging, and more specifically digital imaging, our conceptions of how images are to be recorded have been challenged. Now, there is no longer a need for a permanent media upon which to record and archive our images. In the digital format, images have become transitory, in their physical form, because of the way in which their integral information is stored. That is because digital images are saved as a set of numerical values that are then interpreted by the computer; the act of duplication of images has become an exact science. However, in traditional photography there are two primary ways to duplicate an image. Either a copy photograph—or contact print/enlargement—of the original film negative or positive is made onto another piece of film, or a copy photograph of the photographic print is made onto another piece of film. In either of these traditional procedures, the process of image duplication degrades the image in terms of such attributes as luminosity, contrast, and color fidelity—where the second method described produces images that are even further degraded than the first.

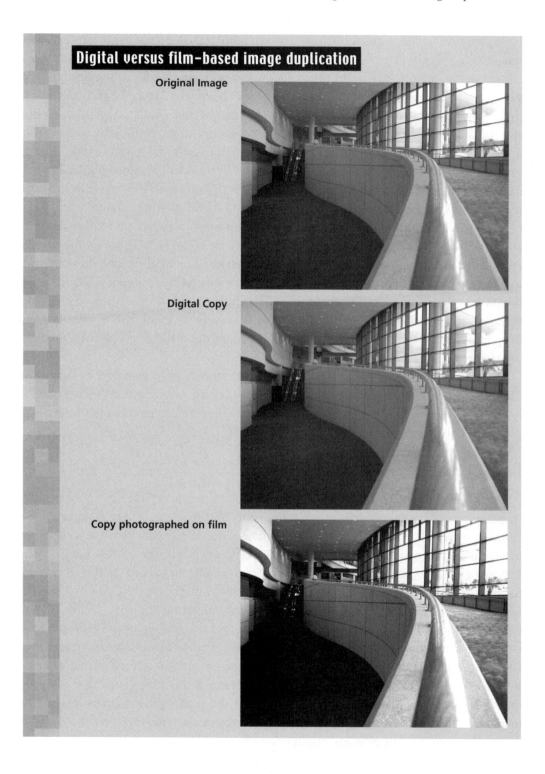

Digital versus film–based image duplication

Original Image

Digital Copy

Copy photographed on film

So, why do we have all of this discussion about copying traditional photographic images at the beginning of a digital camera chapter? Well, quite simply, it is postulated that this is the primary benefit that digital images have to offer to the discipline of photography: the ability to make exact duplications of image data. What this means is that images are no longer bound by the life span of the emulsion of film, or the archival stability of a photographic print. Now images can be continually copied from one media to another—regardless of the life of any given digital media—and the original photographic image data will remain perfectly intact. Therefore digital images, due to their form, have irrevocably changed the discipline of photography because they can survive virtually forever in an uncorrupted and pristine original state. This, of course, is true as long as they are either archived on a media that has a limitless archival life (this technology is not available yet), or someone duplicates the images onto a new media before whatever media they are stored on expires. The most archival media currently available is the Recordable CD produced by Eastman Kodak. Kodak boasts that their InfoGuard™ recordable CDs will last a person's lifetime or one hundred years, whereas various general types of film have an archival life ranging from only fifteen to seventy-five years. This is dependent upon the film type, the processing method, and storage conditions.

The point here is this: now that some digital cameras have matched or surpassed the quality of some photographic film's ability to record information, this new media has taken a significant place in the historical paradigmatic developments of the discipline of photography.

A Brief History of Digital Cameras

Before we discuss digital cameras, we must examine the broader category of electronic cameras. Digital cameras are developments that have evolved from analog electronic cameras. The development of television in the 1940s was the first widespread innovation from which electronic images were produced. In the 1950s, Bing Crosby Laboratories developed the video tape recorder (VTR) to record analog television images to magnetic tape, which was perfected by the Ampex Corporation in 1956. This invention (electronic imaging) revolutionized the television industry. In the 1960s, NASA sent out probes to map the Moon's surface, before landing a manned lunar mission. NASA missions used video cameras and transmitters to broadcast the analog video signals/images, but the transmissions were incoherent due to natural forms of radio interference. Thus, NASA engineers needed to devise a way of enhancing the images into a useable form. They found ways to convert the analog video signals into digital data for computer processing to enhance the images by removing unwanted visual noise. This was the first practical application of digital image processing.

Semantic Clarification: Electronic Imaging and Digital Imaging

So what is the difference?

These terms are often confused, but the distinction is quite simple. *Electronic imaging* deals with any image in any electronic format. This can be a digital file, a static RAM card, or an analog (not digital) encoding of the image on a floppy disk, as with the storage devices in the early Sony Mavica electronic cameras. The term *digital photography* refers to only photographic images that are specifically in the digital form. Finally, the term *digital imaging* deals with any form of imaging that specifically utilizes the digital form as its structural base.

The terms electronic imaging and digital imaging are used in the industry to mean photographic and graphic arts imaging. However, there is a semantic bias that regards both of these terms as implying that the images are of photographic origins.

In 1972 the first patent for an electronic camera was issued to Texas Instruments. Also in the 1970s, Kodak invented several solid-state image sensors. However, this type of camera technology was not popularized until the early 1980s. In 1981, Sony released the Mavica electronic still-video camera—the first commercially available electronic camera. This technology recorded analog video-frame signals to a miniature floppy disk. Then, in 1986 Kodak developed the first megapixel imaging sensor that could capture 1.4 million pixels of information and was capable of producing a photographic quality 5"x 7" print. This camera cost tens of thousands of U.S. dollars when it was released.

In 1990, Kodak again developed a revolutionary technology, the Photo CD. This technology not only allowed photographers to capture images on film, but also to have access to high-resolution digital copies as well. While the photo CD was not a digital camera technology, it popularized digital images and helped to create a demand for digital cameras. Following this development, in 1991 Kodak developed a professional-level digital camera. It was based on the Nikon F3 camera and could capture 1.3 megapixels of information. This camera was marketed as a tool for photojournalists, but because of its very high price tag, only professionals or professional organizations could afford to work with this technology.

At this time other technologies, such as the Sony and Canon still-video cameras, allowed filmless photography; however, the images were low quality. By the mid-1990s, Apple introduced their Quick Take digital camera. This was the first consumer-level camera that made digital photography easy and accessible to the consumer/prosumer-level photographer.

At the professional level, digital scan backs and, later, digital capture backs became available during the 1990s, and virtually changed some photographic industries such as portrait photography and catalog photography.

In the late 1990s, the quality of digital camera images increased and the prices decreased. This led to the widespread diffusion of consumer-level and prosumer-level digital cameras. By the turn of the century, the first consumer /prosumer-level 3+ mega-pixel camera was announced by Nikon, and was soon followed by many other manufacturers. These 3+ megapixel cameras were available for less than $1,000 USD. This was a significant turning point in the evolution of the digital camera because now "affordable" digital cameras were capable of producing images up to 8"x 10" that looked as good as images produced from film. Compared to the +/- $28,000 USD price tag on one of the earliest high quality digital cameras such as the Kodak DCS460. The passage of time had now allowed for a continuing stream of research and made digital cameras affordable. Finally, with the diffusion of 3, 5, 6, and higher megapixel cameras, at the price point of under $1,000 USD, the quality and price of digital camera technologies spurred a revolution in the first years of the new millennium in the way consumers think about photography.

Digital and Traditional Cameras

As discussed, the form that the recorded image takes is of primary significance when comparing digital images to traditional images. Yet, as far as the camera is concerned, there are certain distinctions that need to be made.

The most important camera-based distinction between traditional cameras and digital cameras is in the way in which the image is recorded. With film-based cameras, the recording media—film—is inserted into the camera in roll or sheet form, and the film itself is the physical object that the light, passing through the lens and shutter, strikes to create a latent impression of the image. In a digital camera, this basic premise of recording the image is radically different. Here, the light that passes through the lens and shutter strikes a (or several) computer-technology-based sensing device(s), such as a CMOS (complementary metal oxide semiconductor) chip or a CCD (charge-coupled device), to create electrical signals that are then processed and stored on various types of digital media. This information is not stored in an analog fashion as with film; the representation of the image is not in a form that will be recognizable to the human eye. Rather this information is stored as numerical values that require computer-based algorithmic image processing to interpret the image.

Most significantly, one of the real distinctions between digital cameras/digital media and traditional cameras/film lies in the fact that the dynamic range of various image-recording devices and/or media are radically different. Later, we will discuss the differences of the range of information that can be captured and stored on digital media versus film.

The body:

As for the camera body itself, digital cameras are essentially the same as film-based cameras. They are both available in a wide variety of formats; they both have many shapes, styles, and forms, and have both fixed-lens and interchangeable versions available. The main differences here lie in the fact that some camera manufacturers have decided to change standards for accessories, but this is no different than what occurs with traditional product line replacement models of film-based cameras.

Maximum Print Size and Digital Camera Resolution

Resolution Designation	Pixel Dimensions	Acceptable Print Size (Maximum)
VGA	640 x 480	2.5" x 3.5"
XGA	1024 x 768	4" x 6"
1 megapixel	1280 x 1024	5" x 7"
2 megapixels	1600 x 1200	8" x 10"
3.3 megapixels	2048 x 1536	11" x 14"
4 megapixels	2240 x 1680	11.5" x 15"
5 megapixels	2560 x 1920	13" x 17"
6.1 megapixels	3040 x 2016	14" x 21"

Note that these are the maximum size prints that each of these resolutions will yield. Prints at these resolutions and sizes will begin to show degradation, but should still be acceptable.

The cost:

Another great difference between these types of cameras is their cost. Although there are many very inexpensive digital cameras available, to have a digital camera that can yield print-based results that will match even a good disposable 35 mm camera is still at least as expensive as a mid-level prosumer 35 mm camera (a cross between a professional 35 mm camera and a consumer-level 35 mm camera). In general, a high-quality digital camera will cost significantly more than its traditional media counterpart.

The quality:

In terms of the quality of the recorded image, this is where there is still a great difference between film and digital cameras. Low-end digital cameras will generally capture much less information than film. This is akin to using a very high-speed film that will cause "grainy" results in the photograph. These low-resolution cameras will produce images that are pixelated —they are made up of dots or pixels of information that are large enough to be seen on the print. The more pixelated an image is, the greater the degradation of the image—just as with very grainy traditional photographic prints.

Therefore, the amount of pixels a digital camera can capture is of paramount importance, regarding the resolution of the image. Resolution refers to the camera's ability to faithfully reproduce the tones and hues, as well as the details of the original scene being photographed. This is known as the sampling rate of the camera. Most significant is the need for true resolution in terms of the number of pixels sampled/captured. That is, many manufacturers advertise cameras as having high capture resolutions, but if you read the fine print, you will notice that they may refer to the resolution as interpolated. An interpolated resolution means that where two pixels of information are optically sampled, information is made up to fill the space between the two sampled pixels. This made-up information is the interpolated data that the camera produces. This is not a desirable method of increasing image size. Later we will discuss better ways of "rezing up" image files—to make larger prints from less image information.

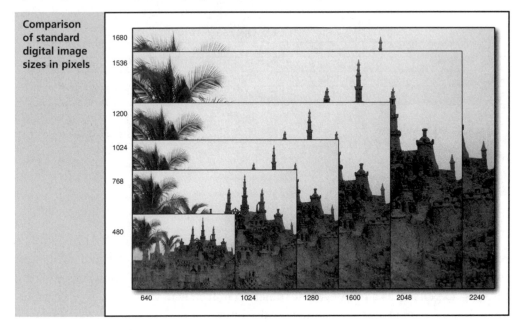

Comparison of standard digital image sizes in pixels

Capture rate:

The rate at which a given camera can record images differs between digital and conventional cameras. With a conventional 35 mm camera which is equipped with a motor drive, you can photograph in a continuous shooting mode and capture many frames of images per second. The lag between exposure times is limited by the shutter speed of the camera and the ability of the motor to advance the film to its next unexposed frame. In this method of shooting, many traditional cameras can capture two, three, or even up to six frames of images per second. The distinction here is that regarding digital cameras, other factors need to be considered with respect to the camera's ability to shoot consecutive frames rapidly.

With digital cameras there are several factors that contribute to the rate at which images can be captured. First, the resolution at which the image is being captured needs to be considered. Here, the general rule of thumb is that the more information there is to be captured, the longer it will take to accomplish several related processes before the image is finally stored and the camera is ready to capture the next image. First, the information that comprises the image is based upon the resolution settings of the camera. Unlike traditional film-based cameras, many digital cameras afford the ability for the photographer to change the amount of information being recorded for individual images. What this means is that some images can be high-resolution, and on the same "digital film" recording media, other images can be captured at low, snap-shot-level resolutions.

Next, the camera's write speed needs to be considered. This is the speed at which a given camera can transfer the captured digital information to a piece of storage media. Which brings us to yet another factor that impacts the cycle time of the digital camera: that of the storage media. Understand that all digital storage media are not created equal. Digital film, as Lexar™ calls it, has certain physical characteristics that restrict the amount of digital information that can be transferred and stored to it in a given amount of time. The speed of the digital film card has a direct correlation to how fast the camera can store images, and therefore how much lag time there will be between pressing the shutter-release and waiting for the camera to be ready to create the next exposure.

When a digital photograph is captured with a digital camera, a process similar to the following generally occurs. When the shutter release is pressed, a degree of lag time occurs. This is because the camera needs to prepare a number of settings before the image can be captured. First, if an auto-focus mode is being used, the auto-focus setting needs to be determined. Then the white balance—color correction—of the scene needs to be determined. Following this, the exposure needs to be calculated and set. Finally, once all of the settings have been determined, the CCD sensor (if present) needs to be charged because CCDs do not retain their charge for very long. At this point the aperture is closed down, and the shutter is opened and then closed, in order to expose light onto the image sensor. As you can see, there are a number of things occurring each time the shutter release is pressed. All of these things require time to accomplish their respective tasks.

Additionally, the LCD display for most digital cameras goes into a sleep mode and the camera powers down when the camera has been idle for a given period time. Some cameras can take upward of twenty seconds to wake up and be ready to shoot again. The technical limitations of a given camera need to be considered if it is to be used for high-speed or action photography.

Storage Media for Digital Cameras

The main types of non-proprietary digital image storage media that are currently utilized are CompactFlash Type I & II cards, Smart Media cards, and Type I & II storage cards, as well as Microdrives.

Beyond these digital storage media forms, there are PC cards that are used for the transfer of information from such media as CompactFlash to various computing devices. Also, there are several types of PC cards for digital imaging; they have been designated as Type I, Type II, and Type III by the PCMCIA (Personal Computer Memory Card International Association). All of the Type I, II, and III cards look the same from a top view, having the same width and length, but they each have a different thickness. Each of these storage media types have a 3.3-mm-thick guide around their edges; however, the Type II and III cards are thicker than the standard Type I cards, at 5 mm and 10.5 mm thick, respectively.

In a computer's PCMCIA slot, the edge guides permit the thin cards to be installed in thicker PCMCIA slots. For example, in a notebook computer's PCMCIA slot, you can insert two Type I or Type II cards on top of each other, or the same slot may be used to hold only one Type III card.

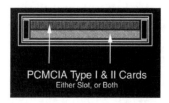

PCMCIA Type I & II Cards
Either Slot, or Both

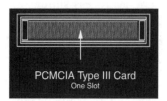

PCMCIA Type III Card
One Slot

The most common types of digital storage media are CompactFlash cards and Microdrives. In part, their popularity is due to their compact size.

However there are significant differences between these two types of storage media. The Microdrive technology allows for significantly more storage space. The main problem with them, though, is that they are generally more fragile than other types of digital image storage media, since they have rotating heads as part of their built-in disk drives. Media such as CompactFlash,

on the other hand, is a solid-state memory technology; it has no moving parts. Many photographers believe that the higher cost of CompactFlash media, in comparison to Type III Microdrives, is offset by the fact that high-quality CompactFlash cards are extremely durable.

A final note about digital storage media: each digital camera utilizes a specific type of storage media. You must first establish what type of media the digital camera uses before purchasing digital film—just as you would when purchasing 35 mm, 120, or 4" x 5" film, based upon the media that the traditional camera accepts.

Digital Cameras and Image Transfer

There a number of ways that images can be transferred from the digital camera to your digital darkroom—the computer. Above, we have discussed the media upon which digital images are stored in the camera. But how do we transfer the image from the digital camera to the computer? Well, there are two primary ways in which images go from the digital camera to the computer. The first method involves a direct link from the camera to the computer. The second method involves the use of an intermediate computer peripheral device to accommodate the digital film media.

In terms of transferring images directly from the camera to the computer/digital darkroom, a direct link must be established between the camera and computer. This link can be in the form of a hard-wired, tethered connection between these devices.

USB-enabled Compact-Flash Reader

Connections to the computer ports such as the serial, USB, FireWire (IEEE 1394), and such are established to allow the computer to directly download information from the camera. This can occur either while shooting or after, based upon the model of digital camera. In addition to a physical tethering of these devices, infrared "wireless" ports on both the camera and the computer can also be utilized for data transfers.

Beyond the direct transfer of images from the camera to the computer, peripheral devices can be used as an interface that allows the computer to access images on various types of digital film media. For example, media such as CompactFlash can be accessed by a computer via a PCMCIA Type I or II adapter, or through proprietary readers such as the Lexar JumpShot™ CompactFlash reader cable/adapter.There are other adapters available for transferring images directly from digital film media to the computer; one example is a PCMCIA-to-CompactFlash adapter.

This device allows the user to insert a CompactFlash card into a standard PCMCIA Type I or Type II card slot on a computer. Then the images, or other data, on the CompactFlash card can be accessed just as though it is on an additional hard drive on the computer system.

It is significant to note that like computer disks, digital film storage cards must be formatted for DOS/Windows before they can be used. The majority of digital film storage media are pre-formatted for DOS so no formatting is necessary for use on a media reader that is attached to a DOS or Windows computer. Macintosh users must have the PC-exchange system extension or an equivalent extension installed, in order to allow the Mac computer to read the Windows-formatted digital film media cards.

How Digital Cameras Work

Zone I - 0%   Zone II - 10%   Zone III - 20%   Zone IV - 30%   Zone V - 40%   Zone VI - 50%   Zone VII - 60%   Zone VII - 70%   Zone VIII - 80%   Zone IX - 90%   Zone X - 100%

There are essentially two different types of digital camera technologies. The first uses a CMOS sensor device, and the second uses a CCD image sensor device. Most cameras use CCD chips to record digital images; however, as technology changes this may change as well. First, remember that all of the information we are capturing is in black-and-white tones, even though an image appears to be in color. This is akin to the ten zones of Ansel Adams' Zone System.

All digital images are captured as measures of luminosity; these tonal values are captured on a gray scale with 256 levels of distinction.

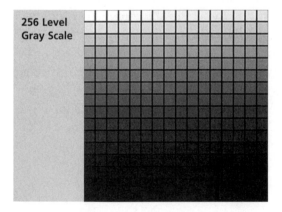

256 Level Gray Scale

With color images in a digital camera, however, each of the areas of the spectrum representing red, green, and blue light are separated through a filtering system integral with the camera or its image sensor. There are three primary ways in which to separate the visible spectrum and then recombine it through a digital photographic representation:

1. Individually filtered and separate imaging sensor devices can be used to capture the red, green, and blue light separately.
2. Individual exposures can be captured, where each exposure uses a red, green, or blue filter to separate the three primary colors of the spectrum—captured on one sensor.
3. The photosites of a particular imaging sensor can be individually filtered in order to capture the red, green, and blue light separately.

CMOS Devices

Devices that utilize CMOS (Complementary Metal Oxide Semiconductor, pronounced "see-moss") sensors comprise both ends of the digital capture spectrum. That is, the highest quality digital capture devices and the lowest level inexpensive digital cameras both use this technology. This paradox occurs because of the way in which the CMOS sensors are being used as devices to capture visual information. Inherent in using a CMOS device as an image capture sensor is the problem that generally these devices produce a greater amount of noise in the form of electronic distortions in the image than CCDs do —especially in the solid or smooth, continuous areas of an image. This noise needs to be countered in the digital camera that uses this type of capture device through the use of reasonably sophisticated, software-based filtering algorithms—generally in the central processor of the camera. At the low-end of the digital camera spectrum, CMOS devices are being used because they are much less expensive than CCD sensors. The problem is that at this level, the internal processing abilities of the camera to enhance the image, and offset the degradation that is being caused by the sensor chip, is not generally sophisticated enough to produce high-quality images.

Before you totally discount the idea of using a digital camera that utilizes a CMOS recording sensor, consider that currently the highest quality digital camera sensor uses a CMOS device.

Foveon's X3 image sensor: the world's first full-color image sensor.

This technology, originally developed by Foveon, is an example of breaking from conventional wisdom to develop truly groundbreaking and revolutionary imaging technologies.

Foveon's 16.8-million-pixel CMOS image sensor

The new design in CMOS technology developed by Foveon incorporates three layers of photodetectors for each pixel. These layers are embedded in silicon, which takes advantage of the fact that red, green, and blue lights penetrate silicon to different depths. This is the basis of the design principle behind the world's first full-color image sensor.

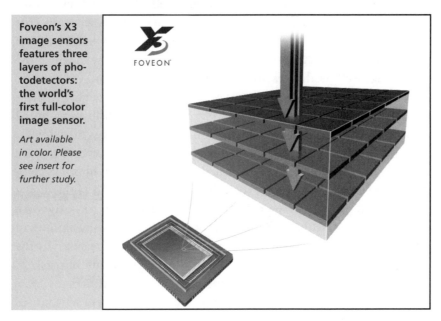

Foveon's X3 image sensors features three layers of photodetectors: the world's first full-color image sensor.

Art available in color. Please see insert for further study.

CCD Sensors

CCD (charge-coupled device) imaging sensors are the most widely utilized forms of digital image capture sensors. This is because they generally produce a high-quality image with little image noise.

CCD Sensor Array

The CCD, however, requires significantly more power to charge the device for image-capture, than does the CMOS sensor. What this means for the photographer is that more batteries will be required when shooting in the field, or an A/C adapter should be used in a studio environment when using CCD-based digital cameras.

There are basically two different types of CCD-based digital cameras. One type utilizes a single CCD chip to record the light levels of the image's red, green, and blue information. With these types of single CCD devices, one third of each sensor's receptors or light sensing elements record the information through a striping technique for each of the respective colors. With a 3 megapixel camera that has a resolution of 2048 pixels x 1536 pixels, the resulting image will comprise 3,145,728 pixels of information. Also, consider that the sensor in the digital camera may be quite a bit smaller than the image capturing area designated for recording images on film.

1/2" and 2/3" sensors compared to a 35 mm negative

Many CCD sensors range in size from those that are 1/2", 2/3", or even 1.125" in size, as compared to the 1" x 1.5" area of a piece of 35 mm film.

Other cameras that make use of CCD image sensor technologies utilize three CCD chips to record an image's information. These cameras employ a prism or beam-splitter to separate the red, green, and blue areas of the spectrum. Each respective color is then recorded on its own CCD chip. This technology is primarily used in cameras for studio use, such as with portrait, or catalog photography. Because these cameras use three CCDs to produce the final image, they require much more power to charge the sensors. Generally these cameras will be powered with A/C, not batteries, due to their power consumption requirements. Also, because these cameras have three CCDs, beam-splitters, and other associated requisites, the manufacturing cost is significantly higher for a three-CCD camera.

DSPs and CPUs

Beyond the image sensors, and before the image is recorded to the digital media, the image needs to be processed. All digital cameras have an internal CPU (central processing unit). This is the onboard computer that processes the digital information that is derived from the CCD/CMOS sensor, and prepares this information to be stored on the digital storage media. More sophisticated digital cameras incorporate a dedicated DSP (digital signal processor). These cameras allow the DSP to handle the processing of the digital image signal information. In these types of digital cameras, the CPU is freed up from the signal processing tasks, and is able to handle all the other camera processing functions such as the exposure calculations, white balance, etc. In cameras that only have a general CPU, the sole CPU processor handles all image and signal processing functions. What this means for the photographer is that a camera with a CPU and a dedicated DSP will generally process the digital image information more rapidly, and, therefore, the camera will be ready to make the next exposure sooner.

Image Aspect Ratios

Due to the fact that image sensors have different aspect ratios than traditional film, the photographer needs to be conscious of the height-to-width ratio of photographs. With traditional 35 mm film, the aspect ratio is 1.5:1, which means that one dimension of the film is 50 percent greater than the other, while 4" x 5" film has an aspect ratio of 1:1.25. However, CCDs and CMOS sensors are usually square; for example, a 3/4" x 3/4" sensor has a 1:1 ratio. These sample ratios translate to print as illustrated in the Aspect Ratios table below.

Aspect Ratios

Width and Height		Dimensions	Width and Height		Dimensions
35 mm FILM:			**CMOS or CCD Image Sensor:**		
1" x 8"	=	8 inches	1/2 " x 16"	=	8 inches
1.5" x 8"	=	12 inches	Final Print size	=	8" x 8"
Final Print size	=	8" x 12"			
4" x 5" FILM:			1.125" x 7.11"	=	8 inches
4" x 2"	=	8 inches	1" x 7.11"	=	7.11 inches
5" x 2"	=	10 inches	Final Print size	=	8" x 7.11"
Final Print size	=	8" x 10"			

As with the change of format in any imaging media, with various digital imaging devices, the photographer's compositions will be affected by the choice of digital camera. In the Aspect Ratio Comparisons table presented here, you can see photographs displayed with varying image format aspect ratios—specifically note the Nikon digital aspect ratio. Not all digital cameras, CCDs, and CMOS sensors have this 1:1.33 aspect ratio.

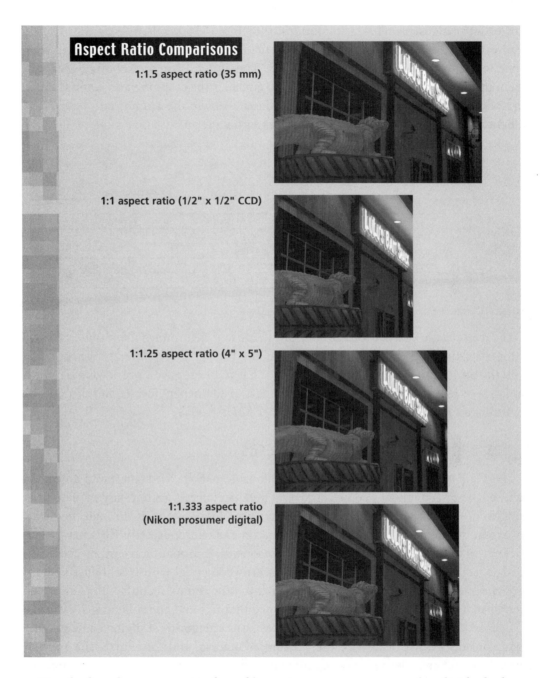

Aspect Ratio Comparisons

1:1.5 aspect ratio (35 mm)

1:1 aspect ratio (1/2" x 1/2" CCD)

1:1.25 aspect ratio (4" x 5")

1:1.333 aspect ratio
(Nikon prosumer digital)

To calculate the aspect ratio of any film or image sensor, you need to divide the larger dimension by the smaller dimension. The result equals the width-to-height factor of the image, where this number is equal to a ratio of one. For example, if a piece of film or an image sensor has a resolution of 2048 x 1536 pixels, the ratio is 1:1.33. Where 2048 /1536= 1.33, and in relation to the number one, the ratio is expressed as a one to one-point-three-three ratio (1:1.33). Therefore, if you are shooting with different models of digital cameras, you need to consider the cropping and compositions carefully before the image is captured, in order to have the appropriate final print dimensions—and without accidentally cropping the image.

Common Aspect Ratios

Image Type	Width x Height	Aspect Ratio
35 mm film	36 x 24 mm	1:1.50
Nikon 5000	2560 X 1920 pixels	1:1.33
Computer Monitor	1024 x 768 pixels	1:1.33
Video (NTSC)	640 x 480 pixels	1:1.33
Photographic Paper	8 x 10 inches	1:1.25
U.S. Letter size paper	8.5 x 11 inches	1:1.29

The aspect ratio of a sensor is important because it determines the shape and proportions of the photographs you create. When an image has a different aspect ratio from the device it is displayed or printed on, it has to be cropped or resized to fit. Your choice is to lose part of the image or waste part of the paper. To imagine this better, try fitting a square image on a rectangular piece of paper.

Types and Levels of Digital Cameras

There are a variety of digital cameras on today's market. With the rapid advancement of these technologies comes an overabundance of new techno-jargon. The first thing to do when considering digital camera technologies is to sift through the techno-jargon, to understand the information that manufacturers supply. This may seem obvious on the surface, but for a variety of reasons, all information regarding the technical aspects of a digital camera is not necessarily presented with true industry-standard specifications. There is some confusion as to how certain manufacturers arrive at their specifications for such factors as megapixel ratings and zoom-factors, for example. Understand, however, that there are three basic categories of digital cameras: the basic consumer/novice cameras, the prosumer cameras, and, of course, the professional level cameras. Beyond these distinctions, there are also super-pro-level cameras. These are the $10,000 USD to $100,000 USD plus models of cameras/camera backs specifically designed for high-end commercial work.

Consumer/Novice

This is the most basic type of digital cameras. Generally, they are point-and-shoot style cameras that have fixed lenses and automatically controlled exposure—with no manual controls available.

Casio's Stainless Steel Wrist Camera Watch

Digital cameras at this level are aimed at the amateur photographer, and generally offer very low-quality images in terms of their resolution and their ability to reproduce light and color values. Often these cameras take the form of multipurpose consumer devices such as Webcam/video/still cameras or MP3 players with video and still camera capabilities. One of the more novel devices in this category is illustrated here: the James Bond-style digital camera watch.

At this level of digital cameras, one should try to get the highest resolution possible for a given price range. Moreover, if it is possible, a camera with removable storage media would be best.

Prosumer

A camera in this hybrid category combines professional and consumer technologies. This is where most affordable digital cameras fall in the spectrum of available technologies. These cameras range from high-end amateur cameras to devices that produce images that equal professional-level digital cameras.

Fuji Photo Film's DS-260 HD digital camera is aimed at outdoor enthusiasts who want to capture their images electronically.

The prosumer cameras encompass those that have both high-level CCD capture devices, and those that offer professional-level optics. Generally, the cutoff between the prosumer designation and the pro cameras lies in the ability to use interchangeable lenses from conventional 35 mm cameras. This is a feature that is generally only found in a professional-level digital camera. Furthermore, all prosumer cameras utilize removable digital film storage media. It is significant to note that currently there are prosumer level cameras that produce higher-quality images than some of the "professional" level cameras that cost up to five times more.

Professional

These are the cameras that look and feel like traditional professional 35 mm cameras. They generally have the ability to store a large number of images on removable media such as microdrives or high-capacity compact flash cards, and will accept standard professional 35 mm lenses. With these cameras, the two most important features regard the resolution of the image and the cycle time of the capture. The professional digital camera represents the level of camera that most photojournalists use to capture news and sporting events. This type of photography requires a camera that can capture images rapidly, and this is where the greatest distinction lies between the high-end prosumer cameras and the professional digital cameras.

Advanced Professional

This type of camera, or camera back, is reserved exclusively for the commercial or professional photographer. Generally, these devices are used in a studio setting, and are quite costly.

They range from full digital studio cameras through medium- and large-format camera backs that will record incredible amounts of image information. For example, one current 4"x 5" digital scanning camera back (in the

$10,000 USD price range) captures an image that is 500 MB to 1GB in size, when attached to the back of a traditional 4" x 5" camera. To get a feel for the massiveness of this image file size, it would require 380 to 760 floppy disks for the storage of one photograph.

As you can see, there is amazing diversity in digital cameras. Choosing the right one for your needs can be quite a chore, especially if you don't understand the manufacturer's techno-jargon that describes the features you are seeking.

Digital Camera Scanning Backs and Inserts

Digital camera scanning backs and film inserts allow conventional cameras to record their images on digital media. These hybrid solutions have much to offer to the photographer, although with limitations. Currently, this type of digital technology has surpassed some conventional film's resolution. Yet, the ways in which some of these technologies work, with medium- and large-format cameras, have certain severe limitations in terms of what and how one can photograph.

This is because, as the name implies, digital scanning backs do just that, they scan in order to capture the image. Because this scanning process occurs over an extended period of time, there are certain obvious limitations on the types of subject matter that can be photographed. One example is that moving objects cannot be recorded.

Digital Scanning Back Considerations

Pros:

- Can be used with standard medium format and 4" x 5" cameras
- Can be used with standard lenses and focal lengths
- Photographer can still compose and focus normally on the ground glass
- All tilt, swing, rise and fall, and shift camera movements can be used
- Instant preview via computer of the final image—no processing
- Saves film, Polaroid, and processing and scanning expenses
- Can be used with many types of continuous lighting such as quartz, tungsten, fluorescent, etc.
- Image quality is as good or better than with film
- Capture a much greater dynamic range than possible with film

Cons:

- Cannot be used with strobes
- Does not allow the photographer to freeze action
- Not practical for photographing people
- All subjects need to be still for the duration of the exposure
- Exposures can take up to several minutes

Scanning backs employ a sensor (CCD) with a row of sensing elements that physically move (scan) across the image area. Thus, image information is captured one row at a time—until the entire area of the image has been covered. The exposure is calculated in terms of conventional exposure times such as 1/15 or 1/60 of a second; this time relates to the amount of time that the light strikes each row on the scanning back. Yet, some of these backs produce more than 15,000 lines (rows) per inch of resolution. Therefore, the total scan time is the product of the exposure time per line multiplied by the number of lines (rows) per scan. Thus, if it takes several seconds (or minutes) to scan the light that is falling upon the CCD array, one would not choose to shoot a "freeze" action type of image, or a portrait, for example.

These technologies are primarily being utilized by commercial and advertising photo studios, especially those that are shooting product photography/still life or copy art. It is important to note that scanning backs need to be used with continuous light sources. What this means to the traditional studio photographer is that they won't be shooting with their studio strobes.

In the realm of large format photography, for example, there are several options available for the photographers who wish to use their current large-format gear in a digital environment. Products such as the Leaf, the Phase One, and the Better Light digital insert/backs enable them to use a traditional 4" x 5" camera, and insert the digital recording device instead of a film holder into the film back of the camera. Currently, the 72 x 90 mm CCD sensor, used in both the Phase One and Better Light devices, offers the highest level of image recording capabilities.

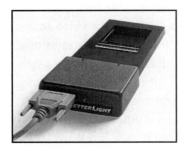

With large-format digital photography, the 4" x 5" host camera must be built well and to rigid standards. Consider first that digital inserts weigh more than traditional film holders. Additionally, note that the depth of field will be reduced because of the darkening effect of the digital UV-A filter.

Alternatives to Still Digital Cameras

Other devices, aside from the types of digital cameras and scanning backs discussed in this chapter, also allow you to capture images in the digital environment, which are closely related to digital still cameras. Digital video cameras, such as those manufactured by Sony, offer such features as high-quality video and still-photo capabilities in a single unit. They also offer the ability to add titles to still images or overlay them with video clips, and have FireWire or IEEE 1394 interfaces for high-speed connection to computers and VCRs for image transfers. Additionally, cameras such as Webcams offer other features: they are inexpensive, they have integrated live video and snapshot capabilities, and they make downloads of still images to a computer easy.

Additionally, the Image Acquisition and Alternative Image Acquisition chapters of this book offer many alternatives to capturing an image with a digital camera.

Video

While this book focuses on the creation of still electronic photographic images, it is important to note that there is a place for mentioning video capture here as well. Because images in the digital form are so easily transportable and adaptable, uses for the photographic image are varied. Beyond the traditional photographic print, video is a platform from which photographic images can be derived, and to which they can be delivered.

In simple terms, video cameras use the same technology to capture images to tape—or digital storage media—as do many still digital cameras.

The CCD is the image-sensing device that is employed in the video camera. These images can be transferred into a computer in a number of different ways, for a variety of purposes. However, these images are low-resolution in form, and will not yield high-quality still photographic images.

There are several ways to acquire a video image for digital photographic use. The most traditional way is to "grab" a frame off the videotape via a specially-designed video capture card, sometimes referred to as a frame grabber. Another way that video images can be acquired is through digital transfer techniques such as direct image capture from a computer through a tethered cable such as a FireWire (IEEE 1394) interface. (See the Image Acquisition chapters in this book for more techniques.) Additionally, many digital video cameras are now available with still image capture capabilities.

Purchasing a Digital Camera

The following suggestions may aid in the decision-making process leading to the purchase of a digital camera.

Novices and Beginners

When examining the manufacturer's specifications for a given camera, check for the cycle rate and make sure that the waiting time to make the next picture is acceptable for your needs. Also, if it is at all possible, get a camera that allows for the use of some type of removable image storage media. This way you won't "run out of digital film" when shooting on location. Finally, make sure that if the camera has a zoom lens, you note the optical zoom factor, and not the digital zoom factor (which will yield poor, interpolated results).

Prosumers and Professionals (who do not require high-speed multiple frames capture)

Look for a camera that has the highest true resolution in terms of the number of pixels to be captured. Next, look for a camera that meets your optical requirements. If the lens is not removable, make sure you know what the optical zoom factor is, and if the manufacturer—not a third party vendor—offers optical accessories to alter the built-in lens for your needs for things like wide angle or telephoto adapters.

Professionals (shooting action or rapid multiple frame exposures)

Most importantly, after you have determined the resolution requirements, verify the burst-mode capability of the camera and its overall cycle time. Also, interchangeable lenses are usually a requirement for professional shooting at this level.

Medium- and Large-Format Scan Backs

Many factors need to be considered here. The size of the sensor and its ability to reproduce luminosity and hue values are the most important factors. Because this technology is changing so rapidly, most specific information written about these technologies will become dated. Therefore, consider the following broad guideline questions.

- Is the scan back compatible with your existing equipment?
- What associated technology will need to be purchased in order to make this scan back functional in your workflow?
- What quality is needed, and does this scan back have the ability to produce images at that quality?
- Will the final product look as good or better than film?
- Because motion is not feasible to capture, will the scan back meet all of your photographic needs? Is the cost of this technology justified?
- If you aren't going to recover your investment in this type of technology within eighteen to twenty-four months, you may want to consider alternatives! Leasing may be an option to consider.

Accessories and Supplies

The following items are gear that you may want to consider when purchasing a digital camera. Although certain items are common to both traditional and digital photography, other items are very specific to digital imaging. For example, digital cameras go through batteries quickly, so much so that you will need at least two fully-charged sets of batteries (or external battery packs) at any given time. For information about common accessories and supplies, see the following table.

Digital Camera Accessories and Supplies

A/C Adapter	If you plan to shoot indoors or anywhere that there is an A/C outlet, this can be an invaluable investment. Digital cameras can have a voracious appetite for batteries. And although you most will assuredly have rechargeable batteries, the process of recharging batteries for many hours—and the wear on the batteries—can be avoided.
Batteries and Chargers	Batteries and chargers are the first thing you should consider purchasing. All digital cameras generally ship with lithium-ion or Ni-MH batteries. However, a second and even a third set of batteries is useful for location shooting. The Ni-MH (Nickel-Metal Hydride) batteries usually last much longer than other rechargeable batteries such as alkaline-rechargeable or Ni-Cad batteries. These types of batteries can be in the form of AA or AAA batteries, specialty camera sizes, or external power packs that plug into the power accessory port of the camera. The best batteries, if available for your digital camera, are lithium-ion batteries.
Transfer Cables	Transfer cables are usually supplied with the camera, but if they aren't, you should consider getting an appropriate transfer cable. These cables are usually USB or FireWire cables on one end, and a proprietary connector on the camera side of the cable. The cable allows the user to download images from the camera to the computer—usually via manufacturer-supplied software.
Lens Filters	As with most every location camera, filters such as a UV filter can help to protect the lens of your digital camera. If the digital camera has an integrated lens, this is crucial, because if the lens gets scratched, it cannot simply be removed and replaced by the user—as with the SLR (single-lens reflex) models. Additionally, as with traditional photography, image enhancement and correction filters can be used with the digital camera.
Supplemental Lenses and Adapters	For digital cameras that have integrated lenses, many manufacturers have produced lens adapters that screw onto the end of the built-in lens —as one would attach a filter —to alter the optical characteristics of the built-in lens. Usually these adapters convert the camera lens into a fish-eye, wide-angle, telephoto, or macro lens.

Digital Camera Accessories and Supplies, continued

Storage Media	When purchasing a digital camera, consider purchasing more of the type of storage media it uses. (See the section on Storage Media for Digital Cameras.)
Media Card Reader	Whether your camera uses microdrives, CompactFlash, or some other type of media, it is a good idea to have a media card reader. This allows for the transfer of the images from the storage media to a computer without the use of the camera.
Cable Release or Remote Control	Unfortunately, most digital cameras do not allow for the use of an inexpensive, traditional cable release. Therefore, if you need to make photographs that require long exposures, you will need to buy a relatively expensive electronic shutter release. The advantage of having an electronic shutter release, however, is that radio-controlled remote controls can be utilized on some of these types of cameras.

Pros and Cons of Digital Cameras

So, why should you, or should you not, use a digital camera to capture images? The answer to this question is multifaceted and has both technical and aesthetic implications and ramifications.

Shadow Details: Film and Digital

Original Photograph as recorded at ISO 100 on film. Here the relative underexposure of the film means that recoverable shadow detail is not available to the photographer.

The photograph as recorded at ISO 100 digitally—and enhanced to bring out midtone and shadow details. Because digital cameras can capture a greater dynamic range of information—especially in the shadow areas of an image—shadow detail can be recovered in the digital darkroom. Note that the original exposure looked exactly like the film exposure shown here. (Continued on next page.)

Shadow Details: Film and Digital, continued

This detail was adjusted to illustrate the information, which is recorded in the black areas of the digital file during image capture. This example shows just how much shadow information can be drawn from the shadow areas of an improperly exposed digital image. With a similarly exposed piece of negative film, this area would be clear and no information could be salvaged.

For the photographer using traditional cameras, such as a Nikon F5, a Canon EOS, a Hasselblad, or a 4"x 5" system, there is usually a period of adaptation when changing to a digital camera, both in terms of the ergonomics and in the dimensions of the new digital camera/camera back. Although quite similar, the digital bodies/backs are generally heavier—and a bit bulkier—than the traditional camera bodies, filmbacks, or film holders.

Another issue is that with the digital camera, one cannot simply buy a faster ISO film to capture images in low light situations. The determination of which ISO range is necessary to use occurs at the time of camera selection, not when purchasing the recording media. Remember, the ISO is determined by the sensitivity of the imaging sensor.

Beyond concern regarding the amount of illumination, a new area of concern for the digital photographer is that of white balance calibration. In traditional photography, correction for color shifts in light was accomplished through the use of color compensation filters affixed to the lens. With digital cameras, the camera's CPU can accomplish this feat internally. Therefore, when evaluating a digital camera, its ability to apply white balance—color correction—manually is significant. This allows the photographer to correct for unusual lighting problems in the field. For example, fluorescent, tungsten, mercury vapor, sodium vapor, daylight, and incandescent light sources can all be reasonably corrected on the fly, with no need for additional filters or other camera accessories.

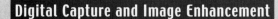

Digital Capture and Image Enhancement

Original digital photograph. Notice the lack of shadow detail.

The photograph as enhanced to bring out midtone and shadow details.

This detail was adjusted to show how much detail was recorded in the black or shadow areas of the digital file.

Another problem that needs to be considered with the digital camera regards the quality of its exposure. It has already been stated that most digital cameras capture a much greater dynamic range of tonal information than traditional film. However, there is one problem with traditional negative film, the main exposure problem that faces the photographer is that of capturing enough shadow detail. If an exposure is made that does not allow enough light to be recorded in the shadow areas, the film negative will be clear, and no detail will result in the shadow areas of the print. This type of problem cannot be corrected to any significant degree by altering processing. With digital capture this same problem exists, only at the opposite end of the spectrum;that is, the main exposure problem with digital camera exposures usually occurs in the highlight regions. Just as a lack of shadow detail in the traditional negative exposure cannot be easily compensated for after the initial exposure is made, the digitally captured image can easily have highlight areas that are washed out, which have no detail to recover, similar to the problems that occur when exposing slide film. Therefore, when evaluating digital cameras, the EV range and metering system need to be considered carefully.

For rapid succession photography, such as sporting events, the speed of capture can become a significant problem. Even with a high-end digital SLR camera, the first five or ten photos may be captured at a motor-drive style rate of three to four frames per second, but at some point the camera will need to pause for time to process and save the images to the digital film media.

An area of great concern with location digital photography is that of battery consumption. With digital cameras, the photographer needs to actively set up a battery usage policy. For example, three replacement sets of Ni-MH or lithium-ion digital camera batteries (or battery packs) should be sufficient on all location shoots. Also, these sets of batteries need to be rotated, in terms of the order of their usage, to extend their life. Finally, the highest priority needs to be placed on always keeping these batteries charged—because it takes anywhere from one to several hours to charge a set of batteries.

Pros and Cons of Photographing with a Digital Camera

Pros: Of course, the best part of digital photography is that you no longer have the following:

- No more film developing—or waiting on a lab to process (and scratch) your film
- No more scratches on your negatives or slides
- No more dust on your prints
- No more dust in your film holders
- No more need for a specialized darkroom facility—and no chemicals on your hands (and clothes) anymore
- Instant access to your images for printing, publishing, and sharing
- An incorrect exposure doesn't necessarily mean a missed shot
- You can delete outtakes while you are shooting

Cons: On the other hand, there are trade-offs with digital photography as well.

- More complicated to produce basic prints
- Requires a lot of expensive, technical apparatus to facilitate the processing and printing of images
- Digital images cannot be viewed with the naked eye
- An expensive camera is required to produce high-quality enlargements

Conclusions

Throughout this chapter we have discussed digital cameras and the related technologies. Although the discussion has focused on digital cameras, mention of technologies such as digital camera backs and digital film inserts has illuminated the vastness of the field of digital photography.

As we have seen, there are many technical issues that the photographer is confronted with, when deciding to become involved with digital photography. This is true, whether it is the decision of which camera to acquire, what type of storage media is appropriate, or even if the digital camera can accommodate your specific photographic requirements. Therefore, just as with traditional photography, the level at which you work as a photographer is directly associated with your ability to know your medium. It is this understanding of the medium that will always separate the professional photographer from the novice. Just as a traditional, professional photographer understands aesthetics, design and visual communications concepts, optics, film and emulsion-types, chemistry, light, perspective control and so forth, the digital professional photographer will understand all of these things. However, in addition to that, the new professional photographer must understand their new medium, too. Now, we are at a point in the evolution of photography where, to be successful and competitive, the photographer must also understand pixels, flash cards, DSPs, CPUs, clock speeds, CMOS and CCDs, interpolation, and a multitude of other new-media technical terms and concepts.

The sword here is double-edged. On the one side, a plethora of new opportunity is available to the photographer. On the other side, there is almost an entirely new discipline of information to acquire, in addition to all of the traditional requisite knowledge that is required to be successful in the field of photography. Due to the advancement of digital photographic technologies in this age of devalued digital stock photography, and royalty-free digital photographic collections, it is easy for the uninformed individual to believe that the photographer's job is easy now because of digital photography. On the contrary, the professional photographer's job has just increased exponentially.

With the diffusion of easy digital cameras and image processing software, the need for well-trained visual communicators has become even more essential. Just as the introduction of the microcomputer allowed relatively untrained individuals to contribute poor design through desktop publishing, digital cameras—and computer-based image processing—have also brought forth their own problems. These problems go beyond the technical issues.

The significance of the digital image lies in these two areas. The image can theoretically last forever in an unaltered form, and the photographer has near-unlimited potential to manipulate the image to achieve an end result. However, it should be noted that if images are created that have no visual merit or value, what is the point of preserving the image?

Therefore because of the accessibility to advanced image-recording devices and manipulation techniques, digital technology developments in the field of photography have created a situation whereby visual literacy is more necessary than any other skill the photographer can possess. But after all, once a photographer has mastered the basics, hasn't this always been the case?

Review Questions:

1 What is the primary benefit that digital images have to offer to the discipline of photography?

2 Which image-recording media yields the greatest dynamic range? In what ways is this significant to the photographer?

3 What are the main differences between prosumer and professional digital cameras?

4 How does capturing an image on a digital scanning back differ from a standard CCD image capture?

5 If you want to make a high quality 8" x 10" inkjet print, what is the minimum number of megapixels required for a digital camera to capture?

Discussion Questions:

1 When is it more advantageous to capture images on film, rather than digitally?

2 When is it more advantageous to capture images digitally, rather than on film?

3 Why is it significant that digital images have 256 levels of tonality? How does this affect the final photographic print?

4 When purchasing a digital camera, what are the most significant factors to be considered?

5 When shooting in the field, what are the key issues that differentiate photographing on digital media from photographing on conventional film?

CHAPTER

3

CHAPTER

Image Acquisition and Properties

Objectives:

This chapter will discuss the various devices and techniques used for image capture. The discussion will enable you to understand and differentiate between the different scanning devices and image acquisition/capture techniques. Upon completion of this chapter, you should have a better understanding of:

- What types of image scanners are available and appropriate for various photographic scanning needs
- Primary uses for scanners
- How scanners work
- How the elements of a digital image represent photographic image information
- How the scanning process works
- How to choose a scanner

Key Concepts

- Scanners are digitizers that convert traditional (analog) photographs into digital information.

- Scanners are used to digitize photographs, line art, three-dimensional art, transparencies, and text.

- There are six basic types of scanners.

- A scanner works like a digital camera and uses a CCD sensor or a PMT to capture the image.

- Pixel is shorthand for Picture Element.

- Resolution is measured in the number of pixels per square unit.

- Resolution is defined as the dots assigned or "mapped" to a given space.

- Image size and resolution need to be determined before an image is scanned so that the resultant image will match the final output requirements.

- Photographs are continuous tone images, and magazine and book illustration photographs are halftone images.

- Bitmaps represent continuous tone photographs in the digital world because they can reproduce the subtle gradations in tone of the original.

- Bitmap images have depth, which is measured by the amount of information assigned to each pixel.

- Bitmaps have four component parts: resolution, dimension, bitdepth, and color space/model.

- There are different types of resolution: spatial, optical, interpolated, and brightness/gamma. Each refers to a different aspect of the scanning reproduction process.

- Each type of scanner is built with a specific intended use. While some are more versatile than others, all have advantages and disadvantages.

- Choosing a scanner requires a careful assessment of your needs, balanced with the specific properties of a scanner—and, of course, your budget.

- After this chapter is fully considered, there will still be certain problems with the scanning equation. This is the nature of the digital imaging medium.

Introduction

s new technologies develop, so does the human capacity to create and invent. As we begin our somewhat technical discussion regarding image acquisition, pay heed to why we are pursuing this thing we call digital photography. In the end, what we are left with is the image, and the importance or lack thereof of the statement we are making as communicators. To illustrate this point, take for example the following quote: "Now at least we know everything that painting isn't." This was said by Pablo Picasso (1881–1973), the Spanish artist, in 1949 in answer to whether painting figures was still possible after the development of the new technological medium, photography (as reported by artist Renato Guttuso in his journals). So what does this mean for today's image-makers? Quite simply, because we are in an age of literal duplication of imagery—through technologies such as digital scanning—now at least we have a glimpse of what photography has not yet achieved.

Image Acquisition

Image acquisition is the process of importing images into the computer from external sources. These sources range from traditional photographic prints, slides, and negatives to three-dimensional objects, electronic photographs, and video. In general, the way we import these images is through the use of various forms of computer peripherals referred to as scanners or digitizers.

Scanners and Scanner Technology

Scanners are digitizers that convert traditional photographic and other images into information that can be utilized by a computer by using a light source, laser, or some other type of electromagnetic radiation. They can range in cost from affordable desktop versions to quite costly professional pre-press devices. Usually, the more precise its capability to duplicate an original, the more costly the scanner will be.

Users of scanner technology include business people, designers and illustrators, photographers, physicians and scientists, service bureau and professional lab operators, and interactive media specialists—to name a few. As input devices that capture visual information into the computer, scanners translate information from print, transparency, drawing, illustration, and text originals into digital information or computer binary code. In one sense, they can work like a slow-motion camera, where the information is captured on a charge-coupled device (CCD) chip. During this process, the information is initially converted to electronic impulses, which are then saved as a digital image.

CCD

Charge-Coupled Device (CCD): a light-sensitive electronic device that stores information in the form of electrical charges. CCDs can be up to one hundred times more sensitive to light than traditional photographic materials. In digital photography, the CCD is used as an analog-to-digital converter, which records information with respect to the light that strikes its surface.

Photographic CCDs are comprised of an array of photodiodes that are mounted on a semiconductor. Once the photodiode is exposed to light, a capacitor stores an electrical current that is relative to the amount of light. Finally, the semiconductor upon which the photodiodes are mounted processes this information.

Some uses of CCDs: Fax machines, digital cameras, video cameras, photocopy machines, digital scanners, and bar-code readers.

 INTERESTING NOTE: In the field of astronomy, photographic film is rarely used anymore. The utilization of CCD imaging technology has all but replaced film—because of its extraordinary sensitivity to light.

A Brief History of Scanners

The first scanners were proposed in 1850 to transmit photos over telegraph lines, while the first facsimile was transmitted in 1863. Also, a precursor to early television was invented in 1884. Wire services for photographs began in 1925, and the first scanned color separations were created in 1937. Now the stage was set for the first affordable desktop scanner. It did not arrive until the mid-1980s, with a price tag of well over $1,000 USD, and it was only capable of duplicating gray scale images. During this same period of time, image-editing software such as Adobe Photoshop was developed to manipulate these digital photographic images.

Key Applications for Scanners

Scanners are used to capture photographs for image manipulation, Web page design, output to desktop printers, and the creation of halftones and color separation. In addition, three-dimensional objects can be scanned or digitized as well. Both high-resolution images for print production and low-resolution images for desktop presentations can be created through image scanning. When Optical Character Recognition (OCR) software is applied to a scanned image of a text page, that text can become editable, in the form of file types such as ASCII text files and word processing documents. Additionally, OCR allows for hard copy material from bulky books to be made faxable, and information forms to be reproduced for easy completion, without the need to rekey text in a word processor.

How a Scanner Works

A scanner is similar to a digital camera, in that it uses a CCD (or PMT, photo-multiplier tube) with sensors to capture an image. On a flatbed scanner, for example, a moving light bar passes under an image that has been placed face down on a glass platen. The light that reflects from the surface of the image is directed to a sensor array consisting of light-sensitive elements that capture the image as it passes across the original. A small, wafer-thin, light-sensitive cell (the CCD) is covered with thousands of photodiodes that measure electrical activity, and the light energy is used to measure the intensity of every part of the original. The measured data is then reconstructed in a computer, pixel by pixel.

Analog-to-Digital Converter (ADC): a device that converts continuous or analog signals into binary or digital data, which then takes the form of 0s and 1s. This is the process that occurs when analog information, such as light, is converted into binary data, such as digital photographs.

The light that is registered is infinitely adjustable in a smooth, continuous analog flow, yet in the digital world, measurements are made in distinct steps. With adequate resolution, the scanned image and the monitor present the visual illusion that the image is as continuous in digital form as it is in analog form. While a CCD in the scanner physically passes over the original image, the driver software allows for image manipulation and adjustments that need to be set prior to scanning.

Six Basic Types of Scanners

The basic types of scanners range from those that can be carried by hand to a library and used with a laptop computer through those used in professional prepress production houses.

Handheld

Film/Transparency

Flatbed

Video Frame Grabbers

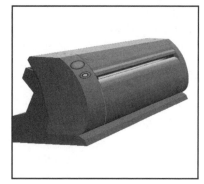

Sheet-fed

Drum

Types of Scanners: An Overview of Advantages and Disadvantages

Flatbed Scanners	Advantages	Disadvantages
■ input flat material such as prints, illustrations, maps, text, and any two-dimensional work ■ glass platen/light source under the surface ■ motor moves the light source and sensor across the surface of the image ■ either linear or trilinear arrays read the image in either one or three passes to create RGB files ■ optionally, offer a transparency adapter for rear illumination of transparent materials	■ can be competitively priced and offer a variety of specifications ■ generally easy to set up and use ■ ideal for OCR and line art ■ work well in a network/group environment	■ large footprint—take up a good deal of flat workspace ■ need special, costly attachments for transparencies which do not always yield high-quality scans of film

Sheet-Fed Scanners	Advantages	Disadvantages
■ work like a fax machine, the image rolls past the light source and the scanning head ■ used to convert paper text to electronic files ■ text may be made editable through OCR software	■ often inexpensive ■ small footprint ■ good for OCR	■ sheets must fit between rollers—width is limited ■ originals must be flexible enough to bend around rollers

Three-D Scanners	Advantages	Disadvantages
■ function like a camera on a copy stand. ■ scan head is focused and adjusted by hand ■ used to scan two- and three-dimensional objects	■ can handle both two- and three-dimensional originals ■ easy to position scanning head	■ require external light source(s), carefully positioned ■ large footprint—similar to a traditional photographic copy stand

Film Transparency Scanners	Advantages	Disadvantages
■ light source projects the slide or negative image onto a sensor ■ motor moves either the light source or the film in one or three passes	■ originals have a wider tonal range, and optimal color saturation ■ quality is preserved when the scan is made from the original, rather than one generation removed	■ film scanners are significantly more costly than flatbed scanners ■ scans may render large files for which larger storage media, more RAM and faster processors are needed ■ specific scanners may not be calibrated for all types of film

Hand-Held Scanners	Advantages	Disadvantages
■ low-level scanners ■ the head contains both the light source and the sensor ■ user drags the head across the image to be scanned ■ scanner fits in the operator's hand or on a stand	■ can scan from items such as oversized books, patterns from fabrics and upholstery, or three-dimensional objects ■ no footprint ■ significantly inexpensive ■ can be used with a laptop for portability	■ scans can appear shaky and unpredictable, as they depend on the movement of the operator's hand ■ the size of the scan is inconvenient for most things, and usually multiple scans must then be "stitched" together with editing software

To Digitize: the process of converting continuous information, such as light waves or a continuous analog video signal, into binary digital image data.

Video Digitizer: an electronic device sometimes referred to as a frame grabber. This device utilizes either a video camera or a special computer interface card to acquire an image and to convert it into digital image data.

Video Digitizers	Advantages	Disadvantages
■ devices that convert signals from VCRs, video cameras, still video cameras, laser disk players, and broadcast TV into digital form by grabbing individual or multiple frames of video ■ operate between a video source and the CPU ■ scanning material originates as electronic signals	■ enables the digitization of analog video signals	■ can often be tricky to make components work well together ■ must have a video source and a computer, in addition to the digitizer ■ even if the equipment may be high-end and costly, true resolution is limited to that of the original video source

Drum Scanners	Advantages	Disadvantages
■ high-end scanning technology, offers the highest possible scan quality of all scanners ■ often larger machines that require highly skilled operators ■ access is more readily available through service bureaus ■ film, photographs, and art work are taped to a cylindrical drum ■ drum revolves and a lamp within focuses a minute spot/laser light through color separation filters ■ photomultiplier tubes (PMTs) attached to each filter convert the light to electronic pulses ■ scan files are typically quite large, and require a computer with a fast processor and plenty of RAM and storage	■ highest possible dynamic range ■ can reveal information impossible to see on an unmagnified original ■ able to achieve highest quality of all scanners ■ fastest speed available, relative to the information scanned	■ high price is prohibitive for small business/individual ownership ■ can only be operated by qualified personnel, and require training for operation, calibration, and maintenance

Elements of Digital Photographic Images

Bitmapped images are a map or grid of bits/pixels, which are pieces of computer information that describe all of the points of information in a grid of dots. Basically, drawing a map of the bits in the image describes the coordinates on both the x and y axis of each sample point. These are the points on a bitmapped graphic that the scanner uses to check for the gray values. The resolution of a bitmap is measured in samples per inch.

Pixels and Bitmap Images

A **pixel** is a picture element (also referred to as a pel). A pixel is one dot in a geometric grid of information that comprises the digital image's information. A pixel is the smallest unit of digital visual information.

All Bitmap Graphics are Made of Pixels

Bitmapped graphics are digital images that are made up of pixels. These images are represented as an array of bits in various computer memory locations, which correspond to the pixels that are displayed on a computer monitor. The individual pixels of information that make up bitmapped images contain all of the image's collective information.

Pixels

Four Basic Characteristics of a Bitmapped Graphic (dimensions, resolution, bit depth, and color space)

The units that image resolution is measured in are pixels. This measure is denoted as pixels per square inch (or other unit of measure) and is also expressed as "ppi." Pixels are data measurements in the computer world, and the equivalent of dots in the nondigital world. The word "pixel" is shorthand for picture element, and represents a data point. On a monitor or printout, pixels look like squares or dots but that shape is dependent on the masking technology of a monitor or printer. The shape of a pixel on screen also depends on how many picture elements exist per area and how much data per pixel (bits per pixel) have been assigned.

As you become more involved with digital imaging, you will notice that the terms dots per inch (dpi) and pixels per inch (ppi) are frequently used interchangeably.

Generally, the greater the number of pixels (dots) that have been scanned in an image, the clearer, sharper and finer the image will appear.

Dimensions:

Bitmapped images are checkerboard-shaped rectangular grids. This grid of pixels makes up your computer screen. However, this does not describe the size of the image. That is, the dimension of the image does not describe how close together the samples are to each other, thus the number of samples is not the sole measurement of an image's size. The dimensions of the image are described in terms of resolution with respect to the height and width of an image.

Resolution:

This is the number of dots (pixels) assigned or mapped to a given space. Resolution refers to the amount of visual information contained in a specific area of an image, where the height, width, and number of pixels per inch determine the overall image resolution. Resolution is described in differing ways:

- scanners use spi (samples per inch)
- printers use spi (samples per inch) and more commonly, dpi (dots per inch)
- display screens use ppi (pixels per inch)
- halftone screens use lpi (lines per inch)

The number of samples in each unit of measurement describes the resolution of a bitmapped image, in units such as inches or centimeters. For example, let's say you have an image at a resolution of 72 pixels per inch (ppi) in a one-inch by one-inch image.

In this case, you will have 72 pixels along each side of the image which means that this image contains 5,184 pixels of information. However, if you change the resolution to 36 ppi, keeping the file size the same, the image size changes to two inches per side where the pixels are twice as large and the image size is quadrupled—an increase of 200 percent both horizontally and vertically—arriving at a two-inch by two-inch image at 36 ppi with a loss of 50 percent of the visual information.

Whereas, if you change the resolution from 72 ppi to 144 ppi, the resolution of the image is doubled and the file size is increased by four, while retaining a one-inch by one-inch aspect ratio. It is significant to note that this will not generate more detail in your image, however.

Yet conversely, if you change the resolution to 144 ppi (from 72 ppi) and resample the image, the resolution is doubled, the file size remains the same, and the print size is reduced—a decrease of 50 percent both horizontally and vertically—arriving at a half-inch by half-inch image at 144 ppi with the illusion of an increase in visual information.

Therefore, remember that although the resolution of the image may have been doubled in your image editing software, the true resolution of an image is tied to the original scan resolution.

In digital photography, resolution seems to be one of the most misunderstood concepts. Yet this is one of the most fundamental issues to comprehend, in terms of achieving a strong base upon which to build an image. Basically, resolution can be defined as a number of dots assigned or "mapped" to a given space.

The objective in choosing the resolution of an image is to match the spi of the scanned image as closely as possible to the requirements for the eventual image output. Most scanner driver software will allow you to set the output dimensions for your image, and the number of dots per inch of resolution you want to have in your image. Driver software is the software that controls the device and is provided by the scanner manufacturer. The following is a formula that can be used to calculate the appropriate resolution at which to scan an image:

Scanning Resolution Formula

$$(O_{tw} / O_{rw}) \times O_{res} = S_{res}$$

First: divide the output width $[O_{tw}]$ by the width of the original $[O_{rw}]$ to equal the resolution factor $[R_f]$

Second: multiply the resolution factor [Rf] by the intended output resolution $[O_{res}]$ dpi or spi

Third: the resultant will be the necessary spi at which to scan the original—Scan Resolution $[S_{res}]$

The formula above is intended for continuous tone images, including photographs. If your output is intended for use as a halftone print, such as a photograph in a newspaper or the printed page of a magazine or a book, you need to increase the size of the output width by 1.5 to 2. Essentially, the rule of thumb here is that you should scan an image at a number of samples per inch (spi) that is one and one-half to two times greater than the halftone screen frequency that is to be used for the reproduction of the image. Generally a factor of 1.5 is sufficient. Your commercial printer or service bureau will usually tell you what their preferred resolution is, based upon their workflow requirements.

Example: Calculating Scan Resolution for Halftone Output

Halftone screen = 150 lines per inch (lpi)

Therefore, the final scan should be at:

225 spi [150 x 1.5 = 225] or

300 spi [150 x 2 = 300]

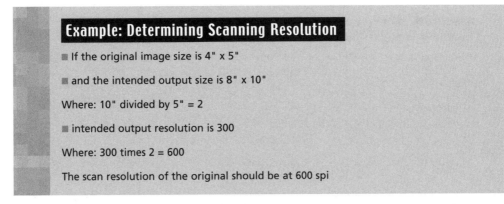

Example: Determining Scanning Resolution

■ If the original image size is 4" x 5"

■ and the intended output size is 8" x 10"

Where: 10" divided by 5" = 2

■ intended output resolution is 300

Where: 300 times 2 = 600

The scan resolution of the original should be at 600 spi

When scanning an image at a specific resolution such as 200 spi, this does not necessarily mean that the final image resolution will be the same. This is because scaling and resampling are also part of the process. For instance, if you place a scanned image on a page and rescale it, you change the image resolution. Each time you rescale an image, you change the resolution unless the image is resampled. Additionally, resizing a bitmapped image without affecting the resolution, or changing the resolution of a bitmap without changing its size, is called resampling. In this process, pixel dimensions are changed and so is the file size,but the resolution can remain the same.

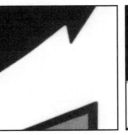

Scan Resolution and Interpolation

300 dpi interpolated image (left)

72 dpi scan (right)

As for the process of downsampling, this process removes samples throughout the image— generally in order to reduce the size of the image. Whereas, the process of interpolation generates sample points in a bitmap where there were none before. With interpolation, pixels are sampled on either side of the generated sample, and an average between the two is chosen. While even though some software has the ability to reduce aliasing— also known as "jaggies"—through the process of antialiasing, the resulting interpolated image may still look grainy or out of focus because this process cannot add detail. Interpolation can only artificially expand the image. Therefore, it is best to determine the resolution needed in the final image before the image is scanned, and to create the scan accordingly (see the table on Aliasing and Resolution).

Aliasing and Resolution

Aliasing, in digital imaging, is the visual appearance of jagged edges, or stairstepping of visual elements—where a smooth appearance is desired.T his is sometimes referred to as "jaggies."

Antialiasing refers to the process of visually smoothing out jagged or stairstepped edges within an image that displays aliased edges.

Resolution refers to the amount and precision f detail in an image. Also, resolution is commonly used to describe the amount of data that can be captured or displayed by various imaging devices such as digital cameras, computer/video monitors, and of course scanning devices.

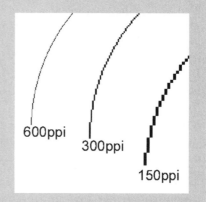

Low-resolution pertains to an image that has a small amount of information to describe its details, and thus appears coarse or grainy.

High-resolution pertains to an image that has a great deal of information to describe its details, and thus appears fine and has a great amount of clarity.

Scan Resolution and File Size

| | | | Image Size in Bytes | | |
Scanning Resolution	Image Size 8x10 inches	Number of Pixels per Image	Color Image 24-bit	Gray-scale Image 8-bit	Line Art Image 1-bit
200 spi	1600x1200	1,920,000	5,760,000	1,920,000	720,000
400 spi	3200x2400	7,680,000	23,040,000	7,680,000	960,000
800 spi	6400x4800	30,720,000	92,160,000	30,720,000	3,840,000

When the scan resolution is being determined, it is important to consider the size of the file versus the pixelation of the image. If the resolution is set high enough to create a high-resolution image of large dimensions, the resulting file size may be so large that all actions in an image manipulation program will be slow and will require a lot of memory. Also, the file will require a large amount of storage space. On the other hand, if the resolution is set too low, the resulting image may appear "grainy" and not very sharp. With digital images, there is always a trade-off between file size and image quality.

Calculating Image Memory Requirements

To determine how large an image will be, you can use the following formula. All you need to know is the height, width, and dpi of the image.

For an 8 x 10 inch image at 200 dpi, the calculation for determining image size is:

(8 inches x 200 dpi) x (10 inches x 200 dpi) = 1600 x 2000 pixels

Then you multiply by the three reserved bytes assigned to each pixel (1 byte per channel) to store its RGB color information. And you arrive at:

1600 x 2000 x 3 = 5.76 million bytes (9,375K or 9.155MB)

Remember: There are 8bits per byte. In this example, this image contains: 46,080,000 bits of information.

Types of Resolution: We have discussed the importance of determining image resolution before scanning to achieve the best possible foundation image from a scanner. The fact is that there are different types of resolution, and each type of resolution refers to a different aspect of the scan quality. The type of resolution we have discussed so far is spatial or optical resolution. This determines the image size and the number of pixels per inch of information from which the image will be composed.

Sometimes a scanner manufacturer will advertise a scanner as having two types of resolution, one higher than the other. The higher resolution is actually an interpolated resolution. It refers to the same idea of generating pixels where there were none, as discussed earlier regarding the resampling of an image. Interpolated resolution is not exclusively comprised of real information. It is information that is generated by the computer to make the image larger, by filling in the spaces between the optically sampled points. Therefore the resulting image may look soft, as if out of focus, and may not have clearly defined detail in the generated pixels. Hence, the true measure of a scanner's ability is the spatial/optical resolution and the gamut or dynamic range of the device.

Dynamic range refers to the brightness aspect of resolution. The number of gray levels your scanner can produce determines the dynamic range of the image. In photographic terms, dynamic range refers to the number of f-stops or zones of tonal information in the image. A scanner's dynamic range is dependent upon the maximum optical density and the number of bits per pixel it can capture, with respect to the detail it can capture from shadow through highlight.

Bit Depth:

This refers to the number of levels of information contained in each pixel or sample. Each sample can be black, white, or a shade of gray, and the indicator is the number of bits used to describe the sample.

- The number of bits of information that determine the image's depth in terms of levels of gray and color is referred to as the image's bit depth.
- Image bit depth is referenced as: 1-bit = 2 levels, 8-bit = 256 levels, etc. (see the table on Image Bit Depth below)
- The bit depth also has an exponential effect on the file size of an (see the table on Color space/model, bit depth, and file size below)

Understanding Dynamic Range

What is Dynamic Range?

Dynamic Range refers to the overall range of brightness or image density. An image's density is measured on a scale of 0 through 4 plus, where 0 is absolute white and 4 is black, but not the theoretical limit. These image densities are measured with a densitometer for sensitometric purposes. With respect to digital scanning technologies, these density values are referred to as Dmax and Dmin—as with traditional photographic imaging. This scale of density is logarithmic in nature. Thus, a density range of 10:1 = 1.0, 100:1 = 2.0, 1,000:1 = 3, and 10,000:1 = 4.0.

To understand this in practical terms, let's say you are considering purchasing a scanner, and the manufacturer has stated that this device has a Dmax value of 3.4 and a Dmin value of 0.2. To calculate the dynamic range for this scanner use the following formula:

Dmax-Dmin = Dynamic Range

So, in this example: 3.4 minus 0.2 = 3.2.

And thus, this scanner has a dynamic range of 3.2.

What this generally means in photographic terms is that the greater the dynamic range of a device, the greater the shadow detail in the scanned image—after all other factors are considered.

Approximate dynamic ranges for images:

A color photographic print: 2.0+/-

A color slide: 3.3+/-

A color negative: 2.9+/-

A color photograph as reproduced in a book or magazine: 2.0+/-

Image depth:

Every pixel is made up of data bits associated with color and luminance information. A bit is the smallest piece of computer information, and the more bits per pixel, the greater the depth of information that can be stored in a pixel. Twenty-four-bit devices produce eight bits of grayscale information per color channel for each of the three primary colors: red, green, and blue (RGB). And, the deeper the bit depth is per scan, the more bits per pixel and image information are acquired. However, keep in mind that more data equals larger file sizes. So, for greater data depth, large storage space and more RAM will be necessary to save and work on these images.

Image Bit Depth

- 1 bit = either black or white
- 2 bits = 4 possible combinations of color or gray levels
- 8 bits = 256 levels of gray
- 24 bits (3 – 8-bit channels - RGB) over 16 million possible colors
- 32 bits (4 – 8-bit channels - CMYK)
- 48 bits (4 – 12-bit channels)

As stated, resolution in the scanner is measured in samples. Here, each sample can be black, white, a shade of gray, or a color. The number of bits used to describe each sample will be fundamental to the image's quality and ability to reproduce tones and color (see the following illustrations on 1-bit, 2-bit, and 8-bit images).

In the table above (Image Bit Depth), the number of bits is referred to as the image's bit depth. One bit would be a flat or bilevel map. More than one bit creates a deeper bitmap—where the number of bits also affects image size. For example, an 8-bit image is eight times the size of a 1-bit image, because eight bits are used to describe each pixel. Full-color photographs are usually scanned, where twenty-four bits is the minimum number required to describe a thee-color (RGB) bitmapped image with eight bits of information per pixel, per color channel—red, green, and blue (see the table on scanner bit depth and color reproduction).

Scanner Bit Depth and Color Reproduction

■ 1 bit scanner	2 levels of gray (2 to the 1st power)—black and white—used for scanning line art
■ 2 bit scanner	4 levels of gray (2 to the 2nd power)
■ 3 bit scanner	8 levels of gray (2 to the 3rd power)
■ 8 bit scanner	256 levels of gray (2 to the 8th power) starting point for high quality scanning
■ 24 bit scanner	over 16.7 million colors (2 to the 24th power) the least number of colors required for an RGB image: yielding 8 bits per pixel per color channel—RGB
■ 36 bit scanner	over 68.7 billion colors (2 to the 36th power)
■ 48 bit scanner	over 281.4 trillion colors (2 to the 48th power)

1-bit Image   **2-bit Image**   **8-bit Image**

Color Spaces and Gamut

Art available in color. Please see insert for further study.

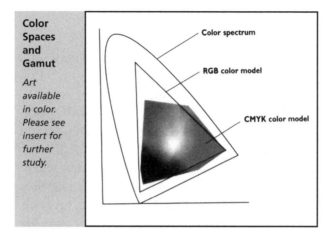

Color spectrum

RGB color model

CMYK color model

Color Space/Model:

This refers to the environment in which a digital image exists, and is defined by the gamut it can represent. An image's gamut represents the range of colors that can be output by a color system. It is significant to note that the human eye can see a greater range than any gamut available for any digital imaging color model that utilizes visible light. One of the most common color spaces for screen display of images is the RGB (or red, green, blue) color space.

Generally, twenty-four bits per pixel represent full color images in this color space, where eight-bits of information for each color channel exists. Another standard color space refers to process colors: CMYK (or cyan, magenta, yellow, black) is generally represented by 32 bits of information, and eight-bits of information for each color channel. The increase does not actually add more color; it is simply a different way of describing colors. The color space or color mode has a direct bearing on file size. As illustrated in the table below, you can see the direct coloration between color space/mode in the bit depth and file size for an image having the same height and width, in different image modes.

Color Space/Mode, Bit Depth and File Size

Image Mode bit depth & file size comparisons for an image of equal dimensions	
CMYK	36.2mb/8bits per channel or 72.4 mb /16bits per channel
RGB	27.2 mb/8bits per channel or 54.3 mb /16bits per channel
Lab Color	27.2 mb/8bits per channel
Indexed Color	9.05 mb/8bits per channel
Gray Scale	9.05 mb/8bits per channel
Bitmap	1.14 mb/1bit per channel

Additionally, there are other color spaces that are created for color management systems. These spaces help systems describe color profiles from one device (such as a scanner or camera) through to the output (print or film). They are described in our chapter on color management.

The Scanning Process

Plug-In Folder: Adobe Photoshop

The way in which different scanners acquire image data varies depending upon the type of scanner and its intended application. Many times, scanner driver software is packaged as an image manipulation program extension, such as a Photoshop plug-in. Once scanned via a plug-in, the image automatically becomes a file in that program. Whereas, a standalone driver will require that the scanned image be saved as an image file, before reopening it in an image manipulation program for editing.

Twain Acquire Module: HP S20 Film Scanner

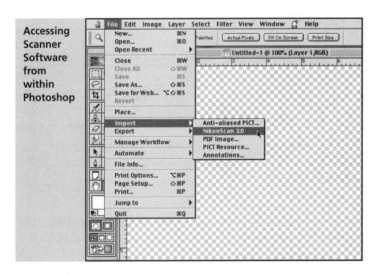

Accessing Scanner Software from within Photoshop

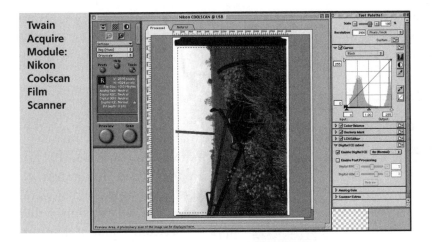

Twain Acquire Module: Nikon Coolscan Film Scanner

The scanning process generally begins with a low-resolution preview. At this point the user can crop and set the image area to be scanned, scale the image, set the number of samples per inch to scan, determine the bit depth of the scan, and adjust the gamma and other settings that are appropriate to achieving a high-quality scan of the original.

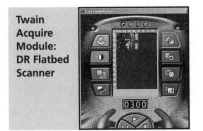

Twain Acquire Module: DR Flatbed Scanner

Then the row or rows of photodiodes can make one or three passes for all three primary colors (RGB). Remember, this is the foundation for your image, and it pays to spend a little time before scanning to make sure you will acquire the highest quality image your scanner is capable of rendering.

Twain Acquire: Adobe Photoshop

The speed of a scan is largely a function of the speed of the scanning head and its sensitivity, the hardware circuitry, and the method used to connect the scanner to the computer. The size and resolution of the scan can also affect the speed of the scanner. Some scanners can be optimized for either speed or accuracy. Usually, when scanning photographs or transparencies, you will want to optimize for accuracy. This is because increased speed is normally less important unless your volume is high and the requisite quality of the image is a lesser issue.

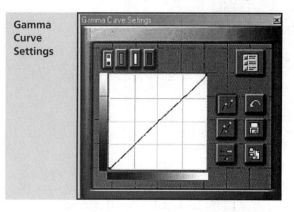

Gamma Curve Settings

Nearly all consumer scanners use solid state sensing devices (CCDs), while high-end drum scanners utilize photomultiplier tubes (PMTs) to scan the image. Regardless of the type of scanner, a software interface is needed to control the optical, electronic, and mechanical functions of the scanner. This software can usually save an image in a variety of formats that can be understood by different image-enhancing software.

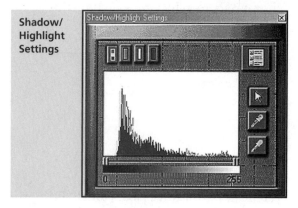

Shadow/ Highlight Settings

Remember, the objective in scanning is to match the spi of the scanned image as closely as possible to the eventual image requirements. This is based upon reproduction size, while keeping the file size as small and manageable as possible.

Choosing a Scanner

The following is a list of questions that need to be addressed in order to determine what type of scanner is appropriate for your needs:

- What is the intended use of the image?
- What is the necessary size of the output or reproduction?
- What level of quality do you need?
- What can you afford to spend?

Note that to match quality of a traditional silver-based image requires scanners that cost more than most individual photographers can normally afford, unless they producing a high-volume work and have an continuing need. Therefore, here are some more specific criteria to consider when choosing a scanner:

- speed
- accuracy
- optical resolution and spatial resolution in terms of spi and bit depth
- dynamic range

Individual requirements:

- two- and three-dimensional film and/or flat art, portability
- level of quality required
- footprint

More issues to consider:

- Speed is usually not the most important factor. However, it may be important if you do high-volume work.
- Accuracy refers to how closely the scan resembles the original and depends on faithful color reproduction, the bit depth, and the resolution capabilities of the scanner.
- Optical and spatial resolution refer to how many bits per pixel the scanner can achieve, and to how many samples per inch the scanner can create.
- The dynamic range of the scanner needs to be adequate enough to capture enough shadow and highlight detail to serve your purpose.

General Rules of Scanning

A Quick Guide to Scanning

The following are general rules of thumb that may aid you in determining scan resolution.

 Note that it is always better to calculate the exact amount of information required for a particular scan. This can be accomplished by utilizing the formulas presented in this chapter.

You need to know the final print size first. Then, if you aren't sure what scan resolution to use, try these:

Line Art: Match the resolution to the dpi output of your printer or output device,i.e. a 720 spi scan, to be printed on a 720 x 720 dpi inkjet printer will reduce aliasing or "jaggies."

Line Art: For **OCR,** 300 spi is a standard setting;much more or less information can cause problems.

Black-and-White or Color Photographs: When in doubt, scan at 300 spi at the final print dimensions. This will give you enough information for four-color offset print reproduction, thermal dye-sublimation printing, high-resolution inkjet printing, etc...

Alternatives to Ownership

The use of **service bureaus** may be worthy of consideration. These are businesses that serve the photographic, graphic arts, and electronic prepress industries—and are often equipped with a range of scanners, including drum scanners. They can range from small shops that service individual photographers and desktop publishers to large operations serving ad agencies and professional publishers (see Chapter 9, Service Bureaus). Additionally, at times it may be better to consider having your negatives and/or slides scanned and written to a picture CD or a photo CD, rather than to invest in a specialized scanner (see the table below on Image Sizes from Kodak Photo CD scans).

Image Sizes from Kodak Photo CD Scans

Image Size (pixels)	Kodak Photo CD Specifications	Image size (bytes)
2048 x 3072	Base*16	18,874,368
1024 x 1536	Base*4 (same resolution as HDTV)	4,718,592
512 x 768	Base (same resolution as TV)	1,179,648
256 x 384	Base/4 (Thumbnail)	294,912
128 x 192	Base/16 (Small Thumbnail)	73,728
6144 x 4096	Base*64 Pro-Photo CD ONLY!	78,643,200

On the other hand, if you own a business with high-volume output, owning a specialized scanner may be more cost-effective.

Additional Factors and Problems with the Scanning Equation

Utilizing the scan resolution formula, as described earlier, is not difficult. All you really need to know is the size and resolution at which the image will be printed, in addition to the size of the original. However, keep in mind that inadequate resolution produces an image that will look grainy and out of focus when printed. If the resolution is set too high for your output device, you will waste computer time and storage space to manipulate and store your image. Whereas, if the image is to be output in several different ways, the scan should be created for the highest resolution output device, and the following generations of the image can be down-sampled.

As discussed earlier, scanners operate by breaking down an image into a grid of pixels. The amount of information contained in a pixel is determined by how many bits or levels of tones a scanner can record. The more bits per pixel, the more levels of gray and the finer the grade of the image rendered. However, more bits per pixel in an image translate into exponentially increased file sizes.

Some scanners have a maximum bit depth that is not based upon the 8-bit per channel model, such as a 30-bit scanner. Of these types of scanners, some can also scan 10, 12, and 16 bits per pixel, per channel. However, keep in mind that, just as important as the bit depth of a scanner is to file size, so too the gamut or dynamic range of a scanner is significant, in terms of its ability to reproduce image fidelity.

There are problems with this equation though. Not all 8-bit and 24-bit scanners can capture the same amount of information. If you scan the same image with two different 8-bit flatbed scanners, for instance, one may do an excellent job of discerning subtle differences in gray levels while showing a good deal of detail in shadow areas. Whereas, another may give you a scan in which all the shadow areas are a uniform black or dark gray. Compared to the first scanner in this example, the second scanner has a poor dynamic range.

The problem here is noise. Just as static on the radio can obscure the quality of music, noise from a bad scanner can obscure important image information in the scanning process—especially in the shadow areas. For example, the first six bits from an 8-bit scanner may be accurate. However, the seventh and eighth bit may be less accurate, where the sensor may have trouble distinguishing between the next 64 and 128 levels of gray. Hence, the final scan may be lacking in shadow detail. Note that most 8-bit scanners cannot actually distinguish between the full 256 levels of gray.

This problem can be managed in high-quality scanners that capture more than eight bits of information per pixel. For instance, if a scanner captures twelve bits of data per channel, the information can be resampled down to eight accurate bits of information per sample point through image-editing software—after the original has been scanned at the deeper bit depth. This technique is known as oversampling.

Conclusions

As you can see, there are a number of technical factors that need to be considered before you commit to a particular type of scanner. Even when the type of scanner has been determined, there are many choices and decisions to be considered. The good news is that once these initial decisions are made, your workflow will actually simplify to some degree—assuming the correct scanner selection choices have been made.

If you consider the choices of the "scanning" or "image acquisition" tools and materials which have been available to the traditional photographer, and their inherent technical restrictions, choosing the correct digital scanning equipment is much akin to choosing what type of film to shoot, what type of developer to use, or which lens to utilize.

In the next chapter, we will discuss alternative ways to acquire images into digital form, and ways in which you can use various acquisition techniques for different production workflows.

Of course, finally, once you have the image in digital form you are ready to begin working in the digital darkroom.

Review Questions:

1 The number of bits assigned to each pixel in a grayscale image determines the number of levels of _____ that are displayed on the screen.

2 What are the three primary additive colors of light?

What are the three subtractive primary colors of light?

What are the four subtractive primary colors used by commercial printers and devices such as inkjet printers?

3 Name the six basic types of scanners.

a. _____

b. _____

c. _____

d. _____

e. _____

f. _____

4 Describe the advantage of making corrections with the scanner software before the scan is completed.

5 What does OCR stand for?

Why would one want a scanner that has OCR capabilities?

6 What are some primary considerations when deciding to buy a scanner?

What are some primary considerations when deciding to use a commercial scanning service?

7 Resolution is an important consideration when preparing up to make a scan. There are three primary considerations when deciding on the scan resolution. They are:

a. _____

b. _____

c. _____

Discussion Questions:

1 High quality scanners and expensive image-enhancement software may be wasted on a poor quality original. Explain why this is so.

2 The magic of the digital darkroom can expand on qualities of photographs that may not have as much merit when printed as they had been in the traditional darkroom. What are some important considerations to keep in mind when transforming images in the digital environment?

3 When do traditional photographs offer more than digital images?

Why?

4 When do digital images offer more than traditional photographs?

Why?

CHAPTER

4

Alternative Image Acquisition Applications and File Management

Objectives:

This chapter will explore alternative devices and techniques, for image capture and image archiving. Here you will learn how to input and archive digital images. Upon completion of this chapter, you should have a better understanding of:

- How to use commercial scanning services to produce Photo CDs, picture disks, and picture CDs
- How to address specialized scanning problems
- How to use image input devices as creative tools
- How to archive digital images using CDs, DVDs, and file management software

Introduction

The computer has bestowed upon photography what photography gave to painting in the middle 1800s: the opportunity to visually expand our creative horizons. Now, in the age of electronic images, we are presented with a new model from which to extrapolate concepts, ideas, and visualizations. This model—electronic media-based imaging—opens up worlds of potential to the visual communicator. This is because we have now passed the point where this new media is trying to imitate traditional photography—it has taken on its own attributes by which it has become distinguished. This means that, as a creative tool, digital photography has opened up exciting possibilities to photographers.

Through alternative image acquisition techniques, new creative possibilities for visual interpretations of subject matter are presented to the photographer. Therefore, in the spirit of innovation and creativity, this chapter will explore alternatives to the traditional models of image acquisition, and different ways to archive and store your digital images.

Alternative Image Acquisition: Photo CD, Picture CD, and Picture Disk

To begin this discussion, let us briefly revisit the ideas presented in the last chapter. In the traditional sense, image acquisition deals with acquiring an image from sources such as a flatbed scanner, a film scanner, or a drum scanner—and obviously a digital camera. Furthermore, some alternative image acquisition technologies were discussed, such as handheld scanners and digitizers, and the Photo CD.

Here, we are going to elaborate upon the utilization and application of such technologies as the Photo CD, the picture CD, and the picture disk. To begin, consider what these three technologies have in common. First, all of these technologies are service-based forms of image acquisition (see Chapter 9, Service Bureaus). Next, all of these technologies involve a hybrid process of image acquisition. Finally, all of these offer the image to the photographer in a digital format that is ready for utilization in the digital darkroom—the computer.

Hybrid Technologies

A hybrid technology is one that bridges a gap between two different technologies. In photography, such technologies as the Photo CD, the picture CD, and the picture disk act as intermediate technologies that enable the cross-pollination of visual information between traditional silver-based photographic media and digital photography.

This essentially means that a photographer utilizing film as a recording media can have that film digitized as easily as the film itself can be processed at a service bureau. What this means for photography is that photographs do not necessarily need to be shot with a digital camera in order to pursue digital photography.

Before discussing the particular details of these forms of image acquisition, some larger issues should be examined. In terms of restrictions, all of these technologies offer varying degrees of limitation, based upon the amount of information that is scanned and the resulting image resolution. Regarding the advantages of each, the shorter amount of time spent by the photographer is one of the greatest benefits. Additionally, these technologies are scalable in that they offer differing levels of visual information based upon specific needs—and accordingly, differing levels of expense. All of these hybrid technologies present interesting possibilities to the photographer.

Photo CD

First developed and implemented by Kodak in 1990, the Photo CD was designed as a consumer-level product that would enable individuals to view their images on a television, and to share these images with computer users as well. The Photo CD was modified in 1992 to accommodate the needs of professionals, and the KODAK Photo CD Image Pac file format became the industry-wide agreed upon digital image file standard.

The Kodak PCD file (or Image Pac) is the basis for the digitally scanned Photo CD image. At the consumer level, scanning any black-and-white or color negative or slide can create this CD. At the professional level, medium- and large-format film —up to 4" x 5" — can also be scanned and recorded to a Photo CD. The Image Pac file format comprises a totally dedicated color-encoding scheme called Photo YCC, developed by Kodak. This is a device-independent, multiresolution image format.

In addition to the Kodak Photo CD, other versions of this technology exist through manufacturers such as Fuji Film.

Photo CD: Format and Size

- Support of Multiple Display Resolutions
- Fast Access to Video Resolution
- Practical Disc Capacity
- Device-Independent Color Encoding

The format was designed to accommodate standard television resolution, High-Definition TV resolution, and a higher resolution for printed "photo" output. Additionally low-resolution images (thumbnails) of all the images on a disc are included.

Pro Photo CD also includes higher resolution images for scanning and storing medium- and large-format film, such as 2-1/4" and 4" x 5" images.

Because a 35 mm RGB image scanned at a resolution of 2048 x 3072 pixels yields an 18MB file, the Photo CD format compresses its images. Additionally, because there are five versions of each image scanned to a CD, there is a need to conserve CD space. Therefore, with the Photo CD format, the base resolution of an image is saved to the CD and the data needed for each resolution is drawn from that base resolution. This creates each of the five different image resolutions from the one base resolution data file.

Picture Disk

This file format was developed to encourage the amateur photo market to become more involved with digital photography. Picture disks let the users have digital access to their photographs without needing to own scanning equipment. This service-based imaging technology provides low-resolution digital scans of film negatives or positives. The files are approximately 50K to 60K in size, are scanned in RGB color, and are saved as compressed jpeg images. This scan produces an image that has a resolution of 768 x 512 pixels at 72 spi. These images are provided to the consumer on a double-sided high-density floppy disk. On the Fuji brand disk, the consumer is provided with an image browsing software application and a user's manual (see following illustrations).

Fuji Picture Disk and Picture CD Online Manual

Contents

Browsing and editing JPEG images is easy using the Image Viewer application. View all images in the current set as thumbnails, run an automatic slide show, or enlarge individual images for editing. Modify the images using the rotation, zoom, or pan tools, and save the changes for future sessions. Copy or save the images in a variety of formats and print them individually or as a group.

The vertical toolbar and the rotation buttons are available in both thumbnail and single-image views, while the remaining editing functions in the horizontal toolbar are available only in single-image view.

The following help topics are available:

Viewing Images

Editing Images

Saving Changes

Running a Slide Show

Saving Images

Printing Images

The primary applications for this type of image acquisition are:

- Consumer digital imaging
- Web sharing of photographs
- Personal Web publishing
- Use in low-resolution publications such as newsletters or "thumbnail" type real estate guides.

The following figures illustrate various views of the software interface, which is supplied with the Fujicolor picture disk and picture CD:

Thumbnail View Window of Supplied Viewing Software: Fujicolor Picture Disk, Software by Walmart Digital Imaging

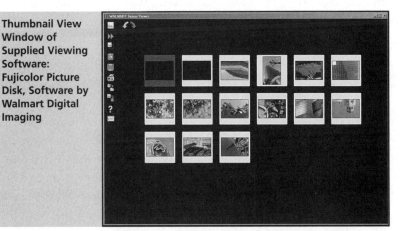

Single-Image Window of Supplied Viewing Software: Fujicolor CD, Software by Walmart Digital Imaging

Sample Image from a Fuji Picture Disk

The "Paris" image is from a picture disk. For low-resolution output, or small reproduction sizes, the picture disk offers an affordable alternative to scanning your own images. Also, it should be noted that although these images are from a "Fuji" picture disk/CD, Kodak and others offer the same services.

Kodak Picture CD

To the left is an illustration of a Kodak Picture CD. This media can store up to 100 image packs, containing five resolutions of each image, derived from one base resolution scan (see the Kodak Photo CD sidebar). Below is an illustration from the Microsoft Picture It! image-editing software, which is supplied for free on the Fuji brand picture CD.

The Fujicolor Picture CD (Windows) comes with Microsoft Picture It! Express software.

Special Scanning Problems

At times, the scanning process may involve more than just laying the original on a scanner and adjusting the software settings. Certain types of images may challenge the technical limitations of the scanner. The discussion that follows explains some common problems regarding images that are difficult to scan.

Removing the Orange Color Negative Mask

Most modern scanners automatically remove the color mask when an image is scanned. Here we will discuss how the scanning process works. Although the following visuals are in black and white, the concept of each of these procedures can still be understood through these illustrations. (Also, see illustrations in the color section of this book.)

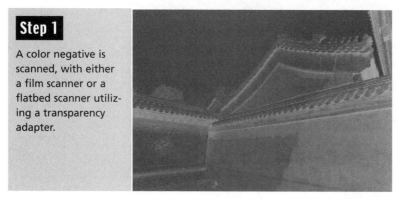

Step 1

A color negative is scanned, with either a film scanner or a flatbed scanner utilizing a transparency adapter.

Step 2

A new adjustment layer is created, in the layers palette.

The layer needs to be a curves layer.

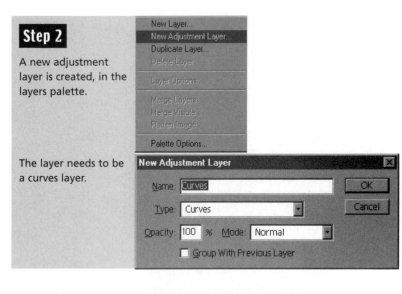

Step 3

With the RGB channel(s) selected, click the Auto button. This will equalize the color in each channel and will remove the orange colored mask.

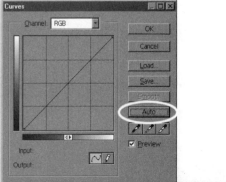

The resulting image will look like this:

Step 4

Next, vertically drag the ends of the curve to the opposite side of the graph, as illustrated.

Now the image looks like a color positive of the negative scan.

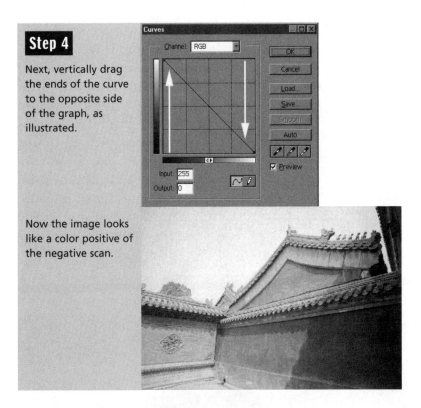

Step 5

Finally, double-click the curves layer and make some fine-tuning adjustments to the image, as illustrated at right.

Manually adjusted image from color negative scan

Here you can see the difference between a manually adjusted image and an automatically adjusted image. The software, in this case the Hewlett Packard S20 scanning software, does quite a good job in correcting for the color negatives orange mask. Our manually adjusted example still needs a bit of work to even match the straight scan that was automatically reversed and color mask corrected with the HP S20 software.

Automatically reversed and Color-Corrected Negative Scan

Alternative Scanning Techniques

Rezing-Up

The process of "rezing-up" (or resing-up) refers to that process which appears to increase the resolution of a bitmap image with aliasing (jaggies). In reality, this process does not increase the image's resolution. Actually, the image's quality is first degraded to blur the stairstepped edges of the bitmap image. Next, the soft gray blurred areas are removed, and the result is an image that contains fewer jagged edges. This is a technique that can save old images or bad bitmap scans. However, it is always best to begin with the highest quality artwork and the best scan possible. The following illustration exemplifies this process.

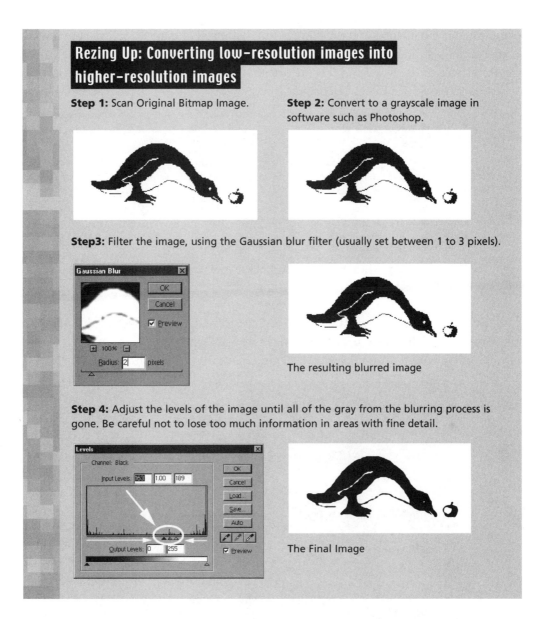

Rezing Up: Converting low-resolution images into higher-resolution images

Step 1: Scan Original Bitmap Image.

Step 2: Convert to a grayscale image in software such as Photoshop.

Step3: Filter the image, using the Gaussian blur filter (usually set between 1 to 3 pixels).

The resulting blurred image

Step 4: Adjust the levels of the image until all of the gray from the blurring process is gone. Be careful not to lose too much information in areas with fine detail.

The Final Image

Halftone Images

When scanning halftone images, the dot pattern of the image will become more visible. The examples that follow suggest ways in which to visually reduce the effect of the halftone screen on the image. The process used is dependent upon the particular image and the type of screen utilized in the halftone. Variables such as the frequency of the screen, the shape of the dots, and the angle of the screen all contribute to the degradation of the image—and the choices you will need to make to salvage the image. Furthermore, distracting patterns can be formed in the image due to the angle of the screen, relative to the way in which the image is scanned. These patterns are called a *moiré* effect (see Moiré Effect sidebar).

Moiré Effect

The effect that occurs when a repetitive pattern like a grid is overlaid on either the same or another repetitive pattern, which produces a pattern that is distinct from the original design or pattern.

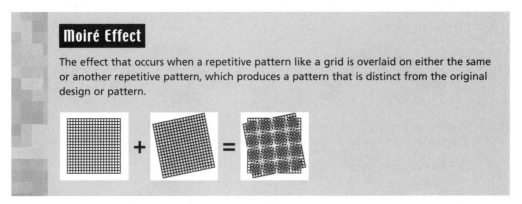

The following figures illustrate two processes to reduce the effect of the halftone screen on images that have been scanned. Figure 1 illustrates the initial scan of the halftone image, and figure 2 shows the distinct pattern of the halftone screen.

**Figure 1:
Original
Scan of
Halftone
Image**

**Figure 2:
Detail of
Halftone
Screen**

This next image illustrates how the Photoshop "despeckle" filter reduces the visual noise of the halftone screen on the scanned image.

Figure 3: Halftone image processed with the Photoshop despeckle filter.

Another method of reducing the effect of the halftone screen involves several steps. First, the image is blurred using the Gaussian blur filter. The amount of blurring required varies from image to image. If the image is blurred too much, it will not be able to be sharpened enough to give a clear appearance.

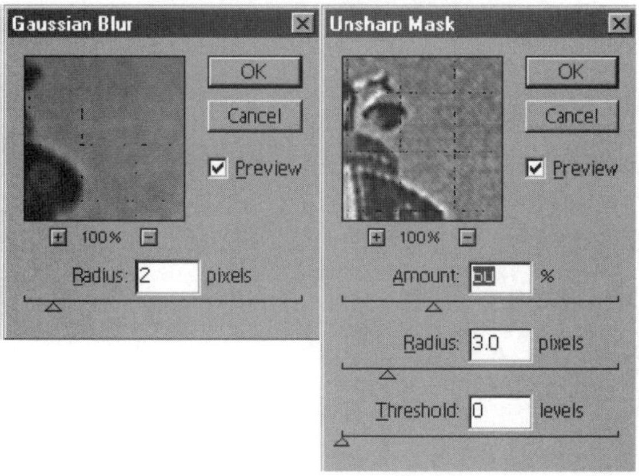

Figure 4: Blur and sharpen method of removing halftone screens.

After the image is blurred, it will need to be resharpened. This is accomplished with the "unsharp" mask filter. Again, the amount of sharpening required varies from image to image.

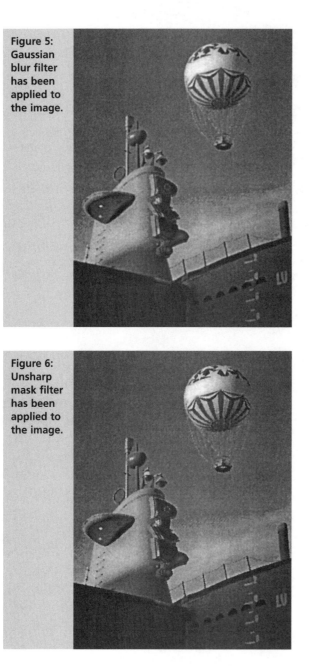

Figure 5: Gaussian blur filter has been applied to the image.

Figure 6: Unsharp mask filter has been applied to the image.

Using Your Scanner as a Creative Tool

Uses for the scanner are only limited by your imagination. Consider that the scanner is essentially a scanning digital camera. Given its unique characteristics, the scanner can be exploited to create unique and unusual images.

Scanning Three-Dimensional Objects

Three-dimensional objects present a distinct set of creative problems—and solutions—when using a flatbed scanner, but new worlds of creative possibilities are opened up when we realize that a camera is no longer needed to create photographs.

While this is similar to traditional photographic techniques such as photograms, the distinction is that these "scan-o-grams" capture image information in continuous and reasonably accurate tones.

Just as with photography, the most important element here is light. Realize that the flatbed scanner is simply a moving light source and image capture device.

Therefore, the first thing to consider is what type of light is being used to illuminate the subject. With a flatbed scanner, the light source is a soft light—a fluorescent tube. Next, the direction in which the light is traveling needs to be considered.

This will determine the way in which the object is illuminated (see the illustrations of the Chinese dragon).

Finally, try to scan an object from two or three different angles, so that you can determine which orientation of the subject will yield the best results.

Keep in mind that regardless of the flatbed scanner being utilized, you can always add additional light sources from behind the object or any of its sides. Also, backgrounds can be changed as well to make it easier to clip out an object, or to give a different visual effect to the image.

Chiaroscuro Modeling

Chiaroscuro, in art, is the distribution and contrast of light and shade in a painting or drawing, whether in monochrome or in color. The term is derived from the Italian *chiaro* ("light") and *oscuro* ("dark") and generally refers to a technique that contrasts bright illumination with areas of dense shadow. The skillful use of light and shade (sometimes called values) for dramatic effect is a particular feature in the works of such sixteenth-century Renaissance masters as Leonardo da Vinci and Raphael and such seventeenth-century baroque masters as Caravaggio, Rembrandt, and Georges de La Tour.

Source: Encarta® Desk Encyclopedia

Backgrounds and Borders

Whether you are trying to create a graphic for a Web page, or to personalize stationary, the scanner can be used to create unique graphics. Below are some examples of ordinary items that have been scanned to produce background or border graphic elements. While these graphics may not be the most exciting images, hopefully they represent an idea of what possibilities are available. For example, consider that each of the following items that have been scanned presents a unique problem and result.

The first item is a strip of holiday ribbon; the original has a shiny metallic surface, yet the silver areas scan as black. The next item is a section of a woven belt; its uneven, three-dimensional shapes show highlights and shadows. A piece of balsa wood was scanned to produce the third image. And the fourth scan is of a cardboard tube that is approximately 2-1/2 inches in diameter; the curved surfaces and the depth (or the height) of the object present several unique scenarios for the scanner. First, the curved edge allows light to fall off, and wrap around, the tube. This produces a chiaroscuro modeling effect, and hence the illusion of three-dimensionality. Notice that in the second (smaller) version of the tube graphic, it is simply a cropped section of the larger graphic, but it presents an entirely different visual statement. Also, based upon the depth/height of a three-dimensional object, you may notice that the scan of the object exhibits a fall off in the depth of field or depth of sharp focus of that object. These same techniques can be used to scan any object to create a variety of patterns, backgrounds, borders, and the like for a number of different purposes.

Three-Dimensional Objects Scanned to create background and border graphics.

Using your scanner to scan objects saves the time and expense of photographing an object, making a print, and then scanning that print. Additionally, the scanner can be used to creatively interpret objects in ways that are not possible with a still camera.

Scan-O-Grams

Similar to how the background and borders were scanned, scanning objects on a flatbed scanner is the method that is usually employed to create scan-o-grams. When creating a scan-o-gram, consider several factors.

- What is the transparency or opacity of the object?
- Can light be burned through portions of this object during the scan process?
- How will motion, or the lack thereof, enhance this scan?
- Why is scanning these objects preferable to scanning a photograph of these objects?

One of the most unique aspects of creating scan-o-grams is the ability to take advantage of the motion of the scanner's sensor and light source. This motion can be used to expand and compress image information, based upon which direction the object is moved and relative to the scanning direction. Furthermore, the addition of light sources during the scanning process, such as a flashlight, a match or lighter, or a bare light bulb, opens up new possibilities. This process can be quite creative. I have seen entire portfolios of work generated by using this technique, and some of the work was quite stunning.

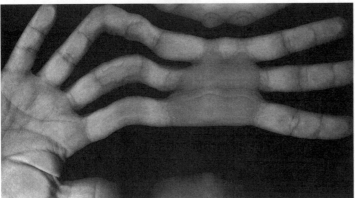

In the example above, only one hand was scanned. The hand was moved in various directions, while it was being scanned, to produce this image.

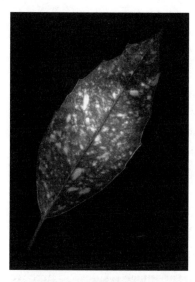

The scan of the leaf illustrates yet another scan-o-gram technique. Here, the leaf was illuminated from the rear with a flashlight.

Notice that from the center of the leaf radiating out, the light falls off. This is due to the shape of the rear illumination light source.

The other two examples were created by placing objects on top of tracing paper on the glass platen of the scanner .

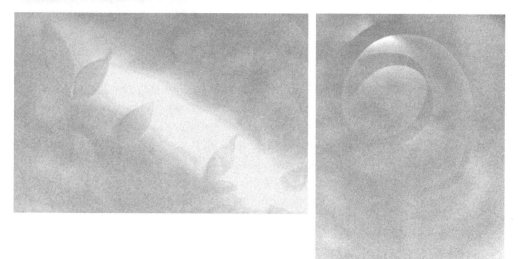

During the scan, the paper and objects were illuminated with a flashlight from varying distances and from varying angles. Keep in mind that the light of the scanner, in addition to any external light sources, illuminates the scan-o-gram subjects.

File Management and Image Archiving

Storage of digital images is of great concern to photographers; the way in which images are stored is significant because digital image files cannot be seen without the aid of a computer or other technological device. The two main areas of concern with file management are accessibility and retrieval. Accessibility refers to the ways in which you can find your digital images. For example, let's say that you have 10,000 images in your image file library. If these were simply files on a disk—hard drive or otherwise—it would be difficult to find a photo you took of a car last year. Unless you know the name of the file, it could take a long time to locate the image file.

In its most basic form, a file management system could be as simple as naming files descriptively. In this way you can search for keywords that you have used in the file-name. For example, if we had a photograph of a Model A Ford automobile that was photographed in New York in the year 2002, we might rename the file from its original name in one of the 2 following ways.

Original Filename: **DSCF0030.JPG**
Renamed as: **Model_A_Ford_2002.JPG**
or Renamed as: **Model_A_Ford_2002-DSCF0030.JPG**

In this example, we would be able to use the Find feature in the Mac OS or Windows to search the disk or folder(s) where we think the image resides. So here we could search for something like "ford" or "model_a." Note that I use underscores instead of spaces in naming files; this aids in moving images between different computer platforms, and is advised.

This is the grass-roots version of file management. It costs nothing except for the time it takes to rename your files. Many photographers use this method of file management. The problem arises when your image library grows. In this example if we had our images on CD and not on a hard drive, 10,000 images at any reasonable resolution will not fit on one CD. So our choice here is to archive the images onto many CDs and search them one at a time, or to use software to keep track of our image discs. This type of software is known as cataloging or image database software. There are many different software applications designed for this specific purpose, such as Cumulus, ActiveShare, iPhoto, and ACDSee. To illustrate how image database software works, we will use ACDSee image management software. Note that this software is available for both the Mac and PC computing platforms. I prefer to use software that is cross-platform; however, if you only work on a Mac with OS-X or higher, software such as iPhoto works quite well.

Image Management with ACDSee

ACDSee is an application that has many useful features for the photographer. It is designed to be reasonably comprehensive in terms of acquiring, organizing, viewing, enhancing, and sharing your images. It has an image-browsing feature that allows you to acquire images from different sources such as digital cameras, scanners, and disks. Additionally, ACDSee allows you to catalog your images with thumbnail views. What this means is that you can visually preview images in your image database library.

Beyond its database functions, this software allows for basic image-editing functions such as red-eye reduction, cropping, sharpening, rotation of images, resizing, file format conversions, conversion of images to sepia tones, and embossing, to list a few of its features.

To see how the file management/database aspects of this software work, we will first look at the main ACDSee window. In this first example, we are viewing the disk folder tree. This allows for browsing of folders on any drives connected to the computer—including network drives. In this illustration, we have selected the View tab for the type of browsing window display. This allows for the viewing of thumbnail images in a folder, and an enlarged view of a selected image at the same time—a convenient way to visually preview images. Note that this viewing method is similar to the image-viewing capabilities built into operating systems since Mac OS-X and Windows XP. The major difference here is that this software provides database functionality.

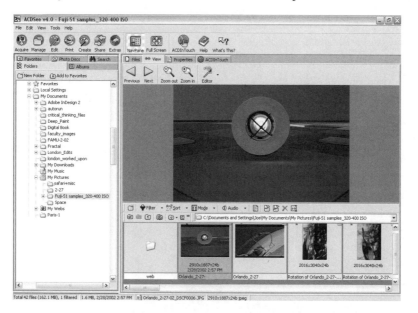

Before we move on, let's take a look at the Mac version of ACDSee. Notice that the interface is quite similar to the Windows version, although buttons and tabs are in different places. Here we are viewing the folder tree, with the thumbnail browser view displayed.

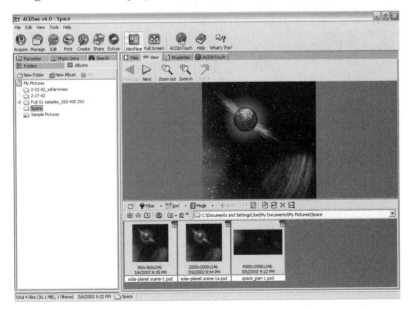

Because this method of file management is centered on the idea that the images are cataloged in a database, we can sort and categorize groups of images in different ways. For example, here you see that albums can be defined for the different jobs, groups of images, or creative projects you are working on.

This appears to work like desktop picture browsing, which was popularized with Mac OS-X and Windows XP. Again, the difference here is that these thumbnail images are cataloged in a database. These images correlate with metadata embedded into the file. This metadata represents the hidden text information that describes such things as the camera, shutter speed, and aperture used to capture the image, as well as user added information, like your name, copyright information, and keywords to be entered into the database. All of this information is then searchable when you are trying to locate your image files.

So, while the picture browsing aspect is similar to Mac or Windows file browsing, the impressive thing here is that every time we are viewing images through ACDSee, we are adding to our image database. The real power here, however, lies in the ability to catalog images from multiple sources; specifically, images on Zip disks, CDs, or DVDs can be cataloged, as well as image information on your hard drive or network drives. To illustrate this, we will add a new CD to our database. Here we simply selected New Disc from the Photo Discs tab on the Browser Bar (left side of the main window, above the directory tree area). Now we can specify whether we want to add all of the images on our disc to the database or only selected folders.

After a moment—longer times for more images—our image thumbnails and metadata are added to the master database file.

Now, when we want to search our database for something like "flying bird," we can see thumbnail images of our bird images, whether or not the actual images reside on the hard drive of the computer that is running ACDSee. If we select an image to be enlarged or edited that the computer is not able to access, we are prompted to insert the disc containing the original image. In this example, our images are on a CD, so we are prompted to insert the CD.

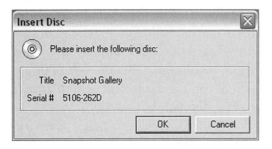

After inserting the disc, we are then able to access the original file—without searching through piles of discs!

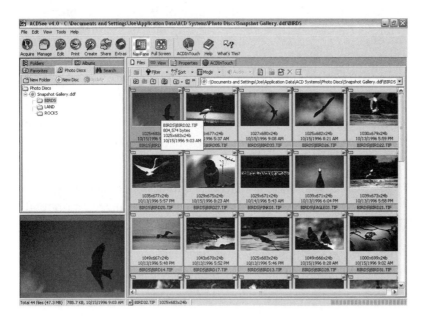

Now, because we are viewing our images within the structure of an image database, we can also sort the images by categories ranging from the name of the image to the description or properties of the image, as illustrated here with our database of bird images.

Finally, as can be seen in many new software applications—as well as in the Mac and Windows operating systems—integrated imaging services are becoming commonplace. Here is one example of integrated online print ordering; just one of the many value-added features offered through software such as ACDSee.

Another very popular image database application is Cumulus. This application functions similarly to ACDSee. The main purpose of Cumulus is also to catalog images into a database for convenient and organized classification and retrieval of archived images.

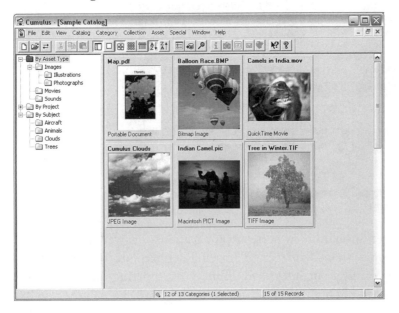

The software you choose to use is an individual choice. Just make sure your choice addresses not only your present needs, but your potential future imaging needs as well.

Finally, both Apple and Microsoft have added extensive imaging functionality into their operating systems since the release of OS-X and Windows XP. This functionality addresses many of the needs of the digital photographer. Integrated OS imaging functions range from direct image capture from digital cameras—where no other software is needed once the camera is attached to the computer—to generating contact sheets, and services such as online print ordering.

Here you can see two examples of OS integrated file browsing in both Mac OS-X and Windows XP.

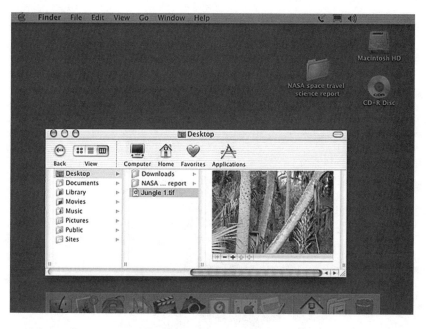

Picture browsing is illustrated in this example from the Mac OS-X. This allows you to simply select an image file, which is then automatically previewed at the desktop level. Notice that in the Windows XP example, the Picture Tasks menu area illustrates some other ways in which image management is integrated into the OS. For example, images in a folder can be viewed as a slide show, prints of images can be ordered online, or the image can be burned directly onto a CD—without any additional software.

One final example: here you can even see that after selecting Print this picture from the Picture Tasks menu, a photo printing wizard allows the user to print picture packages such as contact sheets or enlargements. These prints can be made from one image or from all of the images in a folder. These are OS features that were once only available in specialized imaging software such as Photoshop.

So as you can see from these examples, digital photography is becoming a regular part of our computer environment, even at the consumer level.

Removable Media and Storage Devices

There are a number of different types of storage devices and media for archiving digital images. There are several reasons why the digital photographer needs to become familiar with these options. Due to the constraints of various technologies, each removable media solution presents both pros and cons.

Understanding that any discussion of specific technologies is bound by the time of that discussion, consider the following. Regardless of the specific name or brand of any technologies discussed herein, the following factors determine the usefulness of storage media/devices for the digital photographer: capacity, access time, read/write time, longevity of the media, MTBF (Mean Time Between Failures) of a device, ability to archive the media, and the cost of the storage solution (see Removable Media and Storage Devices sidebar).

Removable Media and Storage Devices

Capacity: That factor which determines how many images can be stored on a particular type of removable media or storage device. In traditional photography, the capacity of a roll of 35 mm film with 36 exposures is equal to 36 images. With digital imaging, capacity is determined by how many megabytes, gigabytes, or terabytes a device or piece of media can store—where the sum of the different sizes of images determines the number of images that can be stored.

Access Time and Read/Write: Refers to the amount of time it takes to search for an image, transfer all of its data, and read and write the image to and from the storage media to the computer. For example, storage technologies such as magnetic floppy/Zip disks have very slow access times because of their slow read and write times. Whereas, technologies such as CompactFlash, smart media, and other types of static RAM media have fast access times.

Longevity and Ability to Archive: Just as conventional photographic film and paper have a limited lifespan, so do digital technologies. For example, CD recordable media currently has a life span that ranges from under ten years to one hundred years. Additionally, the durability of a particular media needs to be considered.

Storage Cost: This is sometimes referred to as the cost per megabyte in computing terms. Essentially, this is a measure of how much it costs to store each digital image, based upon the accessibility of the image and the longevity of the media.

There are many different ways to store digital images. Current options include a range of choices from 1.44MB floppy disks and 100/250MB Zip disks, to one and two GB Jaz and SparQ drives, to two-plus gigabyte ORB drives and recordable CD/CD-RW disks, as well as five-plus gigabyte DVD disks. Each of these solutions serves a purpose; however, remember that all of these technologies might soon be replaced with newer, larger capacity technologies.

Key questions to ask to determine what technologies need to be utilized are:

- Is this technology compatible with my service bureau/client?
- Will this technology preserve the image for the duration of the project, and for as long as the image may be needed in digital form?
- How much will image archiving cost, when utilizing this technology?
- Is access time a factor for image recall from this media?
- These sample questions will serve you in beginning to make choices when building your digital photography lab storage solutions.

Samples of Removable Media

Creating your Own CD or DVD

The process of creating a CD or DVD is relatively straightforward. Disc-creation software handles most of the technical issues involved. However, before discussing this process, there are certain issues that need to be considered.

As discussed earlier, the CD or DVD media itself varies. When deciding to create or "burn" your own CD/DVD, you should first know what type of disc burner is to be used. The reason for this is because different manufacturers utilize different types of lasers and technology in their burners. Because of these differing technologies, different types of media may be preferred. The manufacturer of the burner will generally recommend the best media for their device.

With digital imaging, yet another concern is raised—that of longevity. Because we are dealing with images, the issue of how the storage medium archives becomes paramount. So, before you create a CD/DVD, you need to know what purpose this disc will serve. For example, if a CD is needed to transport your images to a service bureau, and these images are already backed up and archived, inexpensive, short-lived media can be used. However, if the disc is to be used as your digital negative archive, you need to consider using discs with the longest stable life, such as the Kodak media, which has a longer stable life than current color negative or slide films.

Finally, most of this discussion will probably be moot if the present trend of technological innovation persists. Consider that the generally accepted industry standard for computer equipment replacement in the United States is eighteen months to two years. Therefore, new storage media probably will be developed, and your digital image archives will need to be converted from the old media to the new media. So what we are really talking about, in terms of archiving, is ensuring that your images will survive not one hundred years, but two to seven years—until the next media is available for image transfer. Consider the following example:

If you scanned an image in 1988, you probably stored this image on a double-sided floppy disk. If you wanted to use this image in 1991, you probably transferred the image to a high-density floppy disk. In the mid-1990s, the same image was most likely moved to a SyQuest cartridge, and later to a Zip disk. By the late 1990s, the image could likely find itself stored on a Jaz drive as well. Finally, by the turn of the century, this image was most likely stored on CD-R or DVD media.

This example illustrates the trend that technological innovation has historically taken, with respect to digital image storage media.

The Process of Creating Your Own CD or DVD

As stated previously, the process of storing images on an optical disc such as a CD-R (compact disc-recordable), CD-RW (compact disc-rewritable), or DVD/DVD-RW (digital video disc) is quite simple. Most modern disc creation software is very user friendly. The process of creating a CD-R is illustrated below. For this example, we have used Roxio's CD/DVD creator software on a PC, but the process is virtually identical with the MAC version of Roxio's CD/DVD burning software. Additionally, note that CD burning is native in some operating systems, since Windows XP and OS 9+/OS-X.

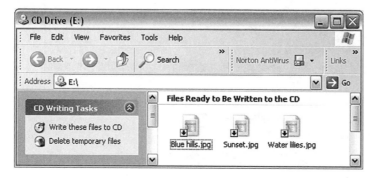

Using Roxio's (Adaptec) CD Creation Software to Burn a CD/DVD

An example of the process of using authoring software to create a CD is as follows:

Step 1

Gather your images (remember the capacity of your recording media, (i.e., CD-R media stores up to 650MB). Place all of your images in a folder on your computer's hard drive.

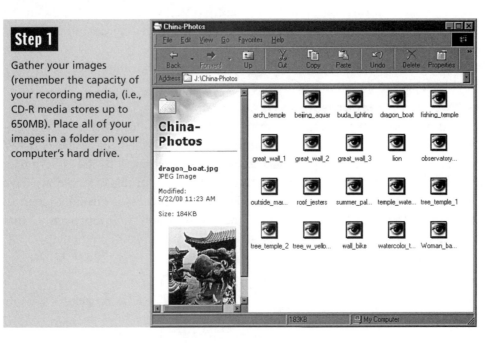

Step 2

Set up the directory structure you wish to have on your disc, if any. Next, define any subfolders that you care to have on your CD; for example, see the following illustration.

Step 3

Adjust the properties of your disc-creation software through a step-by-step, wizard-type process.

The following illustrations exemplify the process of CD creation. Using software such as Adaptec/Roxio Easy CD Creator, designing and burning your CD is as simple as answering a few questions. Remember that it is always best to set up your file and folder structure on your hard drive first.

CD-R Setup and Burn Process

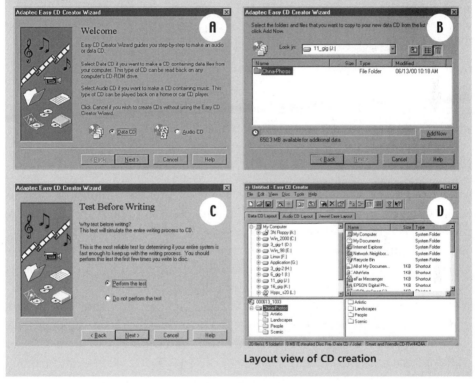

Layout view of CD creation

When creating a CD for the storage of data, such as digital images, two physical formats can be "burned" or written: CD-ROM (Mode 1) and CD-ROM XA (Mode 2).

Generally, the CD-ROM format is used. However, if you want to add more images to the CD later, you will want to make a multisession CD, which will be burned in CD-ROM XA format. If you are not sure if you will add images at a later time, it is best to burn the first session to your CD in CD-ROM XA format, so that potential subsequent burns can be accommodated. It is always best to use only one format on a multisession CD, and not to combine CD-ROM and CD-ROM XA formats on one CD-R.

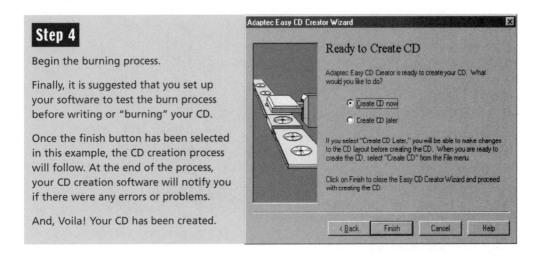

Note, the process is virtually identical when burning DVD discs, with the exception that there is a great deal more storage space on a DVD.

Conclusions

Digital photography is referred to as a new media process. Implicative in this description is that these media and processes are just that, new. Being new, there are no clearly defined boundaries. In one sense, this may be a bit unsettling for those who are comfortable with traditional photographic materials and processes. However, we suggest that you should view the newness and uncertainty of these new media as opportunities to grow, both creatively and technically.

By using such alternative acquisition technologies such as the Photo CD, picture CD, and picture Disk, the photographer's work is already in a form that is inexpensive and easily distributable. Additionally, consider that by creating your own CDs or DVDs, the potential exists to share creative work in ways that go far beyond passing around the traditional page of slides. Now music, narration, and multimedia elements can be utilized to enhance the presentation of your portfolios. Even though we discussed these media as storage media in this chapter, look beyond this and see the potential of this new media—and exploit it. The same is true for the alternative scanning technologies discussed herein.

Creative Vision

It's like driving a car at night:you never see further than your headlights, but you can make the whole trip that way.

E. L. Doctorow (b. 1931), U.S. novelist. Interview in *Writers at Work* (Eighth Series, ed. by George Plimpton, 1988), said of his writing technique.

Source: The Columbia Dictionary of Quotations.

Remember, these are only starting points!

Review Questions:

1. What are the three main types of alternative image acquisition technologies that can be obtained through a service bureau/photofinisher?

a. _____

b. _____

c. _____

2 Hybrid technologies generally bridge the gap between
_____ and _____ technologies.

3 If you don't have access to a scanner, what is the best alternative way to have images scanned, to obtain enough resolution to make a photographic inkjet print?

4 Describe the advantages of creating a Photo CD over creating a picture CD.

5 Why does a photographer need to use removable media and storage devices?
Name six different types of storage media that can be used to store digital photographs.

a. _____

b. _____

c. _____

d. _____

e. _____

f. _____

6 Why would a photographer want to crate a CD or DVD?

7 At the present time, what is the best way to archive your digital image files?

8 Name three alternative scanning techniques that compensate for problems that occur because of the original scan, and briefly state how to correct these problems.

a. _____

b. _____

c. _____

Discussion Questions:

1 Even though I have access to a high-quality scanner, why might I consider an alternative image-acquisition technique, such as having a Photo CD created? Explain.

2 What is the best way to preserve my digital images at present? Also, how can I ensure that my digital files will still be accessible and viable in the future?

3 Which media has a longer life, a magnetic Zip disk, or an optical Kodak Photo CD, and why?

4 How can a scanner be used as a creative device for the creation of imagery? And, why might I choose this method over traditional methods of image-making?

CHAPTER 5

Fundamentals of Image Editing

Objectives:

This chapter will survey basic digital darkroom techniques. It is intended to give an overview of the digital darkroom, but not to serve as the sole source for comprehensive training. You will learn how to deal with photographic images in digital form in a variety of ways ranging from opening and saving images in various digital file formats, through enhancing images. Additionally, you will become accustomed to the digital darkroom environment, as illustrated with Adobe's Mac and PC-compatible software application Photoshop™. Upon completion of this chapter, you should have a better understanding of:

- What conventions are used in photographic image-editing applications
- How to import/open and export/save images in a variety of digital image formats
- How a variety of image-enhancing techniques work in the digital darkroom
- How image masking and selections can be used to improve the quality of images

Conventions Used in Image-Editing Programs

There are a wide variety of image-editing software applications/programs available for the digital photographer which range from the beginner or novice level through advanced commercial and professional applications for the photographic and graphic arts industries. In this chapter, we will discuss concepts that relate to a broad range of software applications. One product will be showcased here for illustrative purposes: Adobe Photoshop. Quite simply, Adobe Photoshop is the industry de facto standard in image-editing applications. There are a number of reasons for this, not the least of which is that it offers the professional photographer a comprehensive toolkit.

While most bitmap image-editing programs offer a group of similar features, many of these programs also include specialized tools. The more successful products available—and the ones that have survived fierce industry competition—have been successful because they have addressed the concerns of niche markets. These specialty markets are an important, and often overlooked, area of concern for many large corporations. Nonetheless, there are times when both digital photographers and graphic designers need solutions to specific problems, which are not easily solved by using just one software package.

The foundation of commonality in these applications is the fact that they all deal with bitmap imagery. That is, the images to be manipulated in these programs are all pixel-based graphics. Pixel images (picture element) are also referred to as bitmap images and raster graphics, as well. Pixel-based images differ from the other broad category of graphic images: vector graphics. Vector-based graphics are defined as mathematical formulas that when processed, redraw the image each time it is viewed or printed. With pixel images, the dots—or more specifically the pixels—are the individual components that make up the image. These pixels are similar to the grain of traditional photographic images, in that if enlarged excessively, the image becomes distorted in terms of its overall quality. One exception to this general rule of thumb is software such as Altamira's Genuine Fractals software. This extension to Adobe Photoshop allows you to save an image into a genuine fractal file format, and when this image is reopened, it is resized based upon vector-based mathematical processing techniques, and converted back into a bitmap image.

Image Editing with Adobe Photoshop®

Although there are many image-editing programs available to the digital photographer, most of the illustrations and discussion in this chapter will focus on using Adobe Photoshop. The reason for this is that Photoshop is one of the most powerful and most widely used software applications for digital image enhancement.

Opening a File

While it may seem a bit basic, opening an image is an important part of the image-editing process. Most of the time, images will simply be opened from the File menu's Open command; however, there are some significant exceptions to this workflow.

One of the handier features offered is the File > Open Recent command. This menu command allows you to quickly open the last several previously edited files.

Next, the File > Open As command is quite useful for times when the actual format or the file type is unrecognized by Photoshop. This allows the user to tell Photoshop what the image's file format should be.

This is useful, for example, when sharing files between Windows and Mac computing platforms. In this situation, the image's file format can become confused because the image either doesn't have the correct three-letter extension, or the conversion software transfers the image to the new platform as a generic file type.

And of course, you can simply open an image file from the File > Open command.

Saving and Closing a File

There are three different ways to save images in Photoshop. The most basic way to save an image is through the Save command in the File menu. The standard Save option allows you to save a new version of a file over the original version on disk. It also allows you to save a newly created image to disk.

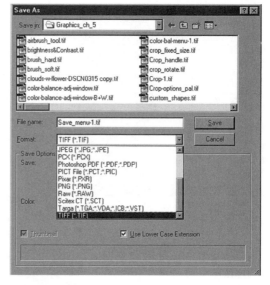

The Save As… command in the File menu allows you to choose different options such as the file format to be saved, and whether or not to save such peripheral information as annotations, alpha channels, layers, spot colors, and profile information.

Finally, the third way to save an image in Photoshop is to use the wizard-like Save for Web… command. This option allows the user to create a screen resolution version of any graphic, with control over the file type (jpeg/gif/png), the amount of jpeg compression, transparency, the color table, the image size, interlacing/progressive scans, dithering, the number of colors to be saved, and even HTML Web page preview/output options.

Saving your files is the most important part of working in the digital darkroom,. because it is here that you either preserve or destroy all of your hard work. It is significant to note that the Photoshop file format is the only image file format that will save all of an image's information, along with its peripheral information such as its editable type layers, channels, and paths.

Image Size and Resolution

When first working with an image in Photoshop—or any image-editing software—you need to determine the actual size of the image. Image size comprises several variables that define the image. First, the resolution of the image determines how much information is represented by an image.

The higher the resolution, the more image data is present; the lower the resolution, the less image information. Next the height and width of the image need to be examined. It is appropriate to change the units in the document size section of the Image Size dialog box to the units that are appropriate to your workflow.

In the illustration presented here, the image is measured in inches, to represent a standard 8"x10" photograph. You will notice that the resolution in this example is set to 300 pixels per inch. This is an appropriate image resolution to derive a photographic print on a variety of materials ranging from dye-sublimation prints to offset commercial printing. Finally, notice in this example that the pixel dimensions of this image are 2400 x 3000 pixels.

These overall dimensions of the image relate to the size of the image on screen, where 8" x 300 pixels/inch = 2400 pixels and 10" x 300 pixels/inch = 3000 pixels. Hence, the image information that comprises this image is equal to 7,200,000 pixels of information, which means that over seven million points (picture elements) of information make up this image. This is like counting the number of pieces of grain in a traditional photograph.

Just as ISO 3200 film produces a grainy photograph, so will a low-resolution image such as a 72 pixel/inch image. Likewise, just as an ISO 32 film produces an image with very fine grain, so will a 300 pixel/inch image be a fine-grain type image.

It is crucially important that before any image editing occurs, the image's resolution, height, and width be determined. As an example, say you have a photograph that was captured with a digital camera. When the image is opened in Photoshop, let's say its initial resolution settings are 1536 pixels x 2048 pixels at 72 pixels per inch. If what you are after is a gigantic screen resolution image, this will be fine.

However, if an inkjet print is desired, the resolution needs to be altered. Knowing that an optimum resolution for inkjet printing is 200 pixels per inch, when the image is resized through the image size dialog box, the result is an image that will be 7.68" x 10.24" at a resolution of 200 pixels per inch, an appropriate resolution for inkjet printing.

Preparing to Work in the Digital Darkroom

There are an amazing number of image-editing tools available to the photographer in Photoshop. Before we begin a discussion of these tools, it is important to first discuss where some of these tools come from. Photoshop has evolved into a program that a wide variety of individuals rely upon. These individuals come from varying backgrounds, and Adobe has added tools over time to accommodate many of these sub-groups of users. For example, Photoshop has tools that are familiar to artists, graphic designers, photographers (of course), graphic artists, graphics prepress people, and more. This is a significant fact to note, because it will alter the way one approaches dealing with Photoshop. One of the greatest problems of dealing with a software application such as Photoshop is that it seems to offer too much, which can be overwhelming to beginners and novices. This should not be the case, given good information.

To approach the tools that are afforded in Photoshop, understand that you do not need to know all of the tools before using this, or any other image-editing program. Rather, I believe a learn-as-you-go philosophy will aid in the understanding of Photoshop. If you try to learn everything about Photoshop before using the software, you will most likely become confused and overwhelmed. If you start with the basics, just as one would in traditional photography, and build upon these basics, Photoshop will be quite easy to understand and use.

To begin a discussion about specific procedures, let us use traditional photographic metaphors. A person's first time in the darkroom doesn't generally produce the perfect Ansel Adams-type Zone System print, right? With that in mind, consider that it has always been the case that through our mistakes, and experimentation, the mystery of the darkroom will unfold. So, too, is the case in the digital darkroom. Until you are comfortable working in a digital environment, changing too many controls at one time can confuse and counter the process of image adjustment in a controlled manner.

Image Modes

Before you can begin working on an image in your digital darkroom, you need to know what image mode you are working within. To make image modes easier to understand, think of them as though they were choices of film, where grayscale is for black-and-white photos, CMYK is for special print reproduction work, RGB is for general color photography, and so on.

In Photoshop there are eight basic modes within which you can deal with your images. For most people—with the exception of professionals—however, there are only two modes that will be primarily utilized: the grayscale and RGB modes, where the grayscale mode allows you to work on continuous tone, black-and-white photographic images, and the RGB (red, green, blue) mode allows you to edit color photographic images.

It is important to always know what mode you are working within in Photoshop, which can be quickly determined by looking at the title bar of the image.

Working in the incorrect mode can have a dramatic impact upon your images—and not necessarily a positive one.

Adjusting for Brightness and Contrast

The first thing that is needed is a digital negative or positive. This will be in the form of an image file, which can be from a wide variety of sources such as a digital camera, flatbed scanner, film scanner, picture CD, Photo CD, etc. Now that we have our digital file—the equivalent of the negative—let's go into the digital darkroom.

Now, just as one would do in a traditional darkroom, we need to determine several key factors in order to arrive at a quality, full-tonal range print. First, in the traditional darkroom, we would make a test strip to determine the proper amount of exposure from the enlarger.

In the digital darkroom, we also need to first determine the overall brightness of the print. While there are numerous ways to do this in Photoshop, the most basic way is to use the brightness/contrast adjustment control: Image > Adjust > Brightness/Contrast.

It is suggested that when becoming familiar with the digital darkroom, you should proceed as you would in a traditional printing process. That is, first determine the proper brightness of the image. Then, and in a separate step, adjust the contrast.

After adjusting the brightness, we have a print that looks like the brightness adjustment-only illustration. This is an image where we have not altered the contrast in any way. Next we adjust the contrast independently. After a while, you will develop a feel for adjusting both of these elements at one time. You will notice that the basic image adjustments remain the same with digital photography as with traditional photography. The main difference here is that these adjustments can now be processed in real time with no more developing, stop-baths, or fixing each test print to determine brightness and contrast.

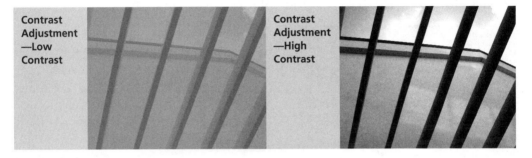

Contrast Adjustment —Low Contrast

Contrast Adjustment —High Contrast

Finally, as with traditional media, we arrive at the final print. Although quite basic, this introduction to the digital darkroom is intended to show how simple, and similar, this process is to traditional darkroom work.

Note that the entire process from digital image (originally acquired image) to final print adjustment took less than 30 seconds to complete.

Adjusting for Color Balance

After adjusting the density (brightness) and contrast of an image, you need to adjust the color balance. What is amazing about dealing with images in the digital form is the amount of control the photographer can have in the digital darkroom. Adjusting color balance is an area that illustrates this point well. In a traditional photographic darkroom, only two factors can be adjusted in the darkroom: density and overall color balance. The film that is shot, or the choice of standard- or high-contrast enlarging paper, determines contrast. Whereas in the digital color darkroom, the photographer can adjust density, contrast, hue, saturation, or even histogram and/or parametric curve information for any area of an image's tonal information—selectively. That is, adjustments can be made in just the shadows, mid-tones, or highlights, for example. And this means that the photographer has an incredible amount of control in terms of adjusting the tonal and color information of an image.

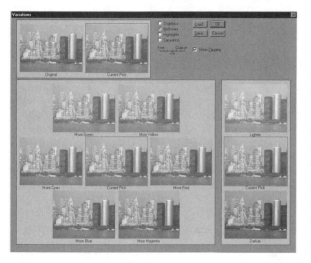

Photoshop offers the photographer a number of tools to aid in the balancing of an image's color information. Notice the Variations illustration. This option—Image > Adjust > Variations—allows for a quick, visual "ring-around" type of subjective color correction. This is similar to creating test prints in the traditional color darkroom, and then visually evaluating the test in order to further correct the image's color balance. However, with Photoshop, six choices are presented at a time, and all of the supporting test prints dynamically change each time you select a new choice.

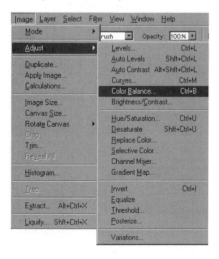

Other, more precise methods of adjusting color are offered as well. For example, the Image > Adjust > Color Balance… menu item offers a tool that will allow for the selective manipulation of color information in specific tonal regions of the image.

Here the color balance can be adjusted for just the highlights, and then a different color balance can be made for the midtones, and finally the shadows can be adjusted independently as well. With this type of control over the color information of an image, the most critical photographer now has the ability to compensate for exposure-related color issues, and to produce the image that was originally conceived.

Finally, the overall color balance of the image can be adjusted—as with the traditional darkroom—by using the Image > Adjust > Hue/Saturation... menu item.

This tool allows for the adjustment of the overall color or hue of the image. Furthermore, this tool enables the photographer to increase or decrease the amount of color saturation (the richness/vibrancy) of an image's chromatic information.

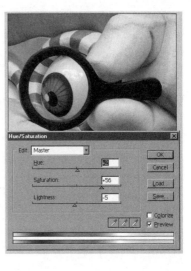

The ability to adjust saturation in this way enables the photographer to more precisely control the image's information, so that it may be reproduced with the finest fidelity to match the requirements of different delivery platforms.

Rotating and Cropping the Image

Cropping the image can occur either at the end of the imaging process or the beginning. This is similar to making a decision to crop the image on the easel in the darkroom, or to print it full frame and cut away the parts of the image that are unwanted, after the fact. In the digital darkroom, however, cropping deals with more than simply slicing off unwanted areas of the image. Here, one can have an advanced degree of control with their cropping.

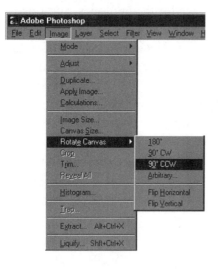

To begin, let's rotate a vertical image that was shot on a digital camera. Of course, because the camera was turned on its side to capture the image, the file displays the image on its side—just as with 35 mm or 120 film.

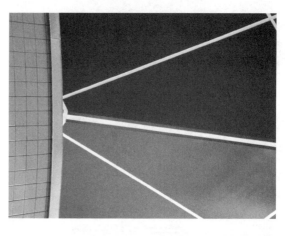

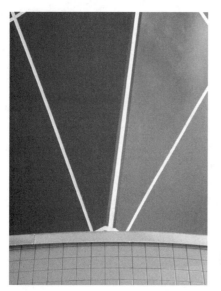

After performing the rotate task (Image > Rotate Canvas > 90° CCW), the image is righted, and we can begin our normal image processing and editing tasks.

Now, we will choose to crop the image at the beginning of this process. First, we need to select the crop tool. Next, we click the mouse on a point on the image and drag out a box without releasing the mouse button, then release the mouse button when the size is established.

Now the crop box can be adjusted. The handles on the sides of the marquee-bounding box can be dragged to adjust the size of the box.

When the crop is exactly as desired, simply double-click inside the bounding box, and the shaded areas of the image will be discarded.

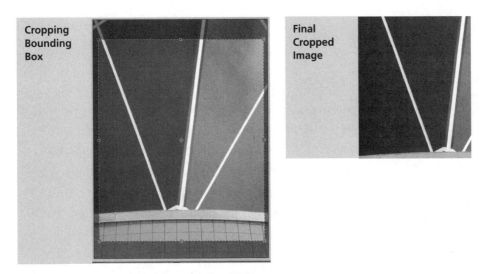

Beyond the basic crop though, there are more advanced features available to make your work more precise. For example, the crop tool allows for setting the definition of precise variables, such as width, height and resolution.

This is significant to the photographer in that the exact image size can be precisely set, and duplicated.

In this example, you can see that we have set a fixed width, height, and resolution of the image to be cropped.

Finally, the crop tool can also be used to rotate an image during the cropping process.

This can be quite useful, especially for correcting tilted horizons. Beyond the crop tool itself, images can be cropped with the Crop command (Image > Crop) and the Trim command (Image > Trim). These commands can be used to crop an image down to a selection, or to crop an image based upon the tonality of a select pixel color (i.e., to trim away a white background).

Defining the Tools

Here, you can see the basic Photoshop toolbox. Before we begin discussing some of the various tools, let's first discuss certain key features of the toolbox. The first functional thing to note about the toolbox is that some tools are single-tool selections, such as the magic wand and the crop tool. Other tool selections access multiple context-sensitive tools. This is done to save screen space, so you can see more of the image that is being worked on. To access a single tool, click once on its icon in the toolbox.

 To access one of the multiple tools in a context-sensitive tool selection, click and hold the mouse down on any tool that has a triangle in the lower-right corner of its icon.

As illustrated, a context-sensitive subpalette pops up and allows for the selection of other tools, which are not shown on the main view of the toolbox palette.

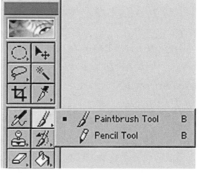

This first example illustrates how the clone (rubber stamp) tool can be used to manipulate an image.

 More often than not, this tool is used as a retouching tool; it works quite well to duplicate a textured area to eliminate dust or scratches, for example. In this illustration, the usage is intentionally more obvious, in order to demonstrate the power of this. As you can see, this tool offers the image-maker the ability to seamlessly manipulate photographic images.

The main concern here, however, is that of the ethics of such manipulations.

For our next example, the history brush tool can be used to paint from various previous states of the history of the image, while it is being altered.

The first image is the unaltered original. In this example, the second version of the image was altered through a filtering process to add painterly texture to the entire image.

The problem here is that the whole image has been abstracted, and there are no details for the viewer to focus upon. After selecting the history brush, the original unaltered image history state was selected in the history palette, as the state from which to draw with the history brush. Next, the brush size was selected.

Finally, a portion of the image was painted with the history brush to give the illusion that the Key West and several other signs were revealed from behind the brush strokes.

Actually, the clearer information was added back to the image by painting with the original image's history state—rather than with a color.

 In terms of basic image alteration, tools such as the sharpen and blur can be used to selectively focus, or defocus, areas of an image.

Here the pilings of the dock and the water were selectively defocused.

The blur tool can be extremely useful for selectively modifying an image, for example, when you want to decrease the illusion of depth of field, after the fact. In such a case, the background can be knocked out of focus a little bit at a time.

As for the selective lightening and darkening of areas of an image, Photoshop offers the photographer both dodging and burning tools. Just as you would selectively add or subtract exposure to local areas of an image in the traditional darkroom, you can dodge/lighten or burn/darken local areas of an image in the digital darkroom. The real advantage of digital dodging and burning is that you can selectively add or subtract exposure to areas with an infinite variety of sizes and qualities of tools (brushes).

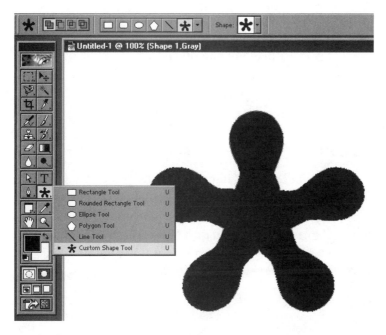

Whereas, illustration tools such as the shape tool allow you to create illustrations or accent images in Photoshop with vector-based artwork.

What this means is that these objects are scalable to very large sizes with no degradation of image quality—until the image is flattened, or the layer is rasterized (converted into bitmap image information). These types of objects, introduced in Photoshop version 6, are handled in the same way as type: as formula-based shapes, not as pixels of information.

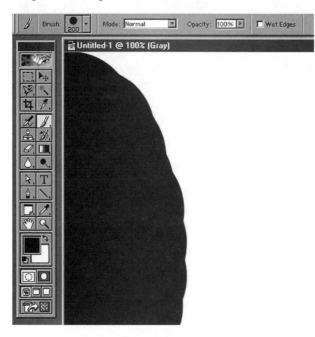

Other basic editing/illustration devices include such tools as the paintbrush and the airbrush tools. The paintbrush tool can have either hard or soft edges—or a custom designed shape.

As illustrated, the hard-edged paintbrush tool shows a crisp and well-defined edge. Whereas, the paintbrush tool can also be used to create a visual effect that looks as though the edge of the painted area is feathered or smoothed.

Additionally, brushes can be used in a variety of ways to edit your images. For example, they can be used to create specialty masks for localized image-editing controls, as well as for such tasks as retouching.

Working with a Selection

One of the most important skills you can develop for a productive workflow in the digital darkroom is the ability to make accurate selections. With digital imaging, a selection is an area of the image that allows you to selectively manipulate a local region of an image.

What this means is that the photographer has nearly unlimited control over the image-enhancement process. For example, let's say that a photograph was taken with a great amount of depth of field/focus, but you want to blur the background, after the fact. With the proper selection, this feat can be easily accomplished.

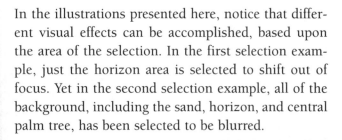

In the illustrations presented here, notice that different visual effects can be accomplished, based upon the area of the selection. In the first selection example, just the horizon area is selected to shift out of focus. Yet in the second selection example, all of the background, including the sand, horizon, and central palm tree, has been selected to be blurred.

In addition to blurring, any number of techniques can be applied to images locally through the use of selections.

In the next example, you will notice that a selection in the shape of a foot has been made.

This selection was then inverted, to show a negative image of the area of the selection; with a bit of brightness and contrast enhancement added to the selection, the final area of the image was then enhanced to produce the finished graphic image.

Although in Photoshop there are a number of ways to make selections, in the end, whether one uses a lasso tool, a magic wand, a quick mask, or any other tool to create the selection, it is the selection that will enable you to have very focused degrees of control over all the local areas in an image. Finally, beyond basic tonal manipulation, the selection forms the foundation for all copying and pasting, compositing, and other types of physical image manipulation.

In the photograph of the clouds, for example, let's say that we want to composite the image of the flower in the upper-right corner.

In addition, let's say that we want to rotate the flower into the correct position. First, we created a quick and rough selection of the flower. Next, the selection was feathered to a 15-pixel radius, in order to fade the edge of the copy/paste selection.

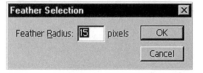

Then the selection was copied and pasted into the new image.

Here the selection on its own layer was transformed, by rotating the image element (the flower) into the correct position.

The final image was then achieved by simply applying the transformation to the pasted flower layer of the image.

These examples only illustrate very limited uses for the innumerable applications of selections as imaging tools. When you begin to use selections, and from the most simplistic traditional example, think of selections as masks to be used just as one would use masks in the darkroom. Just remember, these digital masks can enable you to produce effects that couldn't be imagined before the digital darkroom.

Basic Selection Tools

In order to make accurate selections of a portion of an image, there are a number of different tools provided. These tools enable the user to make selections in a variety of working modes. This is significant, in that it allows the user to choose the right tool for the job. In many less sophisticated image-editing programs, your choices for defining selections are often quite limited. With Photoshop, however, there are many tools that offer differing degrees of subtlety in terms of the way in which control is offered to the image-maker.

 To begin, let's look at the most basic of all selection tools: the lasso tool. This is the general selection tool, which is generally available in all image-editing programs. In Photoshop, the lasso has a number of useful functions, but basically, it is used for outlining an area in an image, just as though you were tracing an outline with a pencil.

 To use the lasso tool, simply click on a beginning point, and trace the area to be defined, while continuing to hold the mouse button down. In this illustration, you can see a detail that illustrates the marquee that defines an area in the image.

Next, the magnetic lasso tool functions much like the lasso tool, with one special exception.

 This tool will snap to boundary areas, based upon the luminosity and contrast of the area in the image. This is useful for quickly selecting an area, when dealing with an image that has clearly defined areas of contrast to be selected, as shown in the illustration.

Beyond these basic selection tools, the magic wand allows the user to select an area of an image by clicking one point, and letting the computer determine the area to be selected, based upon the number of gray levels that the user has predefined.

In this illustration, notice that the shadow area of the image has been easily selected with one simple click of the mouse. Here the Photoshop default of 32 levels of gray was used, and an extremely quick and accurate selection was made.

For more complex selections, or selections where geometric accuracy is required, the pen tool can be quite useful.

This tool is based upon a classic digital illustration tool that allows one to create Bezier curves.

 These curves are vector-based outlines, which means they produce smooth lines and curves that are scalable—with no degradation of the selection area boundaries.

Creating a Quick Mask

A very different type of selection device is the quick mask tool. This tool—or more appropriately, masking mode—allows the user to paint the areas of the image that are to be selected. In its default settings, painting with black adds to the mask, and white subtracts from the mask. Shades of gray can also be used to feather areas of the mask. This is very useful in that you can create a relatively sophisticated selection on an area of an image in a very short amount of time. Furthermore, this masking mode allows for the use of any drawing/painting tool to define the selection or protected area(s) of the image. Whether the airbrush is used with a soft-edged brush, or the pencil with a hard-edged tip, the mask can be precisely defined, and then the mode can be changed to turn the mask back into a selection—in the standard editing mode.

In the quick mask mode, a red film is placed over the areas of the image that are to be protected; this can be changed to correspond to the selection areas as well. Also, this 50 percent red color of the quick mask can be changed to a different color and translucency.

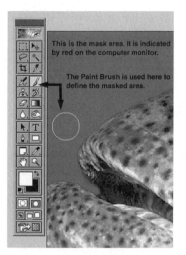

The mask acts like the Amberlith or Rubylith graphic arts materials used in prepress stripping, which would block exposure to orthochromatic materials through a chromatic filtering process. Here, however, the simulated litho mask simply allows the user to see the area that is being defined. This defined area, once converted back to the standard edit mode, will act just like any other type of selection.

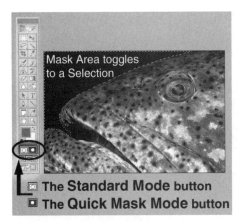

The Standard Mode button
The Quick Mask Mode button

It is significant to note that the quick mask mode can be used in isolation or in combination with any other selection tool or method. These selections can be added to, subtracted from, and modified by any or all selection tools. What this means is that one area might ideally be defined with the magic wand, while another portion of the image can be selected by using the quick mask mode, or the pen tool, or the lasso, and so forth.

Selecting a Color Range

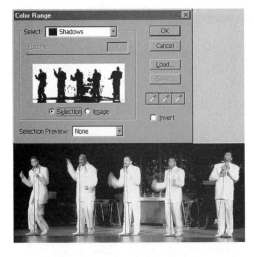

Without discussing every selection tool or mode—Adobe does an excellent job of this in their help documentation—the ability to select a color range has to be one of the most powerful tools available to the digital photographer.

This selection mode allows you to select just the highlights, midtones, shadows, reds, greens, blues, cyans, magentas, or yellows in a layer of an image.

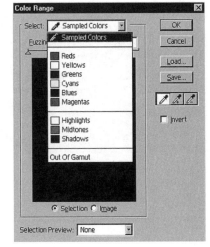

This ability to define regions of an image, based upon tonal or chromatic value, allows for a very specialized and selective way in which to alter an image.

As illustrated, the Color Range selection mode is used to select just the shadow areas of the photograph of the Temptations.

In order to isolate the musicians from their background, the shadow areas of the background need to be darkened.

Here the selection was used to apply more exposure to the background through the brightness and contrast command, and use of the burn tool.

In another example, the image of the tree has had the highlights selected through the use of a color range selection.

Then the highlights were converted from positive image information to negative. The resulting effect is similar to a solarization.

Saving a Selection

Now that you have learned a number of different ways to select portions of an image, wouldn't it be nice to have a way to recall these selections—on demand—at any point in your image-editing session. After all, why go through all the work of reselecting a background or sky again because you forgot to adjust the contrast, for example?

Well, you can save your selections and recall them later. In Photoshop, a selection is saved as a channel. This channel of information is then loaded by the user—and converted by Photoshop into a selection area—when requested through the Select > Load Selection menu choice.

To save a selection after an area has been selected, navigate to the Select > Save Selection menu option.

When the dialog box appears, you will be presented with options of where to save the selection. By default, the selection is saved in a channel in the active image, and the user can name the selection as well.

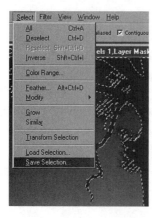

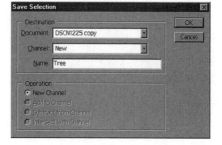

To load a selection, navigate to the Select > Load Selection menu option. When the dialog box appears, a choice of selections is shown. When loading a selection, as with saving a selection, other options are presented.

For example, a selection can be saved to or loaded from either the active document or another document—with the same pixel dimensions.

Consider this new ability to save and 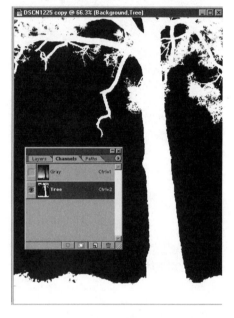 load selections (masks) as another step in the refinement of your ability to have even more control over the development of your images in the digital darkroom.

Conclusions

This chapter has provided an overview of some of the foundational tools and skills that are required to begin working in the digital darkroom. It is not the intention of this book to serve as a replacement for Adobe's documentation. Rather, consider this chapter as a primer, to aid you in beginning to work in your digital darkroom. The concepts discussed in this chapter are mostly universal to all image-editing software applications. The reason for focusing solely on Adobe Photoshop is because it is the de facto standard application for image editing on both the Mac and Windows platforms.

Through the examples presented in this chapter, you can begin to realize just how selective you can be and how much control you can have over fine adjustments and manipulations to your photographic imagery. In the next chapter we will explore some more advanced techniques which will increase your digital darkroom skills even further.

Review Questions:

1 How can an image file be opened in Photoshop when its type cannot be determined by the application? Why is this a significant issue if working on images between Mac and Windows machines?

2 What file format is necessary to use for saving all of an image's information, including layers, channels, paths, and so forth?

3 At what point in the image-editing process should the photographer be concerned with an image's resolution? Why?

4 Does a photographer have more or less control over the tonal manipulation of an image in the digital darkroom, as compared to the wet darkroom? List three significant examples.

a. _____

b. _____

c. _____

Discussion Questions:

1 How has the digital darkroom changed the way we think about tonal control of photographic images?

2 Why does a photographer need to know how the digital image will be used before beginning to work in the digital darkroom? How does this potentially impact the quality of the reproduction of your images?

3 Why is creating and defining selections/masks so important to the photographer? How does this affect one's ability to produce high-quality imagery in the digital darkroom?

4 How has the digital darkroom affected the photographer's ability to control color fidelity, in comparison to traditional, wet darkroom printing techniques?

Advanced Imaging Techniques

Objectives:

This chapter addresses image-editing techniques that range from dealing with multilayer images to advanced techniques such as batch processing. Upon completion of this chapter, the reader should have a better understanding of:

- How and why to use different layer types and effects in a digital image
- How to create composite images, and selectively modify image components
- When and how to use channels for mask and spot color information
- How to use specialized colors such as TRU-MATCH and PANTONE book colors in your images
- How to customize your digital darkroom tools from brushes to textures, through styles and histories and actions
- How to automate repetitive tasks and batch process multiple images
- How to create visual illusions with Photoshop

Introduction

I n the last chapter, we introduced the digital darkroom. The discussion focused around the idea of adapting a working methodology to the digital darkroom. Here we will continue discussing ways to function in the digital darkroom. As with most of this book, the idea of the workflow being central to the digital darkroom will be a focus in this chapter as well.

When speaking of advanced image-editing techniques, we are speaking in subjective terms. That is, what one person may consider to be advanced, another may consider basic. Thus, this discussion will deal with concepts that may be considered advanced by some, but others may simply interpret as fundamental. That being said, understand that all of the techniques that you develop in the digital darkroom are fundamentals, after they are learned.

This chapter will deal with digital image-editing techniques that range from working with images that are composed of multiple layers, to the customization of your working environment, through the automation of tasks and procedures. In this way, we are interpreting the term "advanced" as pertaining to the mastery of the techniques and tools that you can use in your digital darkroom workflow.

We will be discussing advanced image-editing techniques using Adobe Photoshop almost exclusively. Although the attempt in this book is to speak as broadly as possible, Photoshop is the only professional image-editing solution for the photographer that is fully cross-platform. In this way, it doesn't matter whether we are working on a Mac or a PC; we are simply working in Photoshop,

To begin this discussion, we will examine how an image can be edited from a traditional animation perspective using cell-based overlays, referred to as layers.

Layers

When we think of a photograph, we think of a two-dimensional image. Yet when we consider how layers work, we are really dealing with a three-dimensional space. The concept of editing images in the digital darkroom is rooted in historical processes. Specifically, cell animation is the model from which image-editing layers are derived. In cell animation, an artist might paint a background image of a field of flowers, for example, and then continue building the scene where all of the elements that might be in the scene would be illustrated on sheets of clear acetate. These sheets are "laid over" the top of the background image, forming a new composite image, one that is the result of all of the overlay images in combination with the background.

With still digital photographic images in a software application such as Photoshop, the procedure is structurally similar to cell animation, except that the need for motion no longer exists. Here the idea of working on an image's components on separate sheets of clear film allows the digital photographer to work in a way that will not alter the background image. Additionally, the order of these clear (transparent) layers can be changed. This is significant in that it allows for the movement of image components in front of or behind each other. In addition to image components, layers can also affect an image in a variety of other less-traditional, or completely nontraditional, ways.

Types of Layers

There are five basic layer types in Photoshop that can be used to enhance or otherwise modify an image.

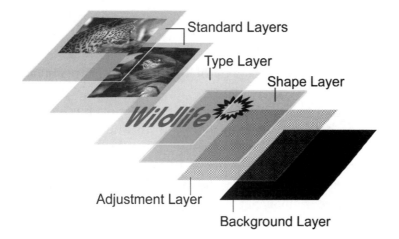

- **Standard Layers:** These layers are images or components of images that can be edited independent of the background image.
- **Adjustment Layers:** This type of layer can alter the images that are beneath it, using attributes such as brightness, contrast, color balance, etc.
- **Type Layers:** This vector-based layer mathematically describes type fonts, and can be scaled with no degradation to the type font.
- **Shape Layers:** This vector-based layer mathematically describes shapes, and can be scaled with no degradation to its components.
- **Background Layers:** These layers are images or components of images that can be edited. This is the default image layer.

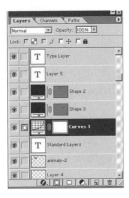

Each of the layer types has a different function that can dramatically aid you when working on digital images.

Standard Layers

To begin, the standard layer is the most obvious type of layer. This type of layer contains bitmapped image information. Generally speaking, when you refer to an image layer, this is the type of layer that is described—a portion of the visual image's information that when composited makes a final image.

When editing image components, the standard layer acts as a piece of clear acetate, with enhanced features that go beyond what is possible with traditional film. This combination makes layers somewhat magical, in that they can be used not only for the isolation of image components, but also for techniques such as pass-through blending and the algorithmic interpretation of tonal and color differences between layers. What this means is that images, or image components, can be visually combined in a variety of ways that far exceed the simple overlaying of image elements of the layer. For example, a simple use of a standard layer might be to combine two elements to create a new image.

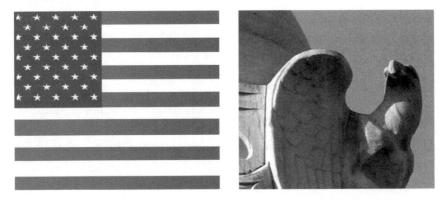

Here we have an image of the American flag that we want to display over the photograph of the eagle. In the most simplistic form, this composite shows the utilization of layers to composite multiple images.

As you can see, the image of the flag is scaled and placed in the upper left corner of the image. If, however, changes are made to the layer's mode, the composite blend can be altered. Here the mode has been changed to Multiply, and the opacity of the top-blending layer has been set to 75%.

This combination illustrates the very different visual effect that is produced by altering the characteristics of a layer. It is important to note that the image components on the layers have not been altered in any way.

Rather, only the layer characteristics have been modified. These characteristics can be reset to the original values (Normal mode and 100% opacity) with no image degradation. Thus, one of the great advantages of using layers to edit an image is that the layers can be duplicated image information, and the ability to experiment with visual problems does not need to degrade the original image. For example, let's say that you want to convert a black-and-white negative to a color image in a traditional workflow. One creative technique that can be used to accomplish this is to paint on your black-and-white negative with colors that are complimentary to the desired outcome. For example, if you want a blue sky, you would paint with yellow in the sky areas of the negative, so that its compliment would be printed in the darkroom. This is a common creative technique that yields unusual results. The problem here is that the original negative will be ruined if you paint on it. Therefore, even in a traditional darkroom, the concept of layers can be employed, in that you can paint on a clear piece of film, which is then overlaid upon the negative before printing. Yet to go one step further, let's say that part of the creative process requires that a negative be scratched to add a new visual element. Here you can see that the original negative will be permanently altered.

This is where the standard layers in Photoshop can be a lifesaver—for your negatives.

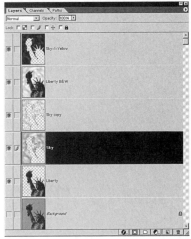

Scratching the negative in Photoshop is as easy as duplicating the image layer, and creating the scratch effect on the new layer.

If it doesn't look right, the layer can simply be discarded, and editing can begin again on a new copy.

This is where the magic of the digital darkroom can be truly realized.

One of the most common uses for layers is the compositing of image elements to form a new image. This is where selective elements are blended to give the illusion of a new, singular image.

Unlike the example with the Statue of Liberty, montage images often comprise elements from several sources. In this next example, you can see that two source images form the basis from which we will build the next illustration.

Here the image of the alligator and the image of the lake will be composited to create a final illustration that shows a ghosted image of the alligator in the upper left corner of the lake image. To begin, we need to change the resolution of both images so that they are the same. For example, both images here are 300 pixels per inch in resolution. Next, the image of the alligator needs to be copied as a layer on top of the image of the lake. This can be accomplished simply by dragging the layer icon from the alligator image over the lake image. This will automatically create a new layer in the lake image that contains the alligator image's information.

As can be seen in the illustration, the image of the alligator appears to be an opaque rectangular image, which is overlaid upon the lake image.

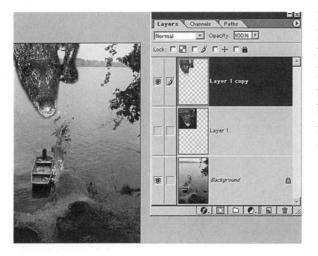

Now we need to alter the alligator layer in a way that will make the blend of these image components look more natural. There are many ways to accomplish this, but in this case a protective quick mask was made around the alligator's head and leg.

On a new layer, the background of the alligator image was deleted by using a soft-edged eraser. This produced a composite image that showed the alligator's head in the upper left corner of the lake image.

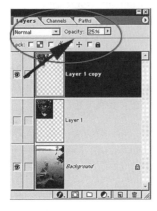

The problem here is that the initial concept called for a ghosted alligator image. To accomplish this, the opacity of the layer was reduced to make a translucent version of the alligator component of the image. It is important to note that the alteration of the opacity of a layer does not alter the layer's image data. It only alters the representation of the image data.

At any point the layer can be restored to its original opaque state. Thus, the final composite of the image shows the blended components from the two different source images, as specified in the concept development stage.

The real power of using standard layers is that each layer is essentially a different image that is saved as part of the whole which can be turned on and off at will, and that can be modified in numerous ways—that do not necessarily permanently alter the original image.

Adjustment Layers

Photo available in color. Please see insert for further study.

One of the more powerful features of the digital darkroom is the ability to have extensive control over the reproduction of images. Specifically, the ability to have precise control over the tonal and/or color control of an image is of special interest to the photographer.

It is the ability to have masterful control over the medium of digital photography that separates the novice from the professional photographer. With software applications such as Photoshop, the ability to control tonal and color information as layers has opened up new worlds of possibility to the creative photographer. The reason that layer-based image adjustments are so significant is because alterations to the image, or portions thereof, can be selectively applied and/or removed at any point in the image-editing process.

Photo available in color. Please see insert for further study.

What this means is that we can apply local contrast, density, color balance, or color saturation controls selectively. Thus, all areas of the image can be controlled independently in terms of their tonal and color characteristics. This is quite significant in the professional photographer's workflow. For example, let's say that an art director wants to see visual variations of an image for a Hard Rock Café campaign. The original photograph showed a palm tree, a guitar and sign with red details, and a portion of a building. The first request was to modify the image so that the color red would be replaced with yellow.

In order to accomplish this, an adjustment layer called Selective color can be used to identify the red areas in the image. These colors can then be altered to produce the yellow replacement color.

Using this method of image color control, the whole layer is affected. In order for certain local areas to be changed, a layer mask is used to selectively control which areas of the image layer, beneath the adjustment layer, are to be affected. The layer mask is simply a black-and-white mask that allows only certain areas of an image to be affected. This works just like a quick mask, which is turned into a selection later, to alter an area of an image.

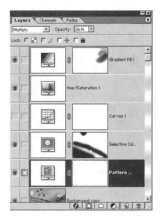

The difference here is that if the mask is linked to an adjustment layer, it automatically applies the variations of the mask to the adjustment layer. Therefore, the layer mask is one way to have precise control over the way in which adjustment layers are applied to selected portions of an image.

In this example, we can see that a mask has been created that will protect the black areas of the mask. Here, the center of the palm tree and the main part of the building are protected (black areas in the mask) and the rest of the image layer is affected by the Selective color adjustment layer—exchanging yellow for red areas of the image.

Next, the art director wanted to see a soft effect that involved the reversal of some of the colors in the image, but not as dramatic as a negative image. The solution was to alter a Curves adjustment layer to produce this effect.

Here, the tonal curve of the image was altered in such a way that the ends of the curve—black-and-white areas in the image—were slightly directed toward a reversal. As for the midtones, the shape of the curve was

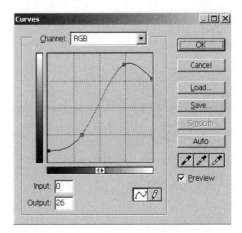

altered at about the one-third point from each end of the curve. This produced an image with a combination of both surreal and real colors.

Next, a hot and saturated neon-style image variation was desired. A Hue/Saturation adjustment layer was used to super-saturate the colors, giving a neon look.

Photo available in color. Please see insert for further study.

Finally, two other variations were sought. First, a fade-out effect was requested, so that text and graphics could be placed over a dark area in the bottom left corner of the image. Here, a gradient adjustment layer was used to fade the image to black from the upper right corner toward the lower left corner.

Photo available in color. Please see insert for further study.

In addition, a layer mask was used to block the gradient from darkening the top point of the guitar too much. Lastly, the art director asked for an alien-type effect. Specifically, a smooth green sky was requested. Additionally, a light alien skin-type of texture was desired on the guitar in combination with parts of the building.

The solution here was to combine the effects of several adjustment layers and layer masks: Gradient fill,Hue/Saturation, Selective color, and Pattern fill layers were used to produce this effect.

Type Layers

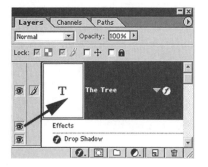

Unlike image layers and image adjustment layers, type layers consist of scalable vector-based type information.

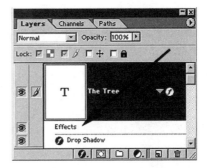

This type of layer is editable and scalable. What this means to the image-maker is that now type can be added to images in Photoshop, and if the file is saved properly—as an Adobe Photoshop file—the text can be modified at a later date without degrading the quality of the image or the type. This is significant because the way most other image- processing software handles text is as bitmap image information. That is, once the text is placed on the image, it permanently alters the pixels of the original image. Another great advantage of handling text on a text layer is that when the image is output, the text will match the highest resolution of the output device—and will not be limited to the pixel resolution of the original image.

As for special effects, because the text is handled as a layer, special effects can be applied to the layer in a manner that will not degrade or alter the original text. Thus, the effects can be turned on and off at will.

Shape Layers

Yet another vector-based tool, the shape layer allows you to create a graphic in Photoshop that is not bitmapped.

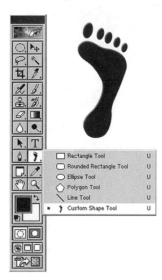

This type of layer/graphic can be scaled with no degradation—just as with text layers. Using a shape layer allows you to create a graphic from a predefined shape or a custom shape. For example, if you wants to make a graphic of a foot on your photographic image, the shape layer is a simple way of accomplishing this task.

Both standard shapes—like rectangles and circles—and custom shapes can be drawn with the shape tool. As with other imaging layer-types, shape layers can also have special effects applied to them without altering the original shape.

The beauty here is that the original vector-based shape can be scaled with no degradation, and so can the special effects.

Layer Effects

A unique way of applying special effects to standard layers, shape layers, and text layers is through the use of layer effects.

A layer effect produces a visual alteration to the information contained on an image layer, without degrading or permanently altering the original image information. Thus, you can experiment with visual solutions without worrying about ruining your image. A variety of visual alterations can be accomplished using layer effects such as adding drop shadows, beveling and embossing objects, adding color and/or texture to layer objects, and more.

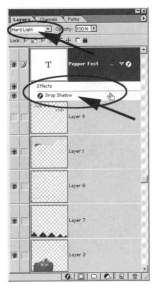

In the example presented here, we can see the layer-effects layer beneath the layer to be affected.

In this case, a drop shadow is being added to a type layer. This was accomplished by clicking on the ⟨⟨icon⟩⟩ icon, at the bottom of the layer palate and selecting drop shadow.

Next, an options window is presented that allows the image-maker to select the particular attributes of the effect to be applied to the layer. Here such elements as the transparency and the color of the shadow can be selected, as well as the shadow's softness, angle, and more.

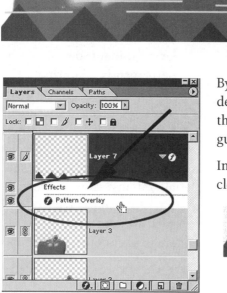

In this next example, the texture of a layer is altered by using an effects layer. In the original image, the triangles are smooth, textureless objects.

By applying a pattern overlay layer effect with a degree of transparency to the layer that contains the triangles, a texture is added to only the triangular shapes at the bottom of the image.

In the detail image, the texture can be seen quite clearly.

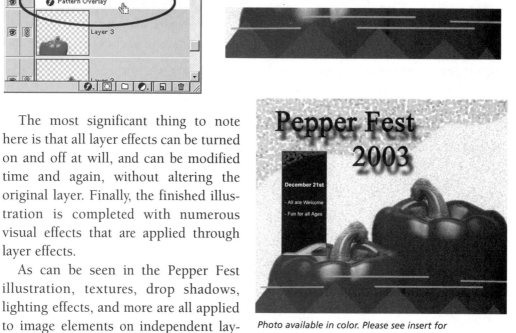

Photo available in color. Please see insert for further study.

The most significant thing to note here is that all layer effects can be turned on and off at will, and can be modified time and again, without altering the original layer. Finally, the finished illustration is completed with numerous visual effects that are applied through layer effects.

As can be seen in the Pepper Fest illustration, textures, drop shadows, lighting effects, and more are all applied to image elements on independent layers. This workflow allows for easy changes after the image is complete.

As anyone who has been in the industry can attest to, clients and art directors change their minds often. By creating illustrations as layers, and not altering the layer information in a permanent fashion, the image-maker can easily modify the image to meet new and changing expectations.

Selecting and Modifying Layers

One of the greatest problems of working on multilayered images is keeping track of which layer you are working on at a given point in the editing process. Because the entire composite image can be seen at one time, it is easy to become confused as to which layer any particular image information is located on. It could easily happen that after making some changes, it appears that nothing has happened, only to then realize that you were working on a different layer than you thought. This is a common occurrence; sometimes this even happens to the professionals. After you become more accustomed to working in this manner, this will occur less frequently.

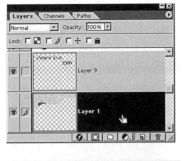

To begin working on a layer, you should first identify which one it is. This is accomplished simply by clicking on the layer in the layers palette.

The layer to be modified is then displayed as white text on a dark background to differentiate it from the other layers.

To modify the layer, edit the image information just as you would with a single background layer image—the default Photoshop image type. The distinction here is that the modifications that are applied will only pertain to the layer that is selected, and not the other image layers.

Thus, you can modify isolated image elements. This gives the image-maker a great deal of control over the articulation of images. For example, let's say that you want to modify an image in a way that removes an object, and additionally alters the color of the image.

Photo available in color. Please see insert for further study.

Photo available in color. Please see insert for further study.

This is a great use of layers because a number of tasks need to be performed. Modifying a layer allows mistakes to have a minimal impact on the overall project. That is, if you are editing an image, and the image is altered in an incorrect way at the end of the editing process, on a one-layer image the ability to go back to various editing points to correct a problem is limited. This is one reason why modifying layers is quite useful in making your workflow more efficient.

In the illustration of the tree presented here, we can see that in the original image, there is a tree on the left side of the image. The first task here is to remove the tree. So a duplicate layer is made from the background image and then modified primarily using the clone tool, to remove the tree.

After this editing step, it was determined that the foreground was too bright. In order to darken the foreground, a Gradient overlay effects layer was created to gently darken the foreground to blend it toward the background.

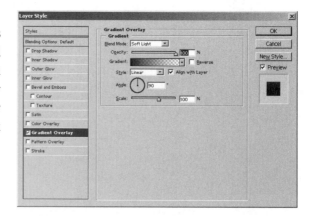

Photo available in color. Please see insert for further study.

This resulted in an image that emphasized the tree, the fence, and the afterglow in the scene. It was then determined that the color cast from the sodium vapor lighting—which illuminated the tree in the original photograph—created a color cast that was not pleasing to the image-maker.

Photo available in color. Please see insert for further study.

The creative solution here was to create an image that fades from a black-and-white foreground to a color background. Additionally, it was determined that the entire tree should be black and white, against the color background, for a dramatic effect. After applying a Hue/Saturation adjustment layer to convert the image from color to black and white, a layer mask was created to let the image's original color information show through the Hue/Saturation layer. This produced the final image's effect of an image that was both black and white and color.

Creating Composite Images

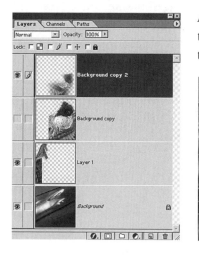

As we illustrated earlier, composite images are those that are created by assembling parts of several images to create one image.

Photo available in color. Please see insert for further study.

Generally, image components are gathered from multiple images, and imported as individual layers. These layers then act as clear sheets of film, which contain various image components. When superimposed, these components form a composite image. Here an image of a guitar, a dinosaur, and a vampire-type image are superimposed to create a rough layout for a CD cover.

Here we will illustrate several different ways to alter composite image components.

Transforming Layers

The ability to transform image information into new shapes has changed the way photographers think about many traditional concepts. This is not because transformations weren't possible with traditional media; rather, it is the accessibility and ease with which we can manipulate image information that makes digital transformations so powerful. In order to accomplish transformations with traditional media, you would need to utilize a view camera, alter the relationship of the enlarging easel to the enlarging lens, or apply other such physical manipulation to the image through optics. However, virtually all of the transformations that could be accomplished in a traditional setting can also be accomplished in the digital darkroom.

Additionally, extreme alterations can be made to the images that go beyond the limitations of the traditional darkroom. Below, four basic image-layer transformations will be discussed: perspective control, distortion, scaling, and rotation.

Perspective Control

Photo available in color. Please see insert for further study.

Perspective control has been accomplished in traditional media by using the camera. Utilizing a large-format camera to optically distort an image to make it appear to be correct has been a challenge for architectural photographers. It's not that it is difficult to achieve corrected perspectives for a skilled photographer; rather, it is a cumbersome process. Beyond perspective control, the idea of post-processing an image to correct it in the digital darkroom offers a few extra features, which are not possible with traditional media. We can quite easily alter the perspective of an image digitally. The distinction here is that we can modify more than just the perspective. In the example here, the first photograph shows an image of a house that displays no perspective control.

Photo available in color. Please see insert for further study.

Additionally, the image of the house has power lines across the façade of the structure: an architect's nightmare. So as a creative architectural photographer, the job presented here is two-fold. First, the perspective needs to be corrected to the true form of the structure, and next the power lines need to be removed. This is the point where we realize that this transformation is essentially impossible with traditional media—unless we have an incredible airbrushing budget.

Beyond this, the tonal range of the image was expanded; this is possible because the original image was captured on digital media. The greater dynamic range of the digital recording media itself has added to the articulation of this image, as well.

In addition to perspective correction, this function can also be used to produce creative visual effects.

Here a photograph of a Washington D.C. Metro station has been altered using the perspective transformation function of Photoshop.

Photo available in color. Please see insert for further study.

Distortion

With perspective control, we have illustrated the correct way to alter an image's appearance, but we do not always need to correct an image. Sometimes the visual goal is quite the opposite; that is, we want to distort the image to produce a creative effect. Here we have an image of the United States Supreme Court.

Let's say that this image is to be used as part of a multiple-image composite, and it needs to look as though it is falling back and to the right. This is the perfect job for the distort transformation. Here each corner of the image can be stretched or compressed to form a new and unique shape for the image. As can be seen in the illustration, the distort function can be used to manipulate the shape of a layer of an image. In this case, the foreground is exaggerated and the building seems to be falling back and to the right side.

Photo available in color. Please see insert for further study.

The distort transformation can also be used for perspective control, to tweak perspective modifications in a more free-form fashion, than the perspective transformation allows.

Photo available in color. Please see insert for further study.

Scaling

Especially when creating multiple-image composites, scaling is an important part of combining the image elements. Instead of scaling each element independently, before importing it into a composite image as a layer, the individual layers within one image can be scaled. This is significant in that it allows for a much more rapid and efficient working environment. Additionally, scaling can be used on a single layer image to adjust its height, width, or both. This can be done in either a constrained manner—where both the height and width are scaled proportionally—or in a way that distorts the image's aspect ratio.

As can be seen in the example here, this image's aspect ratio was distorted to make the image look short and wide.

Rotating

Just as an entire image can be rotated, so too can individual layers be rotated—independent of each other and the base image.

Photo available in color. Please see insert for
further study.

This is especially useful for correcting tilted horizons, and manipulating image elements in composite images. As illustrated here, a layer can be rotated on a transparent background, which allows for the overlaying of layered image elements.

Channels

Image channels allow the image-maker to make sophisticated masks for the precise editing of image information. They also offer the ability to edit an image's component color information. For example, we can edit just the red channel of information of an RGB image.

The main use of channels regards selections. That is, when you make a selection and save it to be recalled later, the selection is saved as a channel. This is significant to the image-maker because this selection becomes a mask. Further, this mask can be edited. With respect to traditional media, this is like making a lithographic mask. Thus, a standard channel mask looks like a lithographic representation of an outline—black and white only.

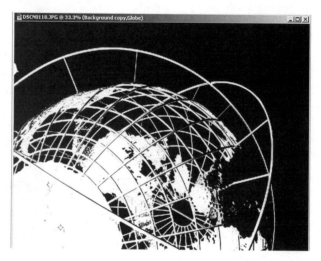

Standard Grayscale Channels as Color Information Channels

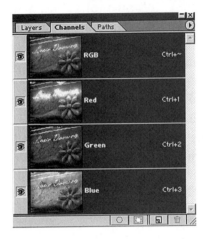

To step back for a moment, let's examine the most basic type of channel: the color channel. In a black-and-white image, this is the grayscale channel. In a standard RGB image, it is the red, green, or blue information that makes up the color components of a color image. As illustrated, the red, green, and blue channels are black-and-white images, which when combined and filtered with the appropriate light, create the full-color RGB composite image. Thus, if each color channel is a black-and-white image, it follows that the black-and-white image can be edited, which will affect the resultant RGB image. We will illustrate this later.

Composite Channel

Photo available in color. Please see insert for further study.

The composite channel is a combination of sub-channels. For an RGB image, the combination of the red, green, and blue channels creates the final composite. Accordingly the combination of the cyan, magenta, yellow, and black channels forms the composite CMYK image. All channels do not, however, need to be utilized to create a composite image. For example, an RGB image that only displays the red and green channels of information will look radically different from a full-RGB image.

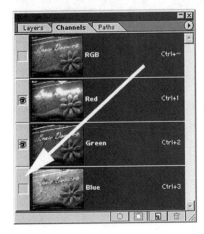

Here you can see the difference when the blue channel of color information is subtracted from the composite image.

Photo available in color. Please see insert for further study.

The colors in the new version of the image are devoid of blue image information. Thus, red and green appear to be emphasized in the resulting image.

This is one way that color channels can be used creatively to create new visual solutions.

By breaking a color image into its component information, we can also modify the color characteristics of an image in very subtle and controlled ways, thus giving the image-maker the ability to be very particular about the way the images are crafted.

Alpha Channels

Simply put, alpha channels are masks. The alpha channel is the place where a selection is stored.

This mask, or stored selection, can then be modified for use as a mask. At the most basic level, alpha channels can conserve much time in the digital darkroom by saving a selection.

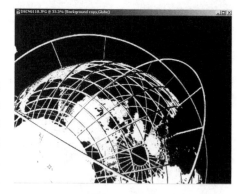

For example, in the illustration of the globe presented here, imagine selecting all of the intricate details of the globe. This could take quite a bit of time, and we would probably not want to go through all of that work again. So, if the selection was saved, to be recalled later, this would make our workflow much more efficient. In order to do this, the selection can be saved as an alpha channel. Once saved, an alpha channel can be converted into a selection. The selection can then be applied to an image, or image layer, to produce a variety of visual effects.

Spot Color Channels

To go beyond the limitations of RGB or CMYK color modes, we can use a spot color to add precise colors to the final, printed image. When printing an image on a commercial printing press, an additional pass on the press is required for each spot color used in the image. Thus, each spot color requires its own printing plate.

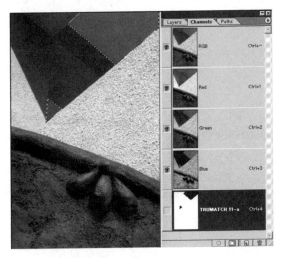

To add a spot color to an image, an alpha channel is created to represent the printed area of the spot color. This channel can be either black and white or continuous-tone in nature.

In this example, the two gray areas in the upper portion of the image are to be replaced with a spot color.

To do this, first, the areas of the image to be printed with a spot color need to be identified and selected. This was accomplished by using the magic wand tool to select both of the gray areas. Then the selection needs to be saved as an alpha channel (mask).

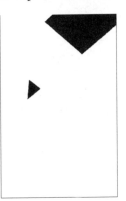

Here, the alpha channel shows these two areas as black graphic shapes.

To convert this alpha channel into a spot color channel, double-click the channel. A Channel Options dialog box then appears, which allows for the conversion of the channel into a spot color channel.

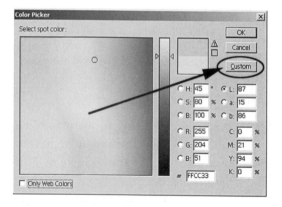

Now the actual spot color for the channel is chosen by clicking on the color swatch. The familiar Color-picker dialog box is then displayed.

To choose a specific color, such as a TRUMATCH or PANTONE color, select the Custom option.

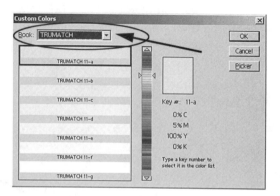

Then it is simply a matter of selecting the color book from which the color is being chosen, and of course the ink color.

Once the selection of ink has been made, the alpha channel is converted into a spot color channel.

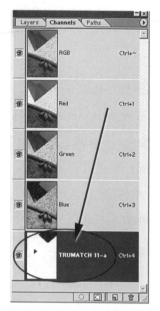

This can be seen in the channel palette. By default, the spot color channel is identified by the ink's name. For example, here we have chosen TRUMATCH 11—a yellow—as the ink to be overprinted on the gray areas of this image.

The fact that spot channels are overprinted after the cyan, magenta, yellow, and black passes on the printing press warrants attention. This is because the yellow TRUMATCH color that we are overprinting here will be on top of the full-color printed image. Thus, it will block out any color printed beneath it, if it is an opaque ink. If, however, we want to see through the spot color ink—and blend its color with those beneath—the solidity of the ink coverage would need to be changed. This is accomplished by altering the ink's coverage characteristics. Double-clicked on the spot color channel to change the percentage of solidity. The result is a lower percentage of ink coverage on the final image.

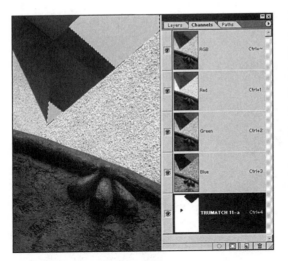

In the end, the final print appears with the new ink overprinted, as per the channel mask(s) that the image-maker has created. This is especially useful for printing out of gamut colors, and inks such as metallic colors that cannot be reproduced with CMYK.

A final note about spot colors: to properly save an image with spot color channels, it must be saved in the native Photoshop file format, the Photoshop DCS 2.0 or higher format (EPS), or as a Tiff (in Photoshop 6 or higher).

Selecting and Modifying Channels (including converting alpha channel masks to selections)

Image channels are very powerful tools for the image-maker. They allow the component-level color information of an image to be altered, and beyond this, they allow for very precise control of image masks. This combination opens up numerous technical and creative possibilities for the photographer.

Before we can discuss selecting and modifying channels, we must first see how to create channels, also known as channel masks or alpha channels. The process is quite simple; elaborating upon our earlier discussion, make a selection in an image, and save the selection.

The process of saving a selection automatically creates a channel in the image. This channel contains a black-and-white representation of the selection. This black-and-white image represents the channel mask, that is, those areas that are protected and those that are affected, when the channel mask is applied to the image.

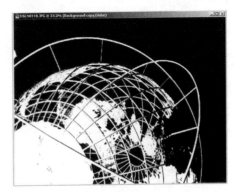

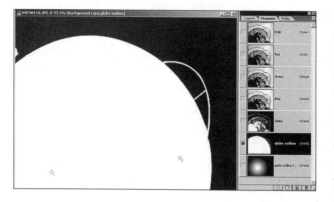

Now that the image contains an alpha channel, this channel information can be used as is, or modified, to apply different effects to local areas within the image. For example, let's say that we first choose to modify the channel information to create a different mask. By selecting the channel, and deselecting the RGB channel, we see the black-and-white mask. Then it is a simple matter of painting or otherwise modifying the image information on the globe channel mask. Here we will convert the mask into an outline mask, by painting all of the interior areas white, and all of the exterior areas black.

Now to convert the channel mask back to a selection, we need to first select the RGB channel in the channels palette, so that we will be editing the whole image, and not just the channel mask. From here, the channel mask needs to be loaded as a selection.

Because we can create multiple channels, the correct channel needs to be identified, to load the proper selection.

In the illustration presented here, the selection of the sky is loaded, and the globe is protected by the mask. Thus, simply hitting the delete key cuts away the sky in the original image.

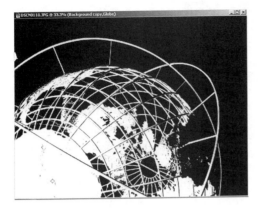

Next, we created a new variation of this image by loading the original channel mask—the one that contained interior information for the globe (shown as a mask here).

This channel was loaded as a selection, and then by simply hitting the delete key, we produced an image that was very low-contrast. Essentially, we deleted all of the dark areas in the globe, and thus created this new image.

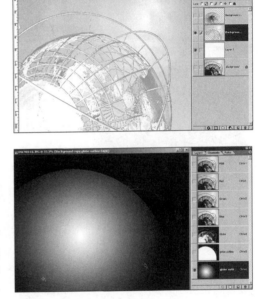

Next we decided to create a more complex mask. We wanted to create a mask that contained smooth gradations of tone. To accomplish this, the globe outline channel was duplicated, and was loaded as a selection. Still editing only the channel, the selected area of the globe outline channel mask was filled with a radial gradient blend.

Next, the channel mask was loaded as a selection, and the selection was inverted—from the Select menu. Now we once again hit the delete key. The resultant image illustrates how selections and channel masks can have a subtlety to them that goes beyond the basic cut out-type selection.

Photo available in color. Please see insert for further study.

Finally, let's examine two more examples of modifying channels. Instead of modifying alpha channels, or spot color channels, let us look back to the basics. First, let's invert just the red channel of information in the globe image.

With no further modifications, we can see that the globe image now appears totally different from the original. By reversing the tones of this channel, we are changing the color relationships of all three primary color channels: red, green, and blue.

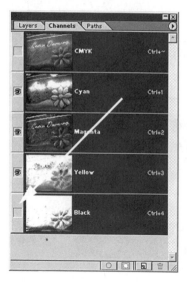

To go one step further, let us revisit the Latin Dancing image. Here we have converted the image from RGB to CMYK. Next we have removed—or disabled—the black layer, leaving only the cyan, magenta, and yellow color channels to represent the colors in the image.

Thus, the final image is much softer looking because the black, or shadow, components of the image have been reduced to gray. This gives the shadow areas of the image a solarized look.

Converting Selections to Paths

As we have already discussed, alpha channels can be converted to selections. This is a very useful way to affect local changes within an image. But what if we could convert channel masks into editable, vector-based outlines? This would open up all kinds of possibilities, regarding the control of local areas of an image. Well, we can!

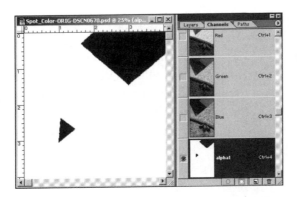

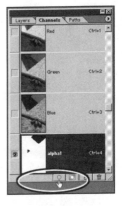

Converting an alpha channel to a path involves several steps. Of course, the first step is to have a channel mask (alpha channel) already created.

For this, we will look back to the image that we used to describe spot colors. Now, on the Channels palette, the icon of the dotted circle needs to be selected.

This will convert the channel mask into a selection. Note that this is the same as loading a selection from the Select menu. Next we need to go to the Paths palette. Now the selection needs to be converted into a path. This can be accomplished by clicking the ⌗ button to Make path from selection.

Now the path can be manipulated, just as though it were a path created with the pen tool. All of the traditional path tools can be used to alter the path, on the Paths palette. In the first path's illustration here, the whole path area surrounding the upper graphic has been dragged down to reveal its shape and points.

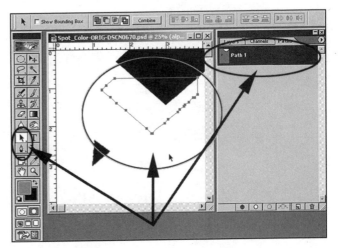

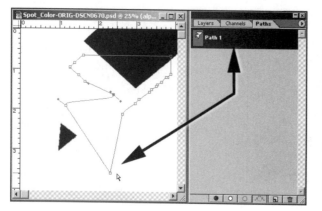

Also, the newly created path can be seen in the Paths palette in this illustration. Finally, the path is altered by dragging out two of its points to create a different shape.

Now the path can be converted back into a selection, and used to modify the graphic as desired.

Custom Colors

Let's face it: color makes the world go around. Maybe not your world, but at least the commercial world is totally dominated by color images. Therefore, it is important to understand color and the way in which you can address color in the digital darkroom.

Using Different Color Palettes
(using TRUMATCH, PANTONE, and other standard color books)

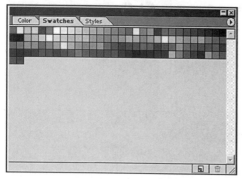

The first thing to consider is how to access different color palettes. One of the greatest needs the photographer and designer face is how to accurately match colors to those that will be reproduced.

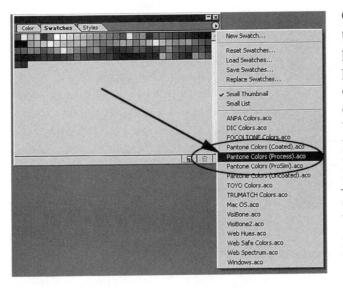

Often you will want to use the same blue from the corporate logo as part of their photographic illustration, for example. So let's say that the corporate blue color is PANTONE 190-1 Process, which has been selected from a PANTONE selection book. Just how do we match this color in Photoshop? Simple! We load the PANTONE process color book into Photoshop, and then select the color. Because we have already illustrated how to select a TRUMATCH color from the color picker, we will discuss an alternate way to choose PANTONE colors here. In this example, the Swatches palette will be used to load a custom book of colors. In this case, we need to load the PANTONE Process Colors book of color swatches.

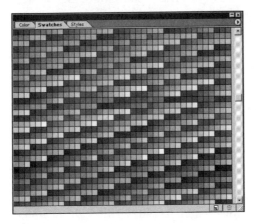

Note that when we load this color book, we will be presented with an option to replace the default colors, or to append these new colors to the end of the default color palette. Here we have replaced the default colors with the PANTONE Process Colors book of swatches.

Now, when you mouseover the swatches, the identifying PANTONE number is displayed in a floating help box, as illustrated. Thus, any TRUMATCH, PANTONE, , TOYO, Web-safe, or other predetermined color can be stored as a color swatch file that can be loaded into Photoshop, for accurate color matching.

Replacing Color in an Image

Photo available in color. Please see insert for further study.

As we illustrated in the adjustments layer section of this chapter, the easiest way to replace a color in a photograph is to use the replace color adjustment layer. If, however, the desired result is to replace a color with a specific ink color, we can use the techniques described in the spot color section of this chapter. Regardless of how the color is replaced, consider the fact that the need to accurately and professionally replace color in images is quite necessary in the commercial field of photography. For example, let's say that an art director wanted the image that you—the photographer—presented exactly as you shot it—except for one thing. Now the cartoon characters are to be red instead of yellow.

Photo available in color. Please see insert for further study.

What do you do? Simple: replace the yellow color with red just as we illustrated in the adjustment layers section of this chapter, and viola! Alternatively, you could create a Selective color adjustment layer, or even a masked color balance layer to accomplish this task. Regardless of the particular techniques you use, you have completed a seemingly difficult task in a matter of minutes—not hours or days.

Custom Brushes

Although modern software provides the digital artist with an incredible amount of tools, there are times when you may still want to make some of your own custom tools. Photoshop allows you to do just that. Suppose you were creating an illustration for a Halloween campaign, and wanted to design a paintbrush to give an appropriate look.

Then, as you examined your images, you realized that the texture of Frankenstein's hair was perfect.

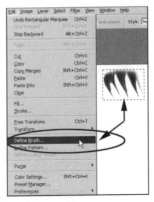

Well, you can easily make a brush from the hair in your photograph. First you need to isolate the element that is to become the brush—in this case, a portion of the hair. Next, the rectangular marquee needs to be used to define the area to become the brush. Now, Define Brush needs to be selected from the Edit menu.

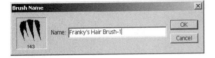

Here, one is given the opportunity to name the new brush.

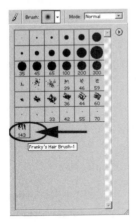

We have named our brush Franky's Hair Brush-1 so that it will be easy to remember why we made this brush at a later date. Once the brush has been created, it can be used in the same manner as any other brush.

Simply select it from the Brushes palette and paint, airbrush, dodge, burn, or do what ever you would with any other paintbrush.

Using a custom paintbrush can also be useful for creating watermarks of such things as corporate logos, or copyright notices.

Consider the use of a brush that was made in the shape of the Yahoo!™ logo, for this travel and leisure photograph.

Photo available in color.
Please see insert for
further study.

Custom Textures

Just as we can create our own brushes, we can also create individualized patterns and textures.

The procedure to produce custom textures is quite simple. First, to create a pattern, an area of the image needs to be identified by using the rectangular marquee tool.

 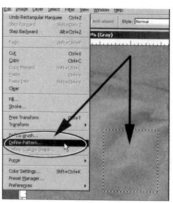

Once the area has been defined, it needs to be defined as a pattern, as illustrated.

The pattern can then be named and stored in the Patterns palette for recall at a later time.

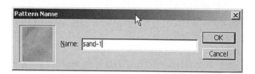

Note that patterns can be saved as sets, so one can create their own pattern libraries.

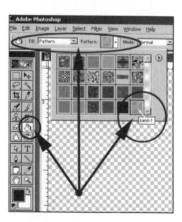

To use a pattern, a tool that allows for a pattern ink option needs to be used. For example, here we have used a paint bucket tool to apply our pattern.

You will notice that the fill type has been changed to Pattern in the tool options bar. Next, by selecting the down-arrow tab next to the pattern icon, the Pattern palette is displayed. Here the newly created pattern is selected. Finally, when the paint is dumped into an area, the pattern is applied, as shown here. This technique can be very useful for creating textured backgrounds, for example.

Styles

As we begin a discussion of automating repetitive tasks, a good starting point is the creation and usage of styles forms. This is because styles allow us to design a set of layer attributes that can be applied to another layer with the click of a button. This is a significant tool in facilitating our workflow in a more streamlined manner.

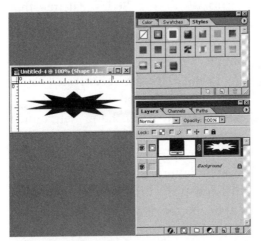

Let's say, for example, that in your workflow, you constantly need to design graphic shapes to be overlaid on your images.

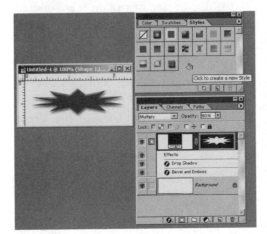

Furthermore, these graphics always have to be on a layer that has 80% opacity, a layer mode of Multiply, have a 120° drop shadow with a specific color and fade, as well as a bevel and emboss effect with its own specific criteria. Because you know that the graphics you will create will be on layers, your workflow can be dramatically improved by the simple creation of a style that defines all of these particular attributes. As we have illustrated here, the initial graphic has no special style or layer effects applied. So the first step here is to create all of the layer effects, layer mode changes, and opacity settings.

Once this is done, a new style can be created—based upon the attributes in the selected layer. On the Styles palette, you only need to click on a gray area—not a button—to create a new style. Here one is prompted to name the new style.

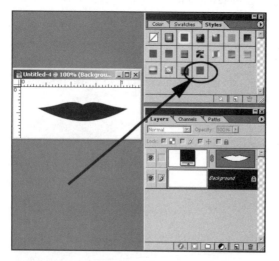

Now a new swatch, or button, will be displayed in the Styles palette—that represents the newly created style.

To use this style any time is quite a simple process. First, select a layer in the image. Here, we have created a new graphic shape layer of a pair of lips. Now to apply all of the predetermined attributes—that have been saved as a style—simply click the appropriate swatch/button in the Styles palette. At this point, all of the layer attributes are applied to the new layer—the lips layer in this case.

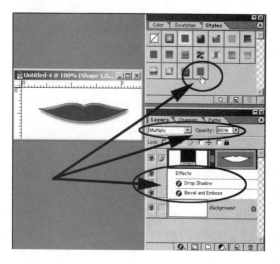

In the illustration below, one can see that by selecting the new style swatch/button, all of the settings are now the same for this new graphic.

Furthermore, styles can be used to automate a portion of your workflow, while the layer is still left editable. What this means is that the first eight steps of ten may be automated through the application of a layer style, but the last two steps of an editing process might be to subtlety alter the drop shadow effect and the layer's opacity—based upon the new graphic's look and feel.

History Palette

Wouldn't it be nice if you had a time machine, and you could go back into the past to change your mistakes? Well, now you do—at least as far as the digital darkroom is concerned. This magic can be performed with the aid of the History palette. Here we can revisit any of a number of image-editing steps, based upon how the workflow has been set up.

There are basically two ways to use the History palette as an image-editing tool. One way is to go back to a particular point in the editing process, and then to continue in an entirely different direction. The other way is to go back to a particular point in the editing process, and remove a step in the middle. These two methods of utilizing the History palette are known as linear history and non-linear history.

Before utilizing the History palette, it is important to set up the default number of History States to be saved at a given time.

This basically defines the number of procedures to be recorded. By default, this is usually set to save 20 history states, but up to 100 states can be recorded at a time. Just remember, the more states there are set to be recorded, the more RAM will be required. Here, we have set the number of states to be recorded to 30—in the Edit>Preferences Menu.

Linear History

The default way of working with image histories is in Standard mode. What this means is that each action is recorded as it's completed. For example, opening an image is the first completed action, while adjusting the image's brightness and contrast may be the second, and so on. This is significant to the image-maker's workflow because these procedures are being recorded; the real beauty is that they can be revisited later. Thus, depending upon how many history states are set to be recorded in a given image-editing session, you can go back to any point in the editing session, and begin editing again.

For example, let's say that after working on an image for a while, we look at the progress and realize that the last dozen or so things that were done really do not work well for this image. Well, with the History palette it is easy to go back. In our example, we have gone back to the Modify Levels Layer to begin editing the image from this point again. Notice that all of the history states below this point are grayed out, indicating that these are the states to be disregarded.

Now you can begin editing from any point in the history just as if you had saved that individual state's version of the image.

Non-Linear History

A bit more abstract than linear history is the concept of editing an image's history in a non-linear fashion. When editing an image in a non-linear fashion, you can randomly alter any given history state.

To change to a non-linear editing mode, first select History Options from the History palette menu. Then select the Allow Non-Linear History option.

Now you can begin to edit your work history in a given editing session in a non-linear fashion.

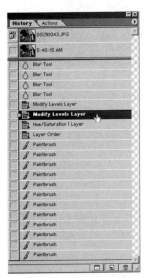

For example, in the illustration presented here, you could go back and remove the Modify Levels Layer without deleting the subsequent procedures that had occurred.

In this way, you can work out of sequence, to further extend your image-editing options. This is yet another example of how to make the workflow more productive. The ability to edit a session history in either a linear or non-linear way allows for increased productivity to address many creative imaging problems in new and creative ways.

History Snapshots

Another way that the History palette can be utilized in the workflow is through the use of captured history states—known as History Snapshots. At the top of the History palette is an area for history snapshots.

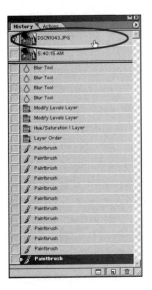

Basically, a history snapshot is a version of the image captured from a given history state. To create a history snapshot, either right-click in Windows or control+click on MAC on a given state in the history palette, and then select a new snapshot from the pop-out menu.

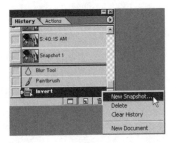

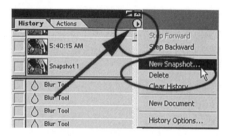

Alternatively, a new snapshot can be selected from the History palette menu.

So, for example, at one point an image may have been inverted, and we thought that might be useful later, so we created a snapshot from that image state. Now we can switch—on the fly—between an image's history state (any step) or any snapshot of the image.

This means that we can switch between numerous variations of an image in a click of the mouse to creatively interpret, or reinterpret an image.

Using the History Palette as a Creative Tool

As you can see, working with an image's editing history can be quite a powerful tool. To go one step further, however, consider that through the History palette you have the ability to edit a portion of an image from a given history state or snapshot—without affecting the entire image! This opens up countless new possibilities in terms of creativity.

Photo available in color. Please see insert for further study.

Let's take this image of the locomotive, for example.

Assuming that the art director likes the basic image, but wanted to do away with the blue of the sky and replace it with a textured black and charcoal surface, the history brush can be useful. We can process our idea of what the background should look like in the same image, and then paint from the history state or snapshot of the modified version. Here, the image of the train is modified in a way that creates a reversed, textured image.

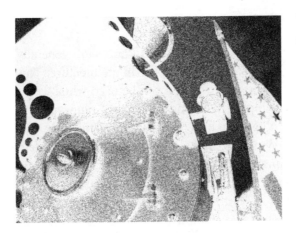

This was then saved as a history snap-shot.

At this point, the history brush icon was selected next to the graphic pen-inverted snapshot. This identifies which history snapshot, or history state, will become the palette from which the history brush will paint.

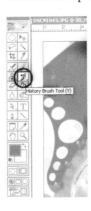

Now, select the history brush from the Tool palettes.

Finally, select areas are painted with the history brush so that the areas from the graphic pen-inverted snapshot become part of the final image.

Photo available in color. Please see insert for further study.

While this is only a simple example, there are many ways in which the use of the History palette and all of the associated history tools can dramatically increase productivity, and enhance the creative work process in the digital darkroom.

Third-Party Plug-Ins

Software that can be used from within an application such as Photoshop generally interfaces with the main software through a system called a plug-in architecture. This allows third-party software developers to create products that can be used while working in the primary application. Here we will discuss using third-party plug-ins with Photoshop, but the Photoshop compatible plug-in architecture is also used by other software applications such as Paint Shop Pro (Windows) and Color It (Mac), to name a few.

To use these types of software extensions, you will need to place the new software plug-ins into the Photoshop (or other image-editing software) plug-ins folder on your PC or Mac machine. When the application—Photoshop, in this example—is restarted, the new plug-ins are loaded, and become available for use. Examples of plug-ins range from calling on a scanner from a twain import plug-in to exporting files in an unusual file format through using special image effects filters.

In our discussion, we will illustrate just a few of the many plug-ins available for Photoshop. Note that there are free and shareware plug-ins that can be downloaded from the Internet, as well as commercial plug-ins that allow you to extend the functionality of Photoshop—or any application that uses Adobe's plug-in architecture. Also note that plug-ins are different between the Mac and the PC, so make sure you get the correct version of a plug-in. This is unlike actions that can be transported between Mac and PCs.

nik Sharpener Pro

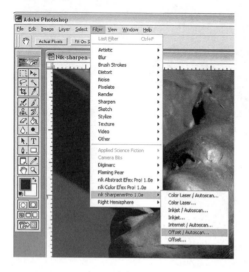

The first example of a third party plug-in we will discuss is nik Sharpener Pro. This is a set of specialized filters that allow you to sharpen images in ways that go far beyond even the best sharpening feature in Photoshop: the unsharp mask. The advantage of using a filter like this is that the algorithms employed allow for smart sharpening through the use of an AI (artificial intelligence) design. In practical terms this means that all areas of the image are not sharpened equally. The software scans the image, and based upon the patterns of the pixels detected, the sharpening occurs selectively. This makes for a very powerful image-processing tool.

When called from the filter menu, several choices of sharpening are shown, which are appropriate for devices ranging from inkjet printers to offset printing presses.

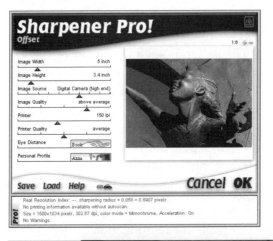

We have chosen the Offset version of Sharpener Pro. After setting the various sliders the way we want for the image, we can see the processed result. We have intentionally started with a preset called Anna (the photo of the eyes on the personal profile setting). This is the gentlest version of the filter.

After processing the image, you can see a before and after version of the image. Notice the degrees of sharpness in both the sharp and blurry areas of the image.

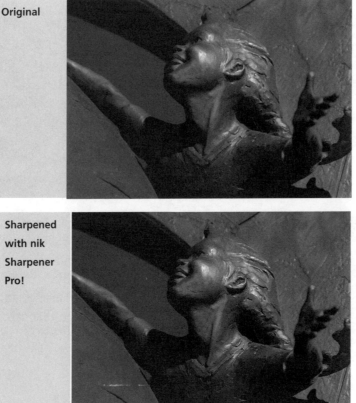

Original

Sharpened with nik Sharpener Pro!

Finally, seeing an original print side-by-side, one sharpened with the unsharp mask, and one sharpened with Sharpener Pro, will tell you more than any words—it's impressive.

nik Color EFEX Pro

Another set of filters produced by nik multimedia is called Color Efex Pro.

These are filters that are made for photographers. The design is such that many of the filters are based upon traditional special effects. So, these plug-ins allow photographers to work with familiar tools. The intention here is not to survey all of the many filters in the Color Efex set, but to illustrate a few examples of what is possible with plug-in filters.

For the first example, we will begin with our original color image (it has been converted to black and white for reproduction purposes).

Now we will run the nik Abstract Efex filter solarization, which will allow solarizing of either a color or black-and-white image in ways that go beyond the Photoshop solarize filter. There are several different methods of solarization that can be applied, all rendering very different results.

Our resulting image looks like a cross between an infrared image and a solarization.

Next we applied the Graduated 0h (Gray) filter to our image.

This is the same as using a neutral density gradation filter on the lens of the camera, but with much more control. The resulting image displays a fade effect that is dark at the top and gradually becomes lighter toward the bottom of the image. Of course, many variables can be changed here, which is true of many filters.

What should be mentioned about the nik filters is that many of these filters do things you can already do in Photoshop. However, for the professional, these filters are an excellent example of third-party solutions that can dramatically improve your workflow.

Deep Paint

If the visual effect you are after needs more of a painterly touch, filters such as Right Hemisphere's Deep Paint allow for the use of specialized artistic tools. When this filter is run, another program is launched and the image is transported from Photoshop to Deep Paint. Then you are able to paint upon your image with a whole new set of tools that go beyond those available in Photoshop.

In our example, we have painted in a fence on the left and right sides of the palm trees image. Of course, this is a simplistic use of this software, but it illustrates the selective control afforded to the user. This is an excellent tool for the digital fine artist.

There are literally thousands of filters and Photoshop plug-in-compatible software available for Photoshop. These examples only begin to illustrate the potential of utilizing third-party additions to your digital darkroom. Also, the intention here is not to value these products as being better or worse than any of the many other products, which are not mentioned.

Automating Image-Processing Tasks

One of the greatest advantages about a digital darkroom, and the digital workflow, is that now photographers have the ability to process many images rapidly and professionally. One of the problems, though, is keeping track of all these images. Conventionally, the photographer would simply make a contact sheet, and place it in a binder with a page of the new negatives. Well, a similar method is available to the digital photographer: contact sheets of images that are kept in specific computer folders, and can be printed for filing with a CD of the images—just as with traditional filing systems. Additionally, because the digital darkroom needs no special environment, it is also effortless to make prints or even multiple prints of different sizes in the home or office. Finally, the Internet can be used to share all of these amazing images. What easier way to show others your images?

In this section we will discuss automated ways to accomplish all of these tasks from within Photoshop™. This is not to say that these are the only automated tasks possible; rather, these are incredibly useful tasks that most photographers will need to use time and again. These features of Photoshop have become practical tools as they have developed since their refinement in Photoshop™ versions 6 and 7.

Creating Contact Sheets

The process to create a digital contact sheet from scratch would be quite tedious. Luckily, there are automated tasks built into the functionality of Photoshop. In this case, we are going to look at the process of automatically making a contact sheet from a folder of digital images.

To create a contact sheet, select Contact Sheet II from the File > Automate > Contact Sheet II menu. You will see a configuration window that allows for the design of the contact sheet.

Here such attributes as the height and width, as well as the number of images horizontally and vertically, can be set up to individual specifications.

Even the resolution of the resulting contact sheet can be determined. This way, the contact sheet can be produced for virtually all needs, ranging from a low-resolution version for the Web to a high-resolution version for thermal dye sublimation output.

The final product acts just as a traditional contact sheet would —as a visual reference to individual negative, or digital files.

Creating Picture Packages

Now that we have created a contact sheet of our negatives, the next logical step is to make enlargements. Photographers often need to make multiple prints of one image, also. In the industry, this is known as a picture package. This is quite common, especially in sports photography, portraits, and school photography.

Let's say that you want to make one 5" x 7", four 2.5" x 3.25", and two 1.5" x 2" prints. Well, making these seven prints can be a bit time consuming. Creating a picture package, however, allows you to print all of these images as one 8" x 10" image. Furthermore, the way they are arranged on the page allows for easy single-pass cutting of images.

As a production aid, the process of picture package automation can be both a time saver and lucrative.

Creating Web Photo Galleries

Beyond printing images, sharing them on the Web has become a common way for people to communicate visually. Whether it is sharing images of their pets with family members, or presenting images to a client for a creative project approval, the Web has emerged as the least expensive and most immediate way to share images with others. One problem is that many people don't have the time to learn HTML, Java, XML, and all of the other languages and tools that were traditionally necessary to build Web pages. This is where the Web photo gallery feature of Photoshop assists the image-maker in publishing images electronically. All of the essential processes related to building a Web-based photo gallery are easily automated by Photoshop.

To begin producing a custom Web gallery, select Web Photo Gallery from the File > Automate menu.

Next, a window will appear that allows for the customization of most settings related to the Web gallery. By altering the Options pull-down menu, you can switch between four areas of Web gallery customization: the Banner, Gallery Images, Gallery Thumbnails, and Custom Colors.

To begin, we will configure the banner for this Web gallery. Here the site name can be customized—this will be shown on all pages in the Web site. Also the owner's name and or date can be placed on all pages; note that any information can be entered into these two fields, not just the name and date as indicated.

The font and its size can also be modified here. On the bottom of this page of options are the two most significant options, which must be entered correctly. Here, in the Files area, the source and destination of the Web images must be defined. The source is simply the folder that contains the original images. Note that these images do not need to be scaled down, or set to 72 ppi before selecting this folder; Photoshop will automate the resizing and scaling of images for you. Lastly, it is suggested that you create a new, empty folder on your hard drive before beginning the Web gallery automation process. This would be the correct folder to select at this point.

Next, from the Options pull-down menu, select the Gallery Images window.

Here such factors as the size and the amount of compression of the images can be set—along with the choice of creating a border or no border (0 pixels).

After these settings have been defined, return to the Options pull-down menu, where we will go to the Gallery Thumbnails window.

At this point, such gallery features as image captions and the layout of the thumbnail grid can be defined. This is similar to laying out the rows and columns in the contact sheet automation task. Note that the Files portion of the window will remain constant once it is set, even while moving from window to window.

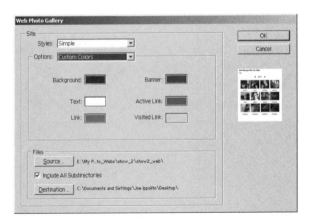

For the last window of options, select Custom Colors from the pull-down menu.

Here the color palette for the Web site is defined. Attributes such as the background, banner, text, and link colors can be defined. This is where you can control the visual feel of the Web site, which is especially important if the image gallery is to be integrated with an existing Web site.

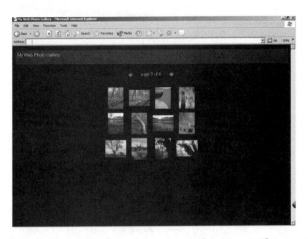

After completing all of the setup options, Photoshop will automatically create a Web site; the HTML pages will be automatically written, and all of the images will be resized twice—to the thumbnail and gallery sizes. The final thumbnail page of the Web site will look like the grid-style illustration presented here. Note that the vertical images are presented as vertical in this illustration. If your Website

has both vertical and horizontal images, the vertical images must be rotated before beginning the Web photo gallery automation task.

Lastly, an individual gallery page will appear as a single page with the image placed upon it. You will note that the style of the page, banner, and buttons remains constant whether viewing a thumbnail page or an individual gallery page.

Remember, once a Web gallery is created, the HTML pages and/or the images may, of course, be further modified to customize the look of the gallery.

Actions Palette

In continuing our discussion of automating processes and tasks, we now turn to the Actions palette. This is where you can record and play back scripts in Photoshop. These scripts can record most of your repeatedly performed tasks, or actions, to use in addition to the default actions in Photoshop. This is significant because these sets of actions can be saved and shared with other computers. Also, you can purchase commercial sets of actions, and numerous actions and sets of actions can also be downloaded from the Internet as public domain or shareware software.

Action Sets

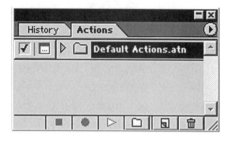

To begin, let's consider the action set. This is basically a grouping of individual actions that can be saved as an independent group of actions.

A set can be transferred between various computers, so you can share your action sets between your home and office digital darkrooms, or you can supply sets of actions to your clients, for example. This is significant if you are in the business of having clients perform repetitive tasks. Take, for example, the role of the service bureau. This is an organization that deals with clients from many different workflows. So let's say that a particular workflow of a given service bureau requires the conversion of an image from RGB to Grayscale, in a customized fashion. This service bureau could create their own action set for their production needs. In this set, one of the actions could be to convert and image from an RGB format to a customized grayscale format. In this way, the distribution of a custom action set can dramatically increase the workflow between the service bureau and its clients.

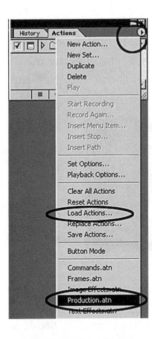

In order to load a new actions set, select Load Actions from the Actions palette menu.

Here is where any action set that is saved on any of your drives can be selected. Then the new set will be displayed in the Actions palette. To expand the folder to see its contents, select the arrow at the left of the action set's folder icon.

Using Existing Actions

To use an action, identify the particular action in the Actions palette. Then simply use the VCR-type controls at the bottom of the palette to play the action (right-arrow button).

At this point the tasks originally recorded in the action will commence in a linear fashion. Some actions complete automatically, while others may require input from the user. In the example presented here, the user needs to modify the Red, Green, Blue, and Constant values to customize the way in which each of the color channels of information will be filtered before they are combined into a single grayscale image.

The final product from using this action is a custom-built grayscale image. So for example, a service bureau might suggest that its clients use a particular set of values when converting certain RGB images into black-and-white images, through the use of this action. The added advantage of actions is that at any point, the action itself can be further modified to create a new version of the action.

Photo available in color. Please see insert for further study.

Creating New Actions

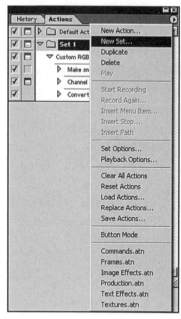

To create a new action, it is usually best to create a new set of actions first.

In this way, you will guard against saving your actions as part of the default Photoshop actions. This can be easily accomplished from the Actions palette menu. Note that at the end of the editing session, the new action set should be saved before exiting Photoshop—from the same Actions palette menu.

Now, to create a new action, select the action set where the new action will be created. Then the action will be created by selecting New Action from the Action palette menu.

Creating an action is as simple as using a VCR. Select the action name to be recorded, and press the record button at the bottom of the Actions palette. At this point, actually perform all of the tasks that you want to be recorded, and press the stop button when you are finished.

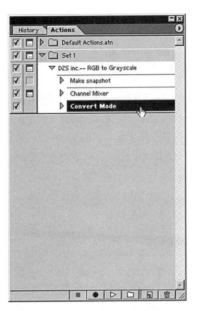

That's all there is to it. You now have a new action that can be played at any time.

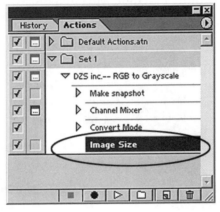

To go a step further, however, let's say you want to modify an existing action; this is just as simple as creating a new action. First select the action to be modified, and then select the point in the action where you want to begin recording new action steps.

Here we want to add an image resolution step to the previous RGB to grayscale action. After pressing the record button, we have selected Image > Image Size, to alter the pixel resolution of the image to 300 pixels per inch.

After this step is complete, press stop on the control bar at the bottom of the Actions palette. Now the action has been modified to include the resolution step (image size), as illustrated.

As you can see, the creation of actions for common tasks can have a dramatic effect upon the efficiency of your workflow.

Droplets

An extension to the action's capabilities of Photoshop, droplets allow for the creation of a small software program. Drag and drop the images onto the icon ✥ of this program to apply an action to the images.

The process of creating a droplet is relatively simple. First, you need to have already selected an existing action—either pre-made or custom. Next, select the Create Droplet command from the File > Automate > Create Droplet menu.

Now, a window will be presented that allows for the modification of such droplet attributes as where the droplet will be saved, what it will be named, and other batch processing related tasks that will be discussed later in this chapter.

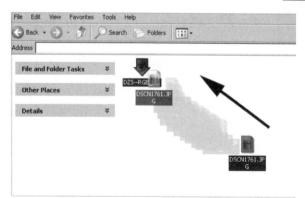

To use your newly created droplet, simply drag the icon(s) of one or more graphic files over the droplet icon. The processes contained in the original action will now be performed on all of the images dropped on the droplet icon.

It is that simple! As you can see, there are many ways to automate aspects of the workflow, freeing up the photographer to pursue more creative work.

Batch Processing

As you can see there are an incredible number of different ways to batch process images. From actions to droplets, and beyond, Photoshop is designed as a professional production tool. A feature named Batch allows for the automation of various tasks in Photoshop. The Batch function acts similarly to the droplet function, except the Batch processing function is called from within Photoshop, whereas the use of droplets occurs at the desktop/finder level.

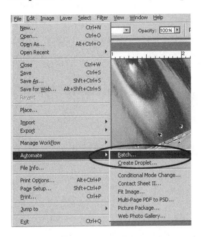

To batch process a group of images, first identify the tasks to be performed. These tasks need to be recorded as an action—just as the droplet was created. Now, select the Batch command from the File > Automate > Batch menu.

This is where we see the Batch options window, and the particular action to be applied as a batch process is designated. Additionally, where the original images are located, and where the newly modified images are to be saved can also be assigned. Once all of the settings are correctly determined, the batch process can be run.

In this example, we chose to make a brushed aluminum frame around all of the images to be batch processed. As seen in the detailed illustration here, the brushed aluminum frame is applied around the outer edges of the image, presenting the illusion of a frame surrounding it.

Although this is a simple example, it illustrates the power of batch processing images. Again, this is yet another way to automate portions of the workflow. For example, if you need to resize an image, alter its pixel resolution, run a minor unsharp mask, and save the image as a level 8 jpeg image, this process might take a minute or two. But if you had 5,000 images in multiple sub-folders, sorted by categories to make these changes to, you can begin to see the significant advantages of using a technique such as batch processing. In this scenario, you basically have two options: hire someone to process all of these images one by one—over the course of several months—or set up one action (which would take only a few minutes), run one batch test on a small folder of duplicate images (another few minutes), and then let the computer batch process all 5,000 images (overnight and unattended). While the batch processing may take several hours, if you set up the computer to perform these tasks overnight, in the morning all 5,000 images will be correctly processed and waiting in their new folder. This is also a practical use for converting collections of high-resolution images into Web format images. This batch processing took approximately twenty minutes of work time instead of many months of potential labor-hours.

Batch processing is certainly one of the most powerful production tools available to the digital photographer today.

Applications of Advanced Image Enhancement

The last section in this chapter will illustrate three different projects: Project 1—Creating Illusions I: Surfaces and Textures; Project 2—Creating Illusions II: The Planet, Light, and Shadow; and Project 3—Building a Composite Image with Lighting Effects. Each of these projects will utilize illustrative techniques that are often used by the digital photographer.

Project 1 –Creating Illusions I: Surfaces and Textures

One of the most common illustrative techniques is to create textures that look like real surfaces. For this project, we will create a brushed-metal texture from scratch. To begin, we need to create a blank canvas upon which we will create our metal texture design.

Now that we have a blank canvas—filled with white—we can begin to define the metal's texture. To begin, we will add noise to the white canvas, to add a random texture to its surface.

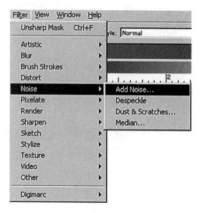

Here we have added a great degree of random noise to overemphasize the effect.

Next we need to change the noise pattern into something that looks more like metal than speckled granite. To accomplish this, we will call upon another Photoshop filter: motion blur.

Here we will streak the speckled pattern, as if we were brushing a rough metal surface with a wire brush.

To finish the illustration, we will bevel the edges of the metal, to give a three-dimensional look. To accomplish this, we will use a bevel and emboss layer effect.

Note that the gloss contour curve is a classic S-curve, and we have modified the size and softness of the bevel, from the Photoshop defaults. This produced a brushed-metal square with a light cast on it from the upper left corner.

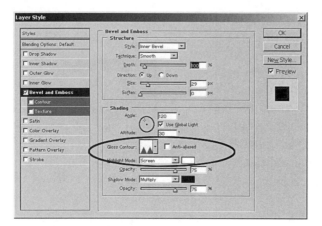

Next we decided to make the metal square look as though it was a black anodized metal surface, with a raised metallic frame. The approach taken here was to modify the gloss contour settings in the bevel and emboss window.

Here the curve was changed from the classic S-curve to a curve with two peaks—indicating that a reversal of tones will occur. The final image displays all of the characteristics we desired to make a black anodized metallic square with raised brushed-metal edges.

Project 2—Creating Illusions II: The Planet, Light, and Shadow

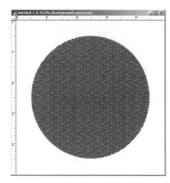

This project illustrates the use of a combination of tools in Photoshop to create several illusions in the final illustration. First we create a circle, which is then filled with a texture—either artificial or from a photograph.

This creates a two-dimensional textured disc. To spice up the texture a bit, we ran the Filter > Brush Strokes > Sumi-e filter to enhance the texture.

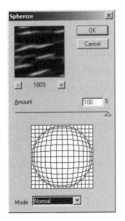

Many other techniques could have been used here. Next, we want to distort the pattern in the disc, to be consistent with the rounded edges of a ball—or a planet in this case. To achieve this effect, we will use the Spherize filter, with a maximum convex warp setting.

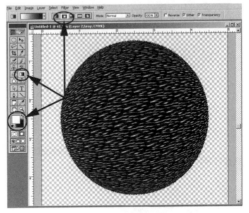

The result is still a two-dimensional looking disk, which has the texture of a three-dimensional sphere.

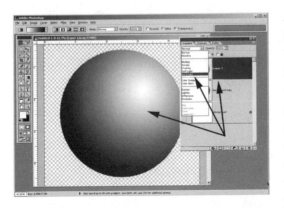

At this point we need to develop the three-dimensional aspects of the planet. The original idea was to use lighting effects to produce a spherical hot spot, where the fade-off from the light would model the surface to appear three-dimensional. Because the disc is still two-dimensional, however, this effect was not as successful as anticipated. Thus, another technique was employed. Here we need to make a three-dimensional sphere the same size as the textured disc, on its own layer. This effect is accomplished with the radial gradient tool.

Here we are able to see exactly what the shape of the sphere looks like. As illustrated, the foreground color is white, and the background color is black. This way we can draw the gradient from the center of the hot spot on the sphere toward the lower left to make the light wrap around the planet. Next, we need to combine this three-dimensional sphere with our two-dimensional disc. To produce the final blended result, we need to alter the layer mode of the sphere layer to something like overlay or hard/soft light—this needs to be above the textured disc layer. The result is a three-dimensional planet with surface textures.

To go one step further, we decided to add some atmospheric rings around the planet. This is easily accomplished by creating a new layer and drawing two very wide, soft-edged lines across the planet, below its center. Then this layer is blurred a bit more with a Gaussian Blur filter. Finally, if color is desired in the planet's rings, the layer can be tinted by using the Hue/Saturation colorize mode.

Photo available in color. Please see insert for further study.

Project 3—Building a Composite Image with Lighting Effects

With the advent of the digital age, numerous situations have arisen that require the assembly of image components from different originals. Now more than ever we need to develop skills that will aid us in the masterful assembly of image components. One of the main areas of weakness displayed in compositing is the lack of understanding of basic concepts of lighting. The key to successful compositing of images is to present the illusion of a single light source. In this project, we will illustrate this point.

To begin, we will start with two different images. The first is lit with artificial light, inside the pharaoh's tomb.

The second is illuminated by natural light.

Photos available in color. Please see insert for further study.

Note that the quality of light is very different between these two images. Also, the direction of light is very different as well. To start on our composite image, we will make the image inside the tomb become the base image. Next, we will import the pharaoh image as a layer—above the tomb image. Now, we need to scale and rotate the pharaoh image to appear as though it is a foreground element in the new composite image.

Once this is accomplished, we need to address the issue of lighting. If we simply leave the new composite this way, it will look very unnatural because the light on the tomb image is coming from the top casting, shadows down and forward. Yet the light in the pharaoh image is coming from the bottom left.

So, we need to alter the lighting on the pharaoh image to match the main image of the tomb. To begin, the pharaoh image layer is selected. Then we select Filter > Render> Lighting Effects.

This will display the Lighting Effects options window. Because the lighting in the tomb image has the character of a spotlight, we will use the default lighting style, which is a broad spotlight. Then we will alter the shape of the light to a more narrow width—more spotlight-like. Additionally, the direction of the light needs to be altered, to match the light in the tomb image more closely. Now, this is where creativity comes into play. For example, we have chosen to not match the original light source exactly.

Rather, we want to make it appear as though the spotlight source from the tomb image is spilling forward onto the pharaoh's head in the foreground—to create a more believable, blended composite image. Here, you can see the difference in the quality of light on the pharaoh's head.

Now, the final composite image appears as though it is one original image, as opposed to a composite of elements from two totally different images. The main goal when combining elements from different images is to make them look believable in the final image.

This takes knowledge of lighting, perspective, and a good general sense of visual design aesthetics. Remember, the digital darkroom is a tool, but you are the artist who will use this tool to produce imagery. The tool is only as good as its user allows it to be!

Conclusions

This chapter has illustrated a variety of different techniques that an image-maker can utilize in the digital darkroom. Remember that these are just a starting point. It has been the intention here to present enough differing techniques to start you off in new directions. Both in terms of creativity, and in terms of realizing the potential of the digital darkroom, this chapter has offered concepts that will enable you to rethink traditional models of workflow. By now, the term darkroom should have a very different connotation: one that goes beyond simply making a print. Rather, darkroom in the twenty-first century is rapidly becoming a concept rather than a specific location; it refers to the conceptual environment where we make images, not just the facility. This is not to devalue the place of wet darkrooms; rather this chapter has begun to illustrate the power of the digital darkroom as yet another tool for the photographer, designer, and image-maker, in general. Through the display of various working methodologies, and creative techniques, the term advanced imaging techniques should now have a new meaning to the creative image-maker.

Review Questions:

1 Why should you consider working on portions of an image on layers?

2 What is the best way to adjust such image attributes as brightness, contrast, color balance, and hue/saturation, so that the changes can later be deleted or modified?

3 How does the use of channels affect the way in which one works in the digital darkroom? List four examples.

4 If you have to perform a repetitive task on many images, what is the best way to approach this in Photoshop?

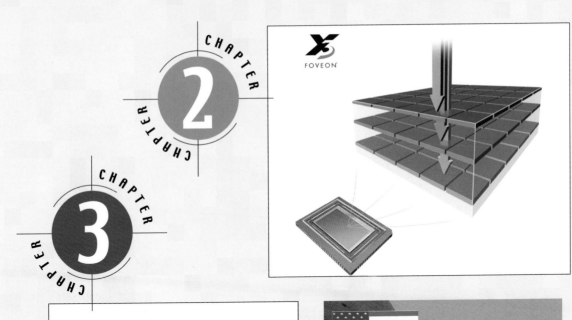

CHAPTER 2

CHAPTER 3

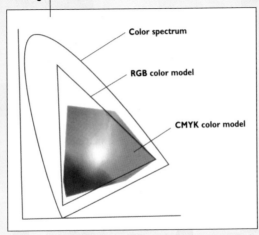

Color spectrum

RGB color model

CMYK color model

CHAPTER 6

CHAPTER

6

CHAPTER

Pepper Fest
2003

December 21st

- All are Welcome

- Fun for all Ages

CHAPTER

6

CHAPTER

CHAPTER

6

CHAPTER

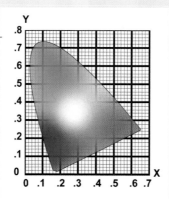

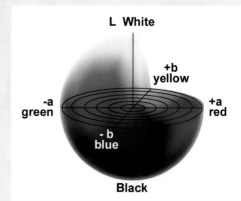

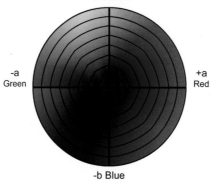

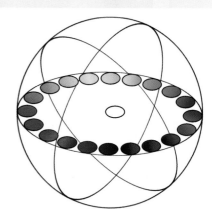

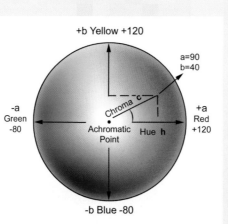

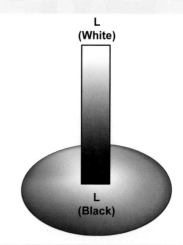

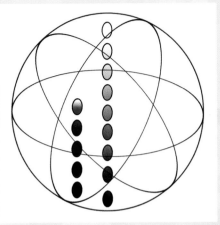

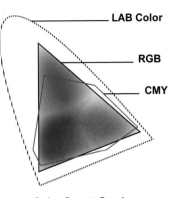

Color Gamut Overlap

- LAB Color
- RGB
- CMY

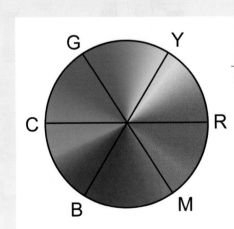

CHAPTER

CHAPTER

7

+15% Yellow +15% Red +15% Magenta

+15% Lighter Current +15% Darker

+15% Green +15% Cyan +15% Blue

CHAPTER

8

CHAPTER

Discussion Questions:

1 How can the digital darkroom be used as a production tool to produce prints of different sizes, galleries of images, and alterations to many images in the same way at one time?

2 As a design production tool, how can Photoshop be used to replace colors in parts of your images? How can specific color book colors (i.e. PANTONE colors) be used in your images?

3 n what ways can digital photography offer more or less control for photographic tasks such as architectural perspective control? Why?

4 How can things such as actions, styles, droplets, batch, and history change the way you think about working in the darkroom? Why?

5 What is the most significant tool—that is not in Photoshop—that you need in order to create successful illustrations and composite images?

CHAPTER

7

Color Management: A Digital Photographer's Approach

Objectives:

This chapter will introduce you to the concepts and practices of color management. Here you will learn about such things as color models, color spaces, and color modes. In a practical sense, you will learn how to develop and implement a color management system in your digital darkroom. Upon completion of this chapter, the reader should have a better understanding of:

- What color management is, and why you need to understand it
- How a color management system works
- How to differentiate between technical terminology that describes color
- When and why to work in different color spaces
- How digital color management is similar to traditional photography techniques
- What color profiles are, and how to create and use your own
- How much color management is necessary for your situation
- How to develop your own personalized workflow

Introduction

One of the most critical areas of concern to a digital photographer is that of achieving predictable and reproducible results. This is no different than with traditional media, but in the digital realm, the ability to have more precise control over the media is more important than ever. This is because, unlike traditional media, digital images are more randomly transportable to various phases of the workflow. What this means, quite simply, is that the process of image production is no longer a linear process.

With traditional photography, the process of image reproduction was relatively straightforward. An example of a standard workflow would be:

1. Image is captured
2. Development of the latent image (slide or negative)
3. Printing on photographic material—if the original image was captured on negative film.
4. Halftone or color separation is made from the original chrome (slide) or print
5. Printing plate(s) made
6. Image is printed on a printing press

With digital photography, the process of image reproduction allows for randomness. An example of a digital workflow might be:

1. Image is captured on film
2. Processing of the slide or negative
3. Image is scanned
4. (or) Image is captured on digital media
5. Halftone or color separation is made from the digital file
6. Printing plate(s) made
7. Image is printed on a printing press

or

1. Image is captured on film
2. Processing of the slide or negative
3. Image is scanned
4. (or) Image is captured on digital media
5. Image is directly printed on a printing press

or

1. Image is captured on film
2. Processing of the slide or negative
3. Image is scanned

4. (or) Image is captured on digital media
5. Image is modified in software such as Adobe Photoshop, and is transported to anther piece of software like Freehand or QuarkXPress
6. Halftone or color separation is made from the digital file
7. Printing plate(s) made
8. Image is printed on a printing press, or no halftone/separations are made, and the image is directly printed on a printing press

As you can see, just these few examples illustrate some of the random processes that can change the direction of a particular project's workflow. Given the number of variables and the potential number of different individuals that can affect the quality of the images, the digital imager's workflow must have implemented some degree of control to achieve consistency.

This is where the concept of color management comes into play. The basic idea of color management is to follow certain procedures to produce dependable and reproducible color in the images. Thus the concept of color management is quite simple. As for the application of color management principles, that requires a bit of preparation.

A NOTE ABOUT COLOR MANAGEMENT

Before we begin discussing color management, as it relates to digital photography, we must first look back to our traditional processes. Consider that in traditional photographic darkroom work, the densitometer, sensitometer, and spectrophotometer all mean one thing to the average photographer: their eye! This is significant to note. In a traditional darkroom, the process of creating a color print involved the subjective interpretation by the photographer to determine density, contrast, saturation, and color balance. Now, we have more sophisticated tools readily available, but in the end, the subjective nature of visual perception needs to be considered. In other words, scientifically right is not always perceptually right. With this thought in mind, let us go continue our discussion of color management for digital imaging.

What is Color Management, Who Needs it, and Why?

So, just what is color management? Simply put, color management is the systematic approach to mastering control over the reproduction of color in our imagery. The reason we hear so much about color management these days is because we, as photographers, are always on the quest toward control over the reproduction of our images. This control is achieved in the digital realm by implementing color management policies into our workflow.

There is much mystique and confusion surrounding color management. Here we will try to demystify color management. One comment I hear often is that "digital photography isn't there yet". I have come to enjoy hearing people make statements like this. Now I know this may sound odd, but I really take delight in empathetically agreeing with them. I then produce a *photograph,* that upon viewing, they generally ask "did you shoot that on 120 film?". Of course I love to watch their expression change as I tell them that I created this 16x20" print from my *consumer-level* digital camera. In disbelief they admittedly say, "You're kidding, right?" Then I smile and say *no,* it's *better* than 35mm film, right? They huff a bit and reluctantly and say… yes. Next of course almost everyone asks "how did you do that?" I then explain how simple the procedure of *resizing-up* my images was. Next they inevitably say, but how did you get the colors so perfect. You must realize that at this point I am grinning ear-to-ear, and I say I just click the print button. Now they really don't believe me, and I usually feel that they have endured enough torture at this point, so I tell them that I work on a calibrated system. Immediately eyes begin to glaze over. Next I briefly explain—in lay-person's terms (even if they are professionals)—how there are only three simple steps involved: calibration of my input device(s), calibration of my system and calibration of the printer.

What is a CMS (Color Management System)?

A color management system (CMS) allows for the transportability of an image between various software applications and/or devices. It acts as an intermediary, or a translator, to transform an image's information from the originating color space to the destination color space. Simply put, if an image is originally derived from a flatbed scanner, its color space is determined by the particular device that has captured it—a flatbed scanner, in this case. When editing the image, in Photoshop for example, the color space is either retained, or converted to an appropriate color space inside Photoshop. Finally, when the image is to be output, on an inkjet printer for example, the color space needs to be converted, or translated, into the new device's color space.

Therefore, a CMS is simply a system that accurately and consistently translates an image's color space to and from any of the following:

- device-to-device
- software-to-software
- software-to-device
- device-to-software

How does a CMS work?

Let's look at the CMS structure utilized by Adobe Photoshop for an example of how a color management systems works. As with most major software and hardware manufacturers, Adobe's color management workflow is based upon International Color Consortium (ICC) conventions. There are three main fundamentals to an ICC color management system: the Color Management Engine, the Color Numbers, and the Color Profiles.

Color Management Engine

The color management engine is the independently developed core of any given CMS that does the actual work of interpreting and translating colors between differing color spaces. This is the software that is designed by individual manufacturers to process color information. Sometimes referred to as a color management module, the color management engine is the part of the CMS that translates colors between different color spaces.

Color Numbers

In any given image document, each pixel is described numerically. This numerical description is called a color number. A color number describes the RGB value, for example, of a particular pixel. The problem arises when the numerical value represents a pixel that cannot be exactly translated to the output device. In other words, an exact red in a flower may not be able to be printed on a given inkjet. Therefore the red color needs to be translated via the color engine into a red that the printer can reproduce—the red that most closely matches the original. Thus, when the contrast, brightness, levels, curves, or color balance is adjusted in an image, or an image is converted into a different color space, the image's color numbers are altered.

Color Profiles

A color profile determines how the actual color numbers of an image will be referenced and translated so that the visual appearance of an image remains the same. Profiles are created from information that is derived from device-specific calibrations. For example, the profile of a digital camera is generated by comparing the colors that are actually captured by the camera with a standard reference. The difference between the actual limitations of a device and the standard then define the particular profile. The ICC profile is used to remap the colors that are incorrect to the correct colors in any given color system.

ICC profiles are generally created for all input and output devices. It is in this way that we can have a calibrated system. The ICC profiles that are relevant are associated, or tagged, to an image. These profiles describe an image's color so that changes to the color appearance can be made to closely represent the correct perceptual color—so an image looks the way you want it to, when output.

Color Models, Color Modes, and Color Management: from RGB to CMYK, through CIELAB

Understand that there are many terms that describe color. For example, color models refer to the theoretical spaces in which color can be described, while color modes refer to the composite information that makes an image. Here we will clarify this often-confusing area of digital imaging's concepts and terminology.

The Basics: XYZ, CIELAB, RGB, CMYK

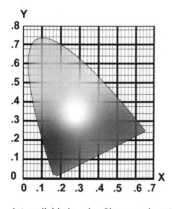

Art available in color. Please see insert for further study.

XYZ

In 1931 the Commission Internationale de l'Eclairage (CIE) created the XYZ color system, referred to as the norm color system. The color space that is represented by the XYZ color system is usually illustrated as a two-dimensional sail-shaped graphic.

When represented in a two-dimensional form, the XYZ system displays green color components on the upper Y-axis, red out on the X-axis, and blue toward the bottom of the Y-axis. In this system, every color can be assigned a numerical value based upon its position on the two-dimensional grid. The intersection point of the X and Y coordinates form the numerical value for any given color in the XYZ system. The limitation of the XYZ system is that it does not take into account the density or brightness of a given color.

With the XYZ system, the colorimetric distances in between specific colors is not directly relational to perceptual differences between colors. For example, when viewing the XYZ system sail graphic, we can see that the blue and green are considerably farther apart than are green and yellow.

This has been a major problem with the XYZ system, for the correct perceptual reproduction of color.

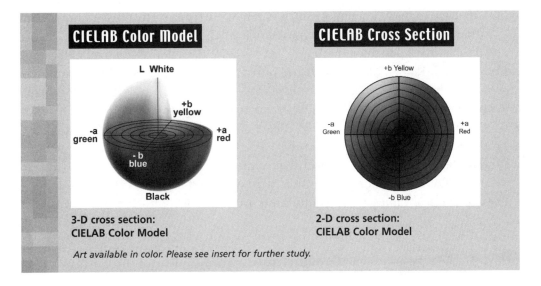

CIELAB Color Model

3-D cross section:
CIELAB Color Model

CIELAB Cross Section

2-D cross section:
CIELAB Color Model

Art available in color. Please see insert for further study.

CIELAB

In 1976 the Commission Internationale de l'Eclairage developed a new color model entitled the **Lab Color** space. The significance of the Lab color space was that now color could be described in a three-dimensional space—thus allowing for the description of brightness in addition to color.

The CIELAB color space allows for the colorimetric measurement of color. In this color space, the **a** axis stretches from green [**-a**] to red [**+a**] and the **b** axis extends from blue [**-b**] to yellow [**+b**]. Additionally, in this color space, brightness (**L**) is increased from bottom to top in a three-dimensional model.

The significance of the ability to describe color in a three-dimensional space is that the CIELAB model allows you to describe color in such a way that what you see is actually what you get. In essence, it's the most basic point of color management.

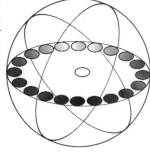

Art available in color. Please see insert for further study.

Because color is described in three dimensions, any given color can be identified in exact terms by identifying its specific **a**, **b**, and **L** values.

Most significant here is the fact that the CIELAB color space is device-independent. That means, quite simply, that this color space represents color in a purely theoretical realm. In this way, the given limitations of any device do not corrupt the color management system. Rather, all devices and colors can be accommodated by the CIELAB color space.

The CIELAB color space is an objective and scientifically accurate color space. All CIELAB colors can be identified in terms of their hue and brightness. This allows us to go from qualitative color descriptions such as bright blue, to a system that allows for the exact numerical and quantitative description of a color.

The reason this is possible is because CIELAB color does not rely on real red, green, and blue values. Rather, the purest values of red, green, and blue are the theoretically pure colors. That is, no device can produce these colors—they are virtual colors. This development of a color model that relies upon virtual-pure colors allows all other devices' gamuts to be contained within the color model. Therefore any color that can be produced can be contained within the CIELAB color model, and can be scientifically quantified with an exact number that references a particular color.

CIELAB color defines hue and chroma by positive and negative values of **a** and **b**.

These numerical values are derived from the **a**, **b**, and **L** coordinates in the CIELAB color space.

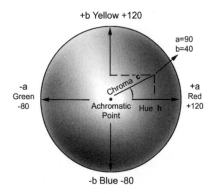

Here, the Hue of a color is the resultant of the arctan, which is expressed as:

b/a=h (hue)

While the chroma of an image corresponds to the distance between the color locus and the midpoint intersection of **a** and **b**, expressed as:

$(a^2+b^2) \times 1/2 = c$ (chroma)

Art available in color. Please see insert for further study.

Finally, the overall brightness/lightness of a color is expressed on a scale **L**, having values that range from 0 (black) to **100** (white).

Key Concepts of CIELAB Color

The chroma of a color equals 0 when the **L** value (brightness) of a color equals either 0 or 100—black or white.

Beyond the traditional CIE color triangle, CIELAB color does not utilize straight lines to connect primary colors. By implementing non-linear lines in plotting colors, the visual equispacing of colors is possible. What this means is that transformations of colors from XYZ values into CIELAB values allows for transformations that account for perceptual changes in color, not just literal transformations.

CIELAB for Color Reproduction

As stated, the CIELAB color space is device-independent. This independence from real-world devices allows the CIELAB color space to act as a universal color space that contains all of the colors that the human eye can perceive, and that devices can reproduce. Hence, this color space can be utilized as a base for transformations from any color space to any other color space. This is because all other color spaces are subsets of the CIELAB color space.

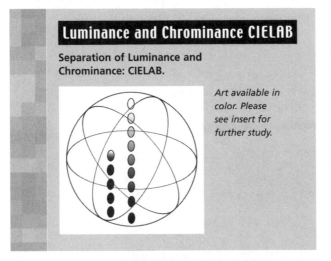

Luminance and Chrominance CIELAB

Separation of Luminance and Chrominance: CIELAB.

Art available in color. Please see insert for further study.

Furthermore, because luminance and chrominance are separate in the CIELAB color space, the chroma of an image can be enhanced in one processing action. Hence, more precise color manipulation can occur, resulting in a higher fidelity image.

The CIELAB color space can represent **all** real color gamuts as subsets of the CIELAB color space.

RGB and CMYK: Device-dependent Gamuts

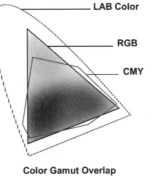

Art available in color. Please see insert for further study.

LAB Color

RGB

CMY

Color Gamut Overlap

In a typical workflow, we work on photographs in RGB (red, green, and blue) mode. This is because the image is displayed on an RGB device—the monitor. When printing the image, it needs to be converted to the appropriate color space of the output device. For example, the RGB image might need to be converted to CMYK (cyan, magenta, yellow, and black) in order to be printed correctly. The problem here is that the two color spaces have neither the same size nor location. Therefore, any CMYK colors that cannot be represented in RGB cannot be printed, unless first converted. Because these colors cannot be produced within the RGB color space, they cannot be directly printed from a RGB image in a CMYK color space, unless these colors are converted from a close color in the RGB color space to the correct color in the CMYK color space. These areas where the two color spaces do not overlap are examples of nonreproducible RGB colors.

To illustrate this, consider the fact that if two color gamuts overlap, only the common color area (referred to as a subset) can be reproduced. Any color outside of the common area will need to be converted to the color of best fit. This simply means that these out-of-gamut colors are not reproducible.

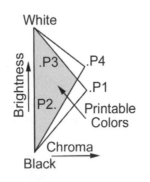

The illustration here shows a section of two overlapping color gamuts: RGB and CMYK. Here you can see that all of the target colors can be reproduced except for P4, which lies outside of the common subset color gamut.

In this example, we can see an image of a flower in the first image as it appears in RGB mode (on screen), while the second image displays the out-of-gamut colors with a gray mask—the colors that will not reproduce with CMYK.

Photos available in color. Please see insert for further study.

Roy G. Biv: An old friend to be forgotten?

As children, many people are taught color theory as follows: RoyGBiv, sounding like the name Roy G. Biv, and standing for Red, Orange, Yellow, Green, Blue, Indigo, and Violet.

Art available in color. Please see insert for further study.

This becomes the basis of color theory for painting, for example.

Photographers and graphic artists use a different color system. This system is based on two specific areas, light theory (RGB) and printing press reproduction (CMYK). Nearly all things that the photographer (traditional or digital) will deal with will relate to RGB, CMY, or CMYK color spaces. So it is time to say goodbye to ROYGBIV, at least for a while.

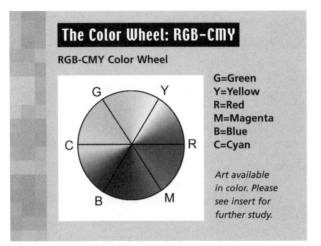

The Color Wheel: RGB-CMY

RGB-CMY Color Wheel

G=Green
Y=Yellow
R=Red
M=Magenta
B=Blue
C=Cyan

Art available in color. Please see insert for further study.

Additive Color Mixing: RGB

RGB Color Mixing

R=Red
G=Green
B=Blue

Art available in color. Please see insert for further study.

RGB-CMY

Here you can see the color wheel that dictates all that happens in photography—digital or traditional. This is the same color wheel that is utilized in traditional color photographic printing. The lines drawn here connect complementary (inverse) colors on the RGB-CMY color wheel.

RGB: Additive Color Mixing

The RGB (red, green, and blue) color space is based upon light theory, where additive color mixing occurs. With the RGB color space, the combination of equal parts of red, green, and blue light—at full strength—equal white light because it is based upon the additive mixing of light. Other basic mixing rules apply to RGB as well.

When two additive primary colors are mixed with equal proportions, new base colors are created as follows:
R=Red G=Green B=Blue

- R+G+B= White
- B+G= Cyan (light blue)
- R+B= Magenta (pink)
- R+G= Yellow

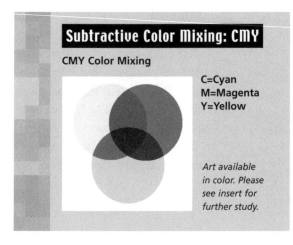

Subtractive Color Mixing: CMY

CMY Color Mixing

C=Cyan
M=Magenta
Y=Yellow

Art available in color. Please see insert for further study.

CMY and CMYK: Subtractive Color Mixing

Cyan, Magenta, and Yellow—and Cyan, Magenta, Yellow, and Black color spaces—are based upon viewing reflected light, where subtractive color mixing occurs. For example, overlaying ink pigments on paper produces the colors that make up the image. Here cyan, magenta and yellow are referred to as subtractive primary colors. That is, these colors are the complements (referred to as *inverse* in Photoshop) of red, green, and blue. In theory, the combination of equal parts of Cyan, Magenta and Yellow ink—at full strength—will create black, the inverse of white light. In practice, however, this is not the case. Rather, a muddy brown color is produced. This is why CMY, subtractive primary colors, are referred to as CMYK with regard to printing images with ink. The K represents Black (the last letter of Black, because **B** refers to Blue—also referred to as **K**ey color). The addition of Black ink to the CMY printing process allows for the reproduction of rich shadows and black areas in a full-color image that is to be reproduced through the use of ink on paper.

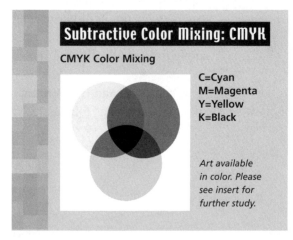

Subtractive Color Mixing: CMYK

CMYK Color Mixing

C=Cyan
M=Magenta
Y=Yellow
K=Black

Art available in color. Please see insert for further study.

As with RGB color, with CMYK, basic mixing rules also apply. When two subtractive primary colors are mixed with **equal proportions,** new base colors are created as follows:

**C=Cyan M=Magenta
Y=Yellow B=Black**

- C+M+Y= (theoretically black)
- C+M+Y+K= Black
- C+Y= Green
- Y+M= Red
- M+C= Blue

Working in RGB or CMYK: Which Choice is Right?

One of the greatest debates you will hear from designers and digital photographers is whether to work in RGB or CMYK, when editing images. First, consider the fact that we generally want to convert an image between color spaces/modes as little as possible. This is because each time an image is converted, some of the colors are interpolated and thus degraded to varying extents. Having said that, we will first suggest reasons for working in CMYK space/mode, and then explain why RGB is generally the best working space.

If we acquire an image in CMYK mode, and simply want to color-separate the image to be printed, it is suggested that the image only be edited in CMYK mode. It is not necessary for you to convert the image to RGB mode, edit it, and then convert it back to CMYK mode. This assumes a very basic level of correction is required. Many functions of Photoshop are disabled in CMYK mode. Thus, CMYK mode is a limited-function editing mode—and should be utilized as such.

Generally, RGB mode is the color space/mode of choice for most color projects. The typical workflow, performed by informed individuals, consists of editing an image in RGB color mode/space, and conversion to CMYK only toward the end of a work session (usually for fine tuning an image)—**if required at all**. This is because there are significant advantages to working in RGB color space/mode. For example:

- RGB mode requires three channels of color information, as opposed to CMYK's four channels of information. For example, a 10MB RGB image translates to a 13.4 megabyte CMYK image: 134 percent of the RGB image. Thus, the RGB image requires less memory and storage, improving performance as well.
- RGB color spaces are not dependent on inks or dyes, thus more device independence is achieved by working in RGB mode.
- The greater gamut of the RGB color space, in comparison to CMYK, allows for finer transitions between various color spaces.
- Most significantly, we can soft-proof CMYK colors in RGB mode. Therefore, the logic of needing to convert an image to CMYK mode to see what the image is going to look like when output, is invalid.

A final note about previewing CMYK colors is warranted. If you are working on an image in CMYK mode because you believe this will aid in proofing the image for CMYK output, consider the fact that the output device being utilized for soft-proofing is RGB—the computer monitor.

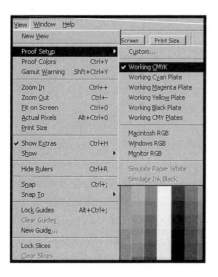

Thus, the image is being converted to an RGB color space during editing. Therefore, it usually makes more sense to edit an image in RGB mode, and soft proof the image.

Color Standards: Transformation for Color-Managed Solutions

Up to this point we have discussed why color spaces work together from a more theoretical perspective. Here we will discuss **how** they work in actual situations. Specifically, we will discuss how to convert between color spaces using a technique known as gamut mapping.

Gamut Mapping

Before we discuss gamut mapping, let us first revisit the concept of color gamut. Simply stated, color gamut refers to that area of a given color space that can be reproduced by a particular device. Therefore, when we discuss gamut mapping, we are simply discussing a way in which colors can be transformed from one color space to the actual gamut of another color space. This process allows for the replacement of colors that cannot be reproduced on a given output device. This replacement, with close matches to a color, is performed through the process of gamut mapping.

Here, a large color space such as LAB or RGB is transformed into a more restrictive color space, such as CMYK. Of course this process can occur when mapping smaller spaces to larger—or color spaces that contain color information that does not even exist in another color space. For example, earlier we discussed that chromatic cyan, for example, exists in the CMYK color space, but not in the RGB color space. This is an example of a color that needs to be remapped to produce a close approximation.

Gamut mapping can occur in a variety of ways. As part of a computer operating system, gamut mapping can manage color transformations between various applications that share image information. This is accomplished by employing ICC profiles to define various color spaces on a given system. For example, Apple Computers has had ICC profiles incorporated into their operating systems since 1995, in the form of ColorSync software.

For gamut mapping to occur, operating system-based profiling does not need to be utilized—it just makes things a bit easier. Rather, individual hardware components and software applications can each be calibrated and profiled with ICC profiles to achieve a color-managed solution.

Color Transformation

When we discuss the transformation of color in a color-managed environment, we are discussing the calibration of all devices and software applications to be utilized in our workflow. This calibration allows for gamut mapping transformations to occur with respect to known standards. Here, standardization is the key.

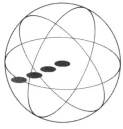

In order to achieve consistency in color output, we need to generate individual device profiles. These profiles describe the limitations of a given device to reproduce color. In conjunction with standard calibrators, these profiles can accurately describe a device's individual color space. This individual color space is a subset of a greater color space, such as RGB or CMY/CMYK.

A standard document can be utilized to profile various digital imaging devices such as scanners, digital cameras, etc.

For example the IT8 subcommittee of the American National Standardization Institute (ANSI) has agreed upon standards to describe colors for graphic applications, known as the ANSI IT8 reference.

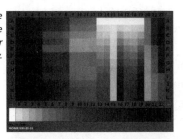

Art available in color. Please see insert for further study.

Individual manufacturers can produce IT8 reference documents that can be used to calibrate these devices. For example, Kodak produced an IT8 target, as illustrated here. This target can be photographed by a digital camera, or scanned, to create a reference file that describes precisely what color the device can capture in a given environment.

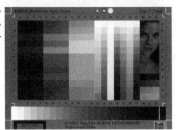

Art available in color. Please see insert for further study.

Here is an IT8 document from Kodak that also includes a flesh-tone sample for subjective evaluation.

The results of the device-specific color values of each of the individual samples (actual values) captured from the standard reference document (such as the IT8 target) are next compared to the theoretical values of a color space—usually in CIELAB. The variations between the theoretical values and the sampled values are stored in a conversion table called a Color Look-Up Table (CLUT). The CLUT table of information is then utilized as the basis for gamut mapping transformations of color.

What is significant here is that the profile information allows for the depiction of a color space in such a way that all deviations from the standard are described. This information can then be compared to any other color space information, where all actual values can be compared and remapped to fit the new color space. This is possible because of the CIELAB color space.

The CIELAB color space provides the perfect environment in which color transformations can occur. This is because the CIELAB color space is a theoretical color space. That is, it contains perfect color values, not just the values that can be reproduced by a given device. Thus, all color profiles contain information that is considered to be a subset of the CIELAB color space. Hence, all other color spaces can be compared to each other within this color space. Here any values that do not match the target color space can then be best fit from the destination color space into the target color space.

It is the global or universal nature of the CIELAB color space that has made it the ideal color space for universal color transformations. For example, all color transformations between color modes (spaces) that occur in Adobe Photoshop are transformed through LAB color because LAB color separates the luminance of an image from the color information.

When profile information is used to convert from one color space to another, interpolation occurs. That is, information from the mismatched profiles is compared and then algorithmically altered in such a way as to calculate any intermediate hues that are not part of the common overlapping color space area. As one can see, the quality of any color management system will be highly dependent upon the algorithms utilized by the software-based color engine.

Device-specific profiles can be saved as data files that can be transported between applications, or between computers. Additionally, many individuals save a TIFF image file of the captured IT8 target, so that various output devices can be later utilized for the production of those image files that have been sampled with the particular device.

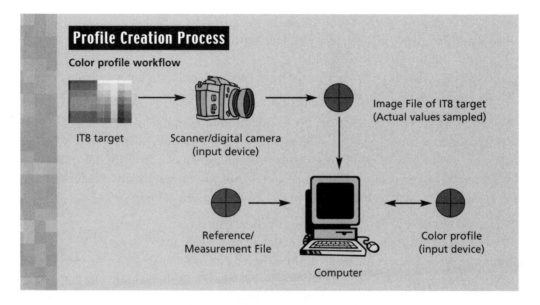

The key to making device profiles function in a workflow is to have consistently calibrated equipment. Devices should be recalibrated on a regular schedule. For example, some photographers will turn on their computer monitor in the morning, and after a warm-up period of 30-45 minutes, they will profile their monitor—each and every morning. Even if you are not that intent on precise quality, you should at least recalibrate a device when changes in the colors of their images become visibly noticeable.

Note that accurate and consistent color transformations can only occur on a completely calibrated system.

Utilizing Traditional Methods for Color Management: a Photographer's Perspective

As mentioned in the beginning of this chapter, traditional methods of custom color printing did not usually employ the use of such devices as densitometers, sensitometers, or spectrophotometers. Rather, the tool called upon for the color management phase of traditional photographic printing was the photographer's eye*. That is, subjective evaluations were made as to the quality of the photographic print in terms of density (brightness), contrast, saturation, and color balance—with subjective control limited to the adjustment of color balance and density. Thus traditional color management techniques involve the following:

- Ensuring that the developer and blix (chemistry) are fresh, or have been replenished properly

- Chemistry is at the correct temperature
- Photographic paper is fresh, and has been stored properly
- Enlarger filtration is not faded
- The photographer's eye is ready to interpret density, and then color information, to make subjective evaluations as to the quality of the image's density and color balance

So how does this methodology apply to digital photography? In one sense, the traditional model of color printing is already the most common way in which digital images are printed. This is because essentially all consumer-level digital photographers do not work on calibrated systems, and do not (intentionally) use profiles. Thus, their typical color management techniques involve the following:

- Ensuring that the ink cartridge in their printer is fresh
- The printer's heads are cleaned (if streaks begin to appear in images)
- Photo-quality paper is utilized, to properly receive inks
- The photographer's eye is ready to interpret density, and then color information, to make subjective evaluations as to the quality of the image's density and color balance

Note: While densitometers are used in traditional photographic printing processes, most photographers use a more subjective means of color evaluation.

Test Strips and Subjective Evaluation

As you can see, this digital printing process parallels the traditional darkroom color printing process. As with the traditional darkroom, here the photographer makes subjective evaluations of the print's density (brightness), and then evaluates its color characteristics. So, if a print's density is correct, but the image looks a bit green, the digital photographer will go back into the digital darkroom, and subtract green from the image's color pack by adding magenta to the print. Next the print (or test strip) would be printed again, and the color would then be subjectively evaluated again. Any necessary corrections would be performed, and the print/test would be printed again until the desired result is achieved—exactly as one would work in a traditional darkroom.

There are several reasons that this method of printing is dominant. First, for photographers that have crossed from film to digital photography, this method allows for a comfortable environment—one that is roughly parallel to what they already know and do on a regular basis. Next, this method of printing does not require any specialized knowledge of any color management tools or techniques—beyond the requisite understanding of basic additive and subtractive color theory (as with traditional photography). Thus, they do not need to properly calibrate their monitor, create a profile for their digital camera, create a profile for their film scanner, create a profile for their flatbed scanner, or create a profile for their printer—for example—in order to print an image.

So if this is the case, why should we bother to learn all of this color management stuff? Simple. Color management allows us to consistently produce high-quality results on one device, or between many devices. To use a traditional darkroom example, how many times have you had a commercial lab make a print, and when you had another print made at a later date, it looked nothing like the first print? This is a common problem with traditional printing methods, and it is because so much of the process is dependent upon the subjective interpretation of the individual who prints the image. The subjectivity referred to here is not creative subjectivity; rather, this is subjectivity related to the misinterpretation of colors.

Here are some things to consider regarding the utilization of the subjective evaluation method of color management:

Pros
- Little knowledge of color management is required to produce a photographic print.

Cons
- Quality is not easily reproducible.
- Image adjustments cannot be easily translated to different output devices.
- Color characteristics of an image are not described in a way that can be utilized by any other software/applications or imaging devices.

Thus, when we discuss utilizing traditional darkroom methods for color management, you can see that this process can yield professional custom results, but is not very efficient or reproducible.

Achieving Consistency Through a Color-Managed Workflow: the Application of Color Management

There are a number of hardware and software solutions that can aid in developing a color management workflow that matches the individual photographer's needs. For example, one digital photographer might never need to share images with anyone else, instead working in a closed-loop system, where the same software, monitor, and printer are always utilized, in the same location and conditions. This individual's color management needs are considerably different from another digital photographer who always needs to share images with others. For example, this second photographer might need to have all images printed on an offset printing press, printed on fine-art inkjet materials, reproduced as part of a multimedia product, output as Dye-Sub prints, and from yet another source even output as LED or Pictography prints. Thus, this photographer's image would never look the same with so many service bureaus involved, and so many individuals making subjective evaluations. This second photographer has much more demanding color management needs than does the first photographer.

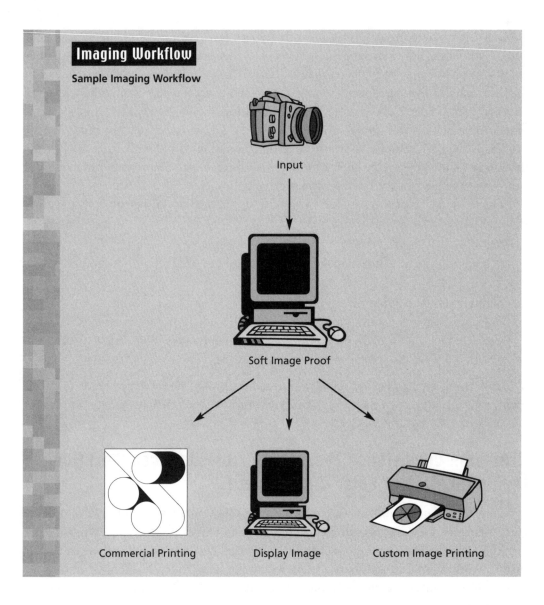

Imaging Workflow

Sample Imaging Workflow

Input

Soft Image Proof

Commercial Printing   Display Image   Custom Image Printing

This is why there are a number of different products on the market to address the differing styles and requirements of various image-makers, with respect to their color management needs. To give a fuller understanding of how color management works, in a practical sense, we will look at how some commercial products address managing color.

Using Test Strip Software

The first product we will discuss here is a software package named Test Strip®, by Vivid Details, Inc. This software package is a Photoshop plug-in that allows the digital photographer to utilize familiar darkroom methods to control the quality of the color, density (brightness), contrast, and saturation in fine steps of control.

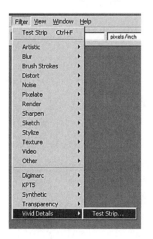

As illustrated here, to use Test Strip, the plug-in is selected from the Filter menu in Photoshop.

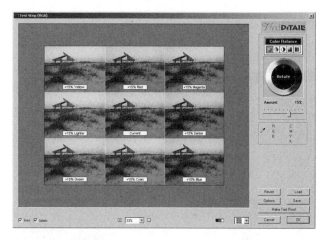

The default screen presented upon running Test Strip is the Color Balance screen.

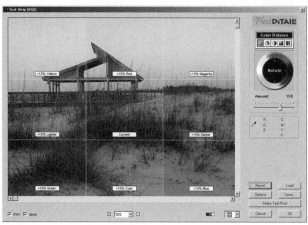

The color balance of an image can be changed using a traditional ring-around swatch method for visual analysis. Here the direction of the color balance can be altered and the degree between the swatches can also be altered. This is the same as adding and subtracting red (yellow + magenta) from the color pack on an enlarger.

The primary difference between this method and the traditional darkroom is that this allows for the whole image to be previewed in the ring-around, instead of small sections of the image which may represent very different color and density information. Notice that a more traditional ring-around can also be produced if so desired.

Next the One Color mode can be used to simulate full test strips across the image. This is like making a full 8" x 10" test strip in the traditional darkroom.

Again, the direction of the color balance can be altered, as well as the degree of change between the strips. As can be seen here, changing the direction of the color correction alters all of the test strips in the preview window. Thus, here we are producing real-time test strips that can be immediately modified and remodified— with no waiting for the print to come out of the processor.

In addition to standard adjustments such as color balance, density, and even saturation, Test Strip allows you to save and load custom filters. This is a very powerful feature: common effects can be applied to an image without wasting time on numerous adjustments each time a change is applied. For example, assume you have images that have been taken under 3200°K (tungsten light) on daylight film (5500°K), and the negatives/slides were scanned into the computer. Even to apply basic color adjustments to get the images close to the correct color balance—to eliminate the heavy yellow-orange cast—would be a time-consuming venture. Because Test Strip allows you to load and save filters, these adjustments can simply be loaded whenever desired. In this example, simply select the load button, and load the 80a filter (supplied by Vivid Details). This will produce essentially the same effect as placing an 80a filter on the lens of a camera—converting warm tungsten light to daylight.

Beyond color correction, such filters as are used for neutral density and polarizing are also available.

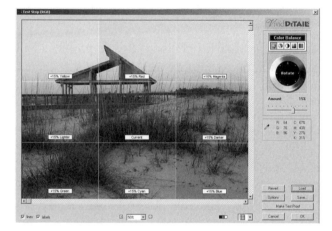

Here, you can see how applying a filter alters the image to look as though a polarizing filter was used. It won't eliminate reflections on glass or water—this needs to be done with an actual filter on the camera.

Numerous other filters, including special effects filters, can also be saved and loaded to affect changes to images.

Here you can see the application of a neutral density filter. While this effect can be achieved using numerous other controls in Photoshop, Test Strip enables photographers to easily work with familiar tools, such as filters.

Finally, the test proof that is generated can be printed. The print is then visually matched to the onscreen display, and appropriate changes are made so that the monitor display will close-ly match the printed image. These changes are then saved as the printer's compensation values. In the future, Test Strip can be used in the normal fashion, but before printing any image, the custom printer settings need to be loaded and applied through Test Strip.

This compensates for differences between the monitor display and what the printer creates. This method of calibration is referred to as *perceptual color compensation*, and is highly individualized, as with custom color printing in a traditional darkroom.

Photo available in color. Please see insert for further study.

Using WiziWYG™ Software

WiziWYG™ is a software package that is used to generate device profiles. This software lets the digital photographer calibrate monitors, printers, and/or scanners. When calibrating each piece of equipment, a device profile is generated that can be saved for use in the future.

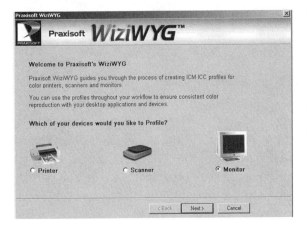

This device information is stored in the form of an ICC profile. WiziWYG™ is designed as a software solution to color management. The only physical object required is an IT8 target. Also, the upgrade version of this software allows the use of a colorimeter when calibrating monitors. Here we will illustrate the wizard-style interface, as related to one of the three calibrations possible with this software: perceptual monitor calibration.

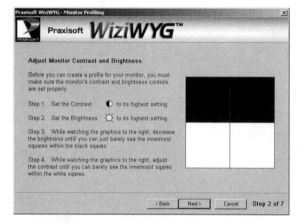

The first thing to note here is that WiziWYG™ functions as a step-by-step wizard.

This approach to color management has been adopted by several manufacturers. The wizard approach helps to reduce the intimidation that many people face when approaching color management.

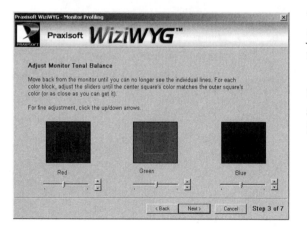

As you can see, the user simply needs to follow the on-screen prompts to generate device profiles. As with Adobe Gamma, which ships with Photoshop, the first adjustment here is to the physical manipulation of the contrast and brightness settings of the monitor. Next, the Red, Green, and Blue guns of the monitor are balanced.

The process here illustrates the subjective visual perception process of monitor calibration.

Following this, the monitor needs to be described to the system, so that the calibration can account for hardware-specific data.

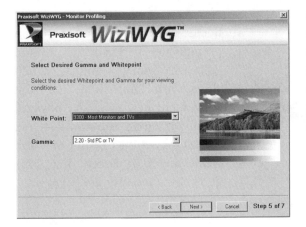

The illustration here shows how a generic monitor type can be substituted, when the actual monitor type is unknown.

Still describing the monitor hardware, the white point and gamma need to be defined for the hardware.

Generally, the Gamma for Macintosh computer monitors is 1.8, and the Gamma for PC monitors is 2.2. After all of the appropriate information is entered, the new profile needs to be generated and saved, so that it can be called upon later.

When saving a profile, it is generally recommended to include the date, or some other identifying information, as part of the profile's file name.

The reason for this is that generating a profile is not a one-time occurrence. Rather, hardware should be reprofiled on a regular basis, resulting in numerous profiles saved for the same device. Therefore, you can see how confusing it can become if a profile name is something like "monitor."

And that's all there is to it. As we will illustrate later, there are other software and hardware solutions that are just as easy to use as WiziWYG™.

Image Environments and Profiles

So now that we have seen how to create our own custom profiles, we need to look at how all of this comes together to form a color management solution. Essentially, this is why we have gone through all of the work of profiling all of our devices—so that we can make our color reproduction more reliable, and quicker. Now after all of the work of building profiles, you are probably thinking, how is this quicker? The answer is two-fold. First, if you are only interested in producing one photographic image, these methods are not quicker. However, when we think of what we do as sort of a production line, then you can see the benefit of standardization. Thus, profiles enable the consistent production of images in a given color-managed environment. This is the goal: consistent, repeatable results that do not require a great deal of individual adjustment or manipulation.

So how do we put all of this in practice? Let us begin with embedding profiles into image documents.

Embedding Profiles

The process of embedding profiles is rather simple in practice, yet extremely powerful in terms of developing a managed solution for image sharing and output. Embedding a profile simply means tagging an image file with additional information that describes the color space, and other variables, from which an image is derived. Thus, if you want to share an image with someone who has an entirely different computer system, where every component is different—for example, transferring an image from a Mac computer with a 21" LCD display to a PC with a 17" CRT—an embedded profile will describe what the image should look like on the new system, after it's been imported and converted. This tagged information represents the image's native environment to the new environment.

Setting Color Preferences in Photoshop

First, before ever opening an image in Photoshop, you need to set up your **color preferences**.

These preferences describe the environment you will be working in. This is a crucial step in managing color, and utilizing profiles for a consistent workflow. To set up color settings in Photoshop, select Color Settings from the Edit menu. Next, a variety of options will be presented. All of these variables are specific to each photographer's environment, workflow, and the job at hand.

In this example, you can see a typical workflow color setup for a system with a Radius monitor where the images are being edited to be output on a standard web offset press (SWOP). Also, subjective color settings such as the Perceptual intent have been selected so that exact color matches will give way to more subjectively pleasing color conversions. Note that these color conversions will be less exact than if Absolute Colorimetric was selected, for example.

Embedding a Profile in Photoshop

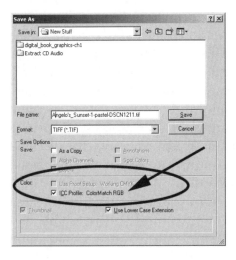

In an application such as Photoshop, we begin the process of embedding a profile by configuring the color setup for a job, and then by editing the images. The next point is saving an image, where the prompt is to save a profile along with the image, as illustrated.

Remember that Apple ColorSync profiles are ICC profiles and, therefore, embedding profiles into an image allows for the sharing of images between all ICC-compliant software, regardless of platform.

Embedding a profile is as simple as that.

From Concept to Final Product: A Color-Managed Environment

The key to designing and working in a color-managed environment is to standardize as much as possible. This standardization allows for the **predictable** and **repeatable** output of digital images. Thus, before you begin dealing with digital photographs, in any form, a color management policy, or workflow, should be established and adhered to by the digital photographer. This personal color management policy will dictate how the working environment facilitates all needs, and slows or speeds the workflow. Additionally, the policies you design and pursue follow the image when it is passed on to others for such purposes as commercial printing, and photographic output.

Begin designing a custom **Color Management Workflow**, by assessing several factors, such as:

- What is the general output for my images? Offset printing, inkjet prints, thermal dye sub prints?
- Do I print all of my images on my own calibrated devices?
- Do I send images to service bureaus to be output? If so, do they understand color management, and can they utilize my embedded profiles?

Only after these kinds of questions are asked, and answered, can you then begin designing your color management workflow.

Form the Concept

Just as you need to identify the particular needs of a project with traditional photography, so too do the needs of a digital project need to be identified—before beginning. For example, if the project is to photograph a still life, that is to be printed as a 30" x 40" poster, the logical film-based choice would be to use 4"x 5" or larger film. The same needs are presented when capturing images on digital media. For example, the particular sensor that captures the image, coupled with the light source—and any interpolation that occurs inside the camera—can have dramatic effects on the rest of the imaging process. Therefore, just as with traditional media, all factors that affect the imaging process need to be considered. This is true regardless of whether a film-based image is being scanned, or the digital image is utilized.

When planning a project, the CMS workflow needs to be considered before images are captured.

Setting Up Your CMS Workflow

There are four primary areas of concern when setting up a color management system workflow (CMS).

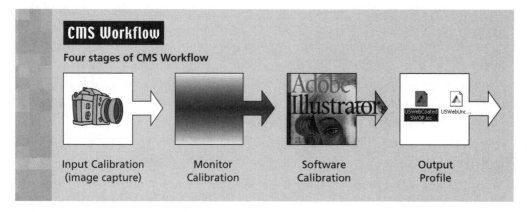

I) Image Capture Considerations

First, the choice of whether to capture images digitally or on film needs to be addressed. This may not always be a choice, and images that were previously captured will need to be dealt with. This is possible, though, under the CMS workflow that will be established here.

Film

When capturing images on film, which will later be scanned into the digital darkroom, some issues to be considered are:

- Does my input device handle this film format?
- If I use a service bureau, will a device profile of their input device be embedded?
- When was this device last calibrated? (Does it need to be recalibrated?)

Digital

When capturing images digitally, issues such as the following need to be considered:

- Is the digital camera (input device) properly calibrated?
- What light source was used to create these photographs? (Does it match the device profile I will use to reference this input source?)
- When was this device last calibrated? (Does it need to be recalibrated?)

Input Device Calibration

As discussed earlier, calibration of the input device (scanner or digital camera) is crucial to an effective CMS. Here we will review an example of calibrating an input device. In this case, we will calibrate a Nikon digital camera.

First, we need an IT8 reference target. Next, the target needs to be photographed under the same lighting conditions we will use to create a device profile.

Art available in color. Please see insert for further study.

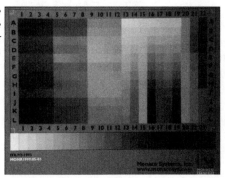

This profile is then compared to the IT8 reference file. The correct reference file must be used if the device profile is to be accurate. All IT8 target documents have a reference number, unique to the batch production of the target. This number can be seen here in the lower left corner of the captured IT8 target.

Here, MONR 1999: 05-03 is the identifier that needs to

be matched to the reference file. Next, the ideal values stored in the reference file are compared with those actually sampled with the camera (or other input device). Depending upon the software chosen, the way this comparison will occur to create the device profile may differ. Basically, a control panel or a wizard is used to generate the actual device profile. Here, we can see the step-by-step progression used in the wizard-based software to develop a digital camera profile. Note that the scanner selection is chosen in the wizard interface. This selection would be more appropriately named *input device*, but most people need to calibrate a scanner as their primary input device.

First, the input device (scanner) is selected. Scanner & Camera profiles are both input profiles.

Next, tips are presented to help the user.

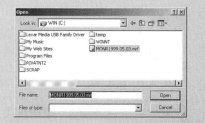

Here, the type of reference document is identified. For cameras and flatbed scanners, this will usually be the reflective IT8 target. For film scanners, this will usually be the transparent IT8 target.

Now the corresponding reference file needs to be selected, based upon the IT8 target reference number.

Because we are calibrating a digital camera, Step 2 refers to photographing the target under the proper lighting conditions.

In Step 3, the image that was photographed of the IT8 target needs to be imported, by selecting Load an Image.

Here, the TIF file that was created by photographing the IT8 target is selected as the file to be imported, which represents the actual values that were captured.

A preview of the image being loaded is then shown for verification.

Step 4 allows the user to verify that the image was scanned or photographed properly.

In Step 5, the absolute position of the target needs to be defined.

By identifying the corner crop marks, the software can align the graphic file in a manner that allows for the geometric matching of colors from the IT8 target.

All four corners must be accurately identified to ensure that the target has been correctly aligned.

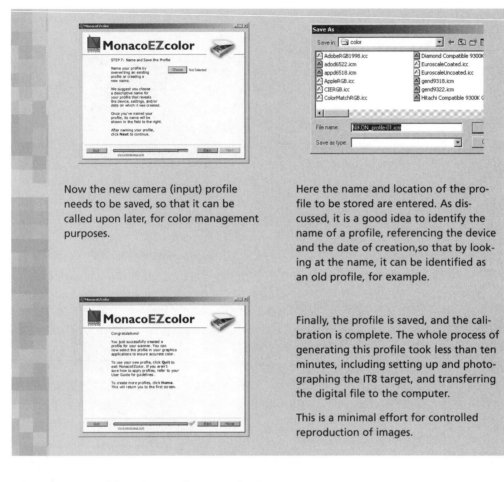

Now the new camera (input) profile needs to be saved, so that it can be called upon later, for color management purposes.

Here the name and location of the profile to be stored are entered. As discussed, it is a good idea to identify the name of a profile, referencing the device and the date of creation, so that by looking at the name, it can be identified as an old profile, for example.

Finally, the profile is saved, and the calibration is complete. The whole process of generating this profile took less than ten minutes, including setting up and photographing the IT8 target, and transferring the digital file to the computer.

This is a minimal effort for controlled reproduction of images.

II) Monitor Calibration Using a Colorimeter

Earlier we showed how to calibrate a monitor using WiziWYG, which functions much as Adobe Gamma. Here, we will go a step beyond calibrating a monitor based on the visual analysis method. We will use a colorimeter to read values from the computer's monitor to build a profile. This method is a purely scientific method for producing a monitor profile; it does not depend on any subjective interpretations from the individual who is calibrating the monitor, except for determining the minimum black point. This is because ambient lighting in different environments will affect how bright or dim the monitor appears. As with the development of a digital camera profile, we will use Monaco EZcolor to illustrate the process of building a colorimeter-based monitor profile.

First, we need to identify the monitor as the device for which the profile will be created.

Unlike our previous example, using WiziWYG software, here we will instruct the software to use a colorimeter to measure the monitor's light values.

Initially, the user needs to adjust the brightness and contrast of the monitor to set the point at which minimal black separation is visible.

Now the sensor (colorimeter) is attached to the monitor with suction cups, over the graphic that looks the same as the colorimeter—as seen on the right side of this illustration.

Next the Gamma needs to be set for the monitor. For Macintosh monitors, this is usually 1.8, and for Windows-based monitors, this is usually 2.2.

The color temperature for the general viewing conditions now needs to be identified. This is usually set between 5000°K and 6500°K.

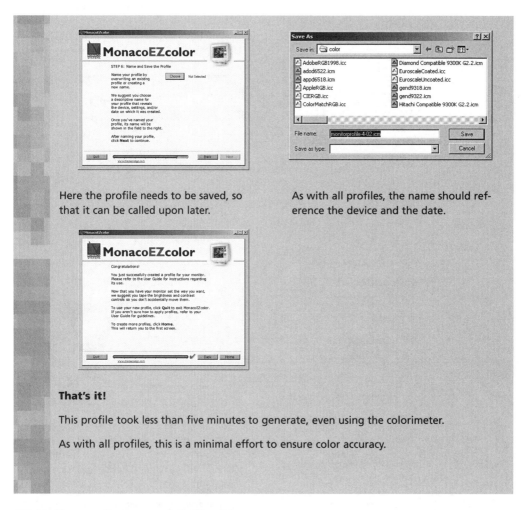

Here the profile needs to be saved, so that it can be called upon later.

As with all profiles, the name should reference the device and the date.

That's it!

This profile took less than five minutes to generate, even using the colorimeter.

As with all profiles, this is a minimal effort to ensure color accuracy.

III) Software Setup and Calibration

Just as physical devices need to be calibrated to identify their characteristics, software applications also need calibration. Here, the initial parameters, or preferences, that you set can have a dramatic impact upon your workflow and color/reproduction accuracy.

Defining Work Spaces

Software applications such as Photoshop have developed predefined color-management settings, referred to as working spaces.

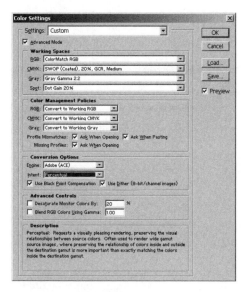

These working spaces are associated with working modes such as RGB, CMYK, and Grayscale. The idea is to predefine a working environment that will use color profiles, which offer color reproduction fidelity for common image output conditions. For example, a working space can define a common RGB monitor color space, along with defining a standard CMYK profile—for common offset printing settings, for example. Additionally, black-and-white image profiles can be associated to the Grayscale working space whether by Gamma or by press dot gain percentage.

The advantage of defining a working space before editing images is that these broad parameters define a general environment that is consistent with your workflow. Furthermore, if images do not contain a profile—untagged images—the working space acts as the image's profile. Thus, the image becomes tagged, or profiled, to the existing working mode's color space.

Before working in a software application such as Photoshop, it is critical that you examine and configure all of the appropriate workspace settings.

IV) Output Profiles

Here we will illustrate the process of creating a printer profile. To illustrate this in a way that most individuals can reproduce, we have utilized a standard desktop scanner as the device that will analyze color differences. The preferred procedure is to use a spectrophotometer to analyze color variations between the target and actual values, but most people do not have access to a spectrophotometer.

With this in mind, we will again use Monaco's EZcolor software. This software uses a flatbed scanner to profile printer output, as illustrated here. As with input device and monitor profiles, device profiles need to be created for all devices that will be used to output images. The process here is essentially the same as creating an input profile, except in reverse.

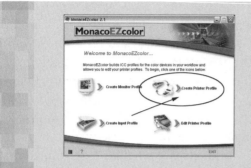

First the scanner and printer selection must be chosen. The reason for this combination is that while the printer profile is being generated here, the scanner is acting as the spectrophotometer—to read the values produced by the printer.

Basic setup and preparation is then shown to the user. Note that the exact type of material to be printed upon must be utilized for accurate calibration. Therefore, if both glossy and watercolor papers will be used, two different profiles need to be made.

The printer type needs to be selected before a profile can be generated. This may seem confusing because an RGB printer is selected, even though the printer uses CMYK inks. This is because most inkjet printers are designed to print RGB images, using CMYK inks. The device's manual can clarify whether a printer is a CMYK or RGB device.

In Step 2, an IT8 target is printed on the chosen printer and material combination. It is essential that all color management and automatic settings for the printer are disabled. These settings would alter how the printer produces the IT8 target, and corrupt the profile.

After the target page is printed, the actual IT8 target needs to be attached to the printed page, for a comparison of the two sets of IT8 values.

In Step 4, the scanner is used to analyze both sets of values. Here, the scanner is acting as a spectrophotometer.

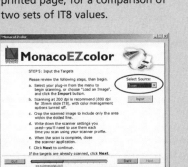

Now the scanner driver is selected, to set up the scanner controls for scanning the IT8 target.

In this case, the VistaScan driver is selected.

The scanner control module is then shown. Here it is important to set the settings properly, as illustrated.

Step 6 allows the user to verify that the target has been scanned properly.

Now, just as with the digital camera calibration, the crop marks need to be identified.

All four corners must be accurately identified to ensure that the target has been correctly aligned.

Step 10 allows you to compensate for problems with your hardware, or to subjectively alter your output results. This is generally contradictory to the idea of profiling.

Next, the scanner profile needs to be saved first, so that it can be called upon later.

Now the actual printer profile is saved.

After committing to the Save command, the software builds the final printer/media profile.

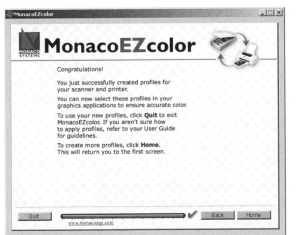

That's all there is to it!

Now your images can be associated with the exact device and media for output purposes.

Finally, how is the printer profile used?

There are two steps involved with using a printer profile. First, the profile needs to be associated with the image, and then the profile needs to be called upon when outputting (printing) the image.

When an image is open in Photoshop, the image needs to be converted to match the new profile.

Here the printer profile that matches both the output device and the material to be printed upon needs to be selected.

Additionally, the color engine and intent of the conversion need to be chosen—these are the suggested default settings for photographs.

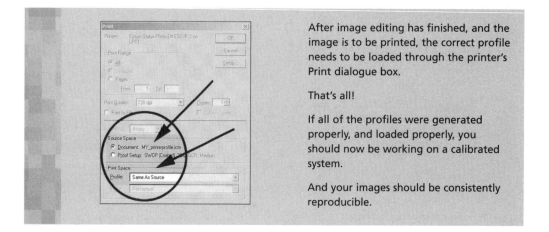

After image editing has finished, and the image is to be printed, the correct profile needs to be loaded through the printer's Print dialogue box.

That's all!

If all of the profiles were generated properly, and loaded properly, you should now be working on a calibrated system.

And your images should be consistently reproducible.

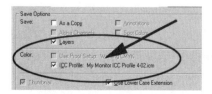

Finally, to share images with others, always be sure to save ICC profiles in your images so that the destination color space knows what to convert—based upon the image's origins.

Profile Editing

Sometimes, even with this degree of control, variables exist that still produce unacceptable output results. If this happens consistently, you will need to alter your device profiles. This can be done with profile editing software. Because we have illustrated this process with Monaco's software, we will use their profile editing software, ColorWorks. The process of profile editing is quite straightforward.

You load the relevant profiles to be edited into the profile-editing software and then adjust settings until the image is output as desired.

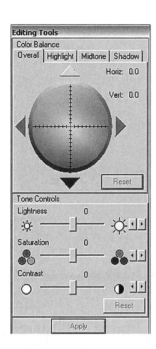

There are many variables that can be adjusted and edited to fine-tune your existing profile. These affect both the tonal and color quality of the image output.

While editing your profile, a before-and-after preview mode allows you to make subjective evaluations of the profile adjustments. This assumes you are working on a calibrated monitor.

The final adjustment is accomplished through outputting the image until you are satisfied with the end result.

WYSIWYG: What you see is what you get?

There is great confusion surrounding proofing digital photographs. Simply stated, there are two types of proofs. The first are those that you can't touch. Generally, these are soft proofs, or those that are displayed on a monitor or other display device. The second type of proof takes a tangible form. Generally, this tangible proof is referred to as a hard proof. So when we discuss the idea of *what you see is what you get*, we are really asking a question that involves numerous variables. Of course, the reason for proofing an image is to get a very close idea—if not exact—of what the final product will look like.

Monitor Soft Proofs

Traditionally, a proof meant that a hard-copy print of the image was to be used to determine the accuracy of the color reproduction for a given output device. With the advancement of digital photography came the need for, and development of, the soft proof. A soft proof is a representation of an image on the monitor that is intended to represent what an image will look like if printed on a given output device.

The key to soft proofing images is to have well-calibrated equipment and software, and a consistent working environment. This is especially important regarding the lighting in the room where the monitor display is located.

To display a soft proof using Photoshop, simply select the Proof Setup selection under the View menu, as illustrated. Remember that the initial color settings and preferences need to be defined first, as discussed earlier.

To give an idea of how dramatic the effect of soft proofing can be, we have changed the proof setup from Working CMYK (based upon our CMYK color preferences), to Macintosh RGB.

Here you can see a side-by-side comparison—a before and after comparison for two different output devices. The first output device is set up for a CMYK printing press using SWOP (coated stock) with a 20% dot gain, gray component replacement, and medium black generation, while the second output device is a Macintosh RGB monitor.

Soft Proofs

Comparison of Soft Proofs

CMYK Soft Proof   Mac RGB Soft Proof

As shown, soft proofing can imitate the results of an output image, if the proper profiles are utilized for the soft proofing process. In general, soft proofing will give a reasonably close approximation of what the final product will look like, but nothing is as accurate as a real hard proof.

Hard Proofs

Hard proofs can take a variety of forms. For the graphic arts, a Matchprint is considered to be the definitive hard proof. This is the film that is exposed from the actual color separations. This type of proof does not use the exact inks to be used on press to create the proof, but still yields a close approximation to that which will be reproduced. So in this sense, we can see that the premise upon which soft proofing is based is not a new one.

Other, more basic hard proofs take the form of actual prints off various output devices. For example, a hard proof for an Epson inkjet printer might simply be a print that will be used to visually adjust the color information of an image. Regardless of the type of devices or software used, a hard proof will always yield a tangible copy of the image to be produced.

It should be noted that beyond the software and processes described in this chapter, other profiling solutions exist. For more advanced users, solutions developed by Kodak, and especially those developed by Gretag, offer advanced color management controls, but go beyond the scope of color management we are discussing in this book.

Where to Go From Here...

The full science of color management goes far beyond the scope of this book. The attempt here has been to give an overview of some of the basic theory upon which color management is founded. , Mastering color management is essential to managing the medium of digital photography. Just as a strong understanding of chemistry and physics is essential to the traditional photographer, now the science of color management is also essential for the master photographer. A good basic online reference source is Kodak's Digital Learning Center (DLC), which includes information, tips, and techniques regarding Digital Imaging [Kodak.com]. Another basic online resource with a variety of information related to color management is [about.com]. Finally, there are numerous publications from organizations such as PMA Photo Marketing Association International [pmai.org] and DIMA Digital Imaging Marketing Association [pmai.org/dima], which address color management issues in support of digital photography.

Conclusions

As you can see, there are a number of factors that contribute to the science of color management. However, you do not need to be a photo-scientist to employ color management techniques in your workflow. The application of a basic color management system can dramatically increase the productivity and accuracy of your image reproduction. After all, the point of color management is to use a systematic approach toward mastering control over the reproduction of color in your imagery.

There is, of course, a basic presupposition that in order to employ color management techniques, you need to have a basic understanding of color theory. This rudimentary base is what the color management system is founded upon. Here, basic color theory pertains to light and inks (or pigments). The premise of a color-managed environment, as related to the digital photographer, is that all light theory is based upon the interactions between Red, Green, and Blue light, while all color reproduction with ink, dye, or pigment is based upon the interactions of Cyan, Magenta, and Yellow—or Cyan, Magenta, Yellow, and Black.

From these basic premises of additive and subtractive color theory, come the ideas and tools that form a CMS. Based upon the photographer's workflow requirements, a CMS can be as basic as printing an image, and adjusting the monitor until it matches the image, subjectively. On the other hand, the system can be as precise as having all devices, software, and even the operating system scientifically calibrated.

As we have discussed in this chapter, various techniques, and software systems can be utilized to create a system that is color managed. It is through the consistent and methodical use of these tools, and the application of these techniques, that we can predict what our images will look like when they are output—either on our own device(s), or on some other device(s) that are also calibrated to a standard.

Finally, one should consider the idea of color management as just another area of photographic endeavor. Just as we experiment with a new film and developer combination until the results are consistent, predictable, and pleasing, in the digital realm the same concepts apply. These concepts are not new—only the technology through which they are applied is new. In the traditional darkroom, we would not process C-41 film at 120°F, or E-6 film at 50°F, for example. This is because there are established parameters that are known to produce consistent and reliable results. Thus, even in the traditional darkroom, there are controls within the color management system with respect to wet processes. Therefore, color management in the digital realm regards the development and implementation of a consistent set of rules or procedures that allow us to master the medium of digital image reproduction.

In the end, color management makes the digital photographer's job much easier!

Review Questions:

1 What is Color Management?

a. Who needs it?

b. Why?

2 What is a CMS? How does it have an impact on:

a. Screen display of an image?

b. Printed output of an image?

3 List the two main color spaces in which digital images are usually edited?

a. _____

b. _____

4 Which color model/space allows for a more accurate description of color?

a. XYZ color

b. CIELAB color

5 Which color space describes **all** colors in purely theoretical terms? How does this impact the reproduction of real colors on a tangible medium like paper?

6 List four basic items that **must** be calibrated in order to work within a color-managed workflow:

a. _____

b. _____

c. _____

d. _____

Discussion Questions:

1 Why is a color management system important for a digital photographer?

2 What is the best way to establish a CMS that will allow you to accurately share your images with:

a. commercial printers

b. photo labs

c. other photographers/designers

3 In general, is it better to work on photographic images in the digital darkroom in RGB or CMYK mode?

Why?

4 Why is CIELAB color space so important to the development of a CMS? How does this impact gamut mapping and color transformations? Why?

5 Are profiles significant to the digital photographer?

6 Is it generally a good idea to embed profiles into images, or not? Why?

7 How can you develop a CMS that allows for soft proofing?

8 Which is better, a soft proof or a hard proof? Why?

CHAPTER 8

Output: Creating Image Products

Objectives:

This chapter will survey various output/printing image types ranging from Web sites and PowerPoint presentations through inkjet, dye sublimation, film, and press reproductions. Here you will learn how to prepare images to be printed and output to varied sources. Upon completion of this chapter, the reader should have a better understanding of:

- When to use different printing/output devices
- What differentiates image quality between printing devices such as laser printers, inkjet printers, and dye sublimation printers
- How to prepare images for output on photographic film or for prepress purposes
- How to control the range of reproduction in digital images
- How to output images for various multimedia and file sharing purposes
- How to develop a personal workflow and handle digital photographic images

Introduction

U p to this point, we have discussed ways to acquire and work on digital images. In this chapter, we will discuss how to get your images "out of the box" and back into the real world. Here we will describe both the devices and the methods for producing final image products.

Output Devices

There are a number of physical devices used to create hard copy images from their digital image files. Beyond these devices, there are a number of software applications that can be used to create virtual hard copies of their images, such as with final image content to be delivered as CD/DVD images, or those that are presented on the Internet.

Printers

When discussing printers, understand that there are a wide variety of devices that can be considered as printers. These devices range from the common types, such as laser and inkjet printers, to the more advanced types, like image setters and thermal dye sublimation printers. In this section we will discuss the main types of printing devices that are generally utilized by digital photographers, or anyone that is concerned with the fidelity of their photographic image output.

Laser Printers

At the most basic level, we begin by discussing laser printers. In terms of generating photographic quality images, lasers are at the bottom of the selection range for digital photographers. While the quality of the images produced by laser printers has increased dramatically, the archival life of these images is extremely short.

Therefore, the laser printer is a good choice for short-life products such as a sales report.

This is due to the fact that the cost per print is very low on a laser printer, and the archival quality of the image is not an issue. In the fine art realm, though, the laser printer would not be the best choice.

A laser printer forms the photographic image by focusing a laser beam on to a photoelectric drum or belt, which in turn generates an electrical charge. The belt/drum then attracts toner to the charged areas. The resulting image on the drum is then transferred to the receiver, the paper/film upon which the final print will appear. The toner is then fixed on the paper through the use of a heat transfer process—sometimes pressure is also applied in the fixing stage of the image.

With the reproduction of color photographs, the process described above occurs in four steps. That is, the charging of the belt and the transfer of the image occurs four times—once for each color separation. Just as with commercial printing, a laser printer needs to break an image into Cyan, Magenta, Yellow, and Black (CMYK). This process of color separation allows the RGB (red, green, and blue) image that is displayed on the monitor to be reproduced with ink or toner onto paper or film.

Pros
- Laser printers are quite reliable, and can handle heavy volume production runs.
- The cost per print is quite low, they are fast, and they do not generally require any specialized media upon which to print.

Cons
- For the reproduction of photographic images, other technologies produce higher-quality images.

Solid Ink Printers

Printers that employ solid ink technology also reproduce images in CMYK. The main distinction here is that these printers use, as the name implies, a solid ink to reproduce the image. The ink is in the form of color sticks, which are melted. The melted material is then sprayed onto the receiver, whether paper or film. Finally the paper/film is cold fused between a pair of rollers to fix the final image upon the receiver.

Pros
- Primarily designed for commercial use, these printers have the advantage of being able to print on most types of material. This is useful on a job where a client wants to see what an image will look like on the final stock or material.

Cons
- Most solid ink printers do not work well with transparency materials.
- The archival quality of the image is surpassed by other technologies such as inkjet and dye sublimation prints.

Thermal Wax Printers

These printers are useful for such tasks as printing presentation graphics. While the photographic output looks good, other technologies produce better results.

In the printing process for thermal wax printers, a ribbon is utilized which is coated with cyan, magenta, yellow, and black wax. This wax is transferred to the receiver paper via a thermal print head. The print head precisely melts the wax onto the receiver in four-color passes, producing the final composite color image.

Pros

■ Thermal wax printers offer fast printing at an affordable per-print cost.

Cons

■ The visual and archival quality of the image is surpassed by other technologies such as inkjet and dye sublimation prints.

Inkjet

The inkjet printer has had a surprising evolution, as far as digital image-makers are concerned. At this point, the inkjet printer offers the highest photographic print quality that can be delivered on varied print media surfaces.

Inkjet printing is the media of choice in fine art printing. Its disadvantages are that it is very slow, and the cost per print is relatively high.

The printing process involves the spraying of ink onto a receiver, paper or film. The inkwells are vibrated through the use of piezoelectric crystals. An electronic signal is employed to cause a variance in the crystal between two electrodes. This in turn causes a vibration that induces the spraying of ink droplets through nozzles.

Inkjet technology prints color images with the traditional CMYK inks. However in addition, seven-color technologies are employed with this type of printer as well. Here cyan, yellow, magenta, and black are still used, but in addition, light cyan and light magenta inks are also used. This type of printing technology expands the printing gamut, and greatly increases the subtlety of reproducible color fidelity. Beyond six-color technologies, many third-party manufacturers have produced inks for fine-art image printing such as quadtone black-and-white inks. Here the color inks are replaced with four (or six) different types of black ink—each having its own hue. The combination of these inks to produce black-and-white imagery has, in many professionals' opinions, surpassed most of the traditional fine-art printing methods and techniques.

Pros

- Inkjet printing devices are extremely inexpensive, and offer amazingly high-quality prints.

- Supplies are readily available. Archival inks are available from hardware manufacturers and from third parties for a variety of printing needs. Inkjet printers can also print on most surfaces. Even the low-level (under $100 USD) inkjet printers can produce near-photographic quality prints.
- Finally, inkjet printers, when paired with the right kind of inks and receivers, can produce prints with an archival life that will outlast most silver-halide film or paper's life.

Cons

- Special inks and papers are needed to produce photographic quality and archival prints.
- The cost per-print is quite high.
- The biggest drawback is that inkjet printers are slow, but in a low volume situation, the results are worth the effort.

Dye Sublimation

Initially championed as the choice for digital photography output, the dye sublimation printer has had a slower evolution than inkjet technology. Dye sublimation prints offer archival characteristics coupled with photographic fidelity. In this sense, they are one of the premier imaging output formats. Where dye sublimation prints fall short of such technologies as inkjet prints is that they are limited to the type of media they are printed upon, whereas other technologies, such as inkjet printing, can be printed on almost any media.

As with thermal wax printers, dye sublimation printers utilize a full-sheet-sized transfer ribbon. This ribbon contains cyan, magenta, and yellow dyes.

These dyes are transferred to the special receiver stock through the use of a thermal transfer process, whereby the print head heats the ribbon, and the dye is fixed upon the surface of the receiver. Here the amount of heat produced by the print head dictates how much dye is to be transferred to the final print.

It should be stated that the prints are stunning and surpass traditional photographic prints.

Pros

- Thermal dye sublimation prints look and feel like traditional photographs.
- They offer a combination that produces a subtlety of tonal reproduction, coupled with archival longevity.
- Dye sublimation printing offers high-quality professional looking prints.

Cons

- Special receiver papers are required to print dye sublimation images, therefore the choice of print surface is quite limited.
- The cost per-print is very high.

Film Output

While image-setters output to film, they output only black (and clear) areas to film—they do not reproduce an image as continuous tones. This is why the images need to be broken into halftone dots, or color separations. With respect to continuous tone reproduction of images, however, there are other types of devices that can be utilized.

The most common type of film output device is the film recorder. Film recorders allow for the output of digital images onto such media as:

- 35 mm negatives
- 35 mm positives (slides)
- 120 negatives
- 120 positives (slides)
- 4" x 5" negatives
- 4" x 5" positives (slides)
- 8" x 10" negatives
- 8" x 10" positives (slides)

By using a film recorder, it is possible to output images to traditional silver-halide films such as Fujicolor negatives, Kodachrome slides, or T-MAX 100 B&W negatives, for example. This is significant in that you can begin with either a digitally captured image or a silver-based image, acquire the image into the digital darkroom for alterations, and have a final product on film. This can then be printed or projected as with any conventional film.

The ability to output images to film allows the digital darkroom to become fully integrated with traditional media. In this sense, the imaging circle becomes complete. Presently, there are a number of photographers that shoot film and scan the images so that they can do their darkroom work in the digital darkroom, and then return the images to film—of course, having the advantage of also retaining a digitally archived copy of their images.

Silver-based Photographic Output

Beyond film, digital images can be output to conventional photographic materials. LED printers are an example of this type of technology. Here an image is printed with LEDs or laser diodes onto traditional photographic printing papers. In effect, this type of device acts as a pixel-by-pixel enlarger, whereby each pixel of light is exposed onto the surface of the enlarging paper. The image is then chemically processed as with any traditional image.

Receiver and Donor Process

In addition to wet processes and thermal dye sublimation, printers such as the Fuji Pictography use a two-step process where a photosensitive donor paper receives its exposure from laser diodes.

The dye-based image is then transferred to the receiver paper from the exposed donor material. This is a popular method of printing high-quality, medium-volume commercially delivered photographs. The cost per print for pictography prints is approximately equal to the cost of dye sublimation prints.

Image Setters

For the publishing industry, image-setters are the de facto standard form of lithographic output for digital images. This lithographic output, as related to digital photographers, is usually in one of two forms. Prints are output to either film or paper halftones, or as color separations—for such uses as offset printing.

While specialized in their purpose, image-setters are responsible for the delivery of most of the images people see. That is because most images are commercially printed, and almost all halftones or color separations are generated on an image-setter.

Regardless of whether the image is output to film, paper, or directly to press, the basics of halftones and color separations apply to all images that are reproduced on a printer or printing press.

Note that technologies such as digital presses alleviate the need for film output because the digital image's plate is actually formed on the press—digitally.

Halftones and Screens

To understand how images are commercially reproduced, you must first understand the basics of halftones and color separations. A halftone is a pattern of dots of differing sizes that represents a continuous tone image, through the use of only one color of ink. This is the basis for all continuous tone reproduction on devices ranging from laser and inkjet printers to commercial printing presses.

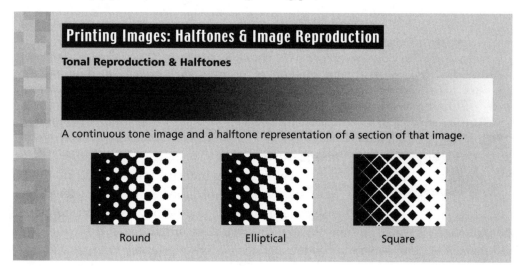

Printing Images: Halftones & Image Reproduction

Tonal Reproduction & Halftones

A continuous tone image and a halftone representation of a section of that image.

Round   Elliptical   Square

To understand half-toning, we must understand the basics of converting continuous tone images into solid ink representations. The following descriptions are the basic concepts that are involved in converting images for image-setters or press —and will even help to explain the workings of an inkjet printer.

- **Screen Frequency/Ruling**: the number of screen lines (rules) per inch, horizontally and vertically.
- **Screen Angle**: the angle from 0°, which defines the direction of the axis of the screen pattern.

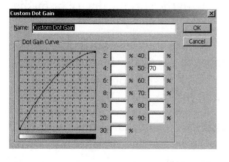

- **Screen Dot Shape**: the form of the pattern of a given screen; usually round, but other shapes can be used for various types of devices and purposes (see illustration).

Dot Size and Dot Gain

Dot size refers to three different aspects of a halftone: the highlight, the midtone, and the shadow.

In order to reproduce an image as a halftone (or as a layer of a color separation), the following must be determined:

- the smallest dot to be reproduced, as a percentage of the white areas of an image
- the largest dot to be reproduced, as a percentage of the black areas of an image
- the midtone/gray dot to be reproduced, as a percentage relative to the midtone areas of an image

Dot gain, however, refers to the amount of size increase of a dot when ink is applied to a page. Generally, software such as Photoshop will calculate a default setting for all of these values, but these settings can be tweaked to match the workflow more accurately (as illustrated).

Precision Output: Setting Target Highlight and Shadow Values

Regarding continuous tone images, you can set your own target values in software such as Photoshop. This enables you to match the range of tone to be reproduced with the output media. For example, let's say an image was to be printed, and it is known that the device has problems reproducing shadow areas. You can alter just the area of the image that contains the shadow information, so that this region will be printed correctly on a given device. The same is true of any area of the tonal range or color spectrum, as well.

For most media that print on standard white papers, the following ranges will usually apply:

- Highlights will normally fall around 2%-4%, where a grayscale value of a 4% dot will be roughly equal to the following values: R-244, G-244, and B-244.
- Shadows will normally fall around 92%-96%, where a grayscale value of a 96% dot will be roughly equal to the following values: R-10, G-10, and B-10.

These are estimates, which will vary depending upon the media used to print the image. The particular target highlight and shadow settings needed also depend upon the specific device that will output the image: inkjet printer, dye sublimation printer, offset printing press, etc.

You can adjust the gamut, and midtones, of an image to more closely match the output device and media, and to counter the limitations with the specific device or media. To illustrate, consider the following examples.

In order to have control over the output of an image, certain tonal corrections need to be made to all images. This is true whether an image is grayscale (black-and-white), or full color (RGB or CMYK). Here we will illustrate the basic process of setting target highlight and shadow values, and adjusting the midtones, as well.

The basic image is opened, and looks like this. Here the image is in its raw format, having no image corrections performed. The problem with trying to print an image like this is that most devices will not be able to print the full tonal range of this image. Just as with traditional photographic prints that can only print five *zones* of tonal information, digital output technologies have their respective tonal reproduction limitations. In this image, there is a great deal of tonal range between the darkest shadows (in the shutters) and the brightest highlights (in the clouds). The first problem for most people is trying to determine where the absolute darkest and lightest points of an image are located. This is often due to perceptual illusion, based on surrounding tones. The human brain is constantly adjusting relationships of tone and color. For example, that is why fluorescent light appears green to daylight film, but white to your eye. Luckily, we do not have to trust our brains for this determination. With Photoshop, the quickest way to determine the darkest and brightest points in an image is to create a *threshold* layer.

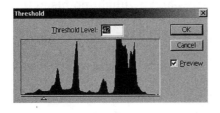

Here the slider can be moved to see the extreme ends of the tonal range.

Now we can set a target point by moving the cursor, which will turn into an eye dropper, over the desired point in the image and shift-clicking the point. The same procedure applies to the opposite end of the tonal range.

This is applicable to both color and black-and-white images. At this point, the threshold layer can either be deleted or turned off in the Layers palette. The image will now have two target points set on it. These will not show when the image is output, even if you leave them on the image.

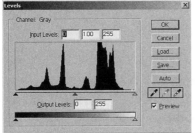

From here, the image's levels will be adjusted. The Levels layer allows you to control the full tonal range of the image, both in terms of the gamut and the relationship of the mid-tones to the highlights and shadows.

This is where we can compensate for the limitations of various output devices. First, the target values need to be set for the shadow and the highlight. This is as simple as selecting the shadow eyedropper (black tip) and clicking on the shadow target in the image. In this example, this is target #1, which was placed on the shutter through the threshold layer. Next, the same procedure applies to the highlight. The highlight eyedropper is selected (white/clear tip), and the highlight target is clicked on the image. That is target #2, in the clouds, which was also set in the threshold layer. The only problem here is that if we follow this procedure, we would have an image with pure black shadows and pure white highlights. While this may yield a spectacular dynamic range, there is no device that can faithfully reproduce this range of tone, while retaining detail. Therefore, we need to *tuck* in the ends of the image's tonal range, so that they can be reproduced. While there are a number of ways to do this, the way that will be illustrated here is one of the easiest and most consistent ways to match an image's gamut to that of an output device and material combination. To go back one procedural step, before we select our shadow and highlight points in the Levels layer (which can also be done in a Curves layer), we need to make two slight adjustments. First, we need to know where the image is to be output. Let's say this image is to be printed on a commercial printing press (although this procedure is exactly the same for an inkjet or dye sublimation printer—for example). Here we would ask the pressperson where to set our highlight and shadow points. Let's assume we are told that on this given press, with a specific ink, on a specific stock, we need to set our shadows to 4% and our highlights to 96%. We would do the following:

In the Levels box, we would first select the shadow eyedropper, but this time we would double-click on the eyedropper. This will open up a color picker menu. Here we would adjust the L value to 4, representing 4% black, and then select OK to set the change.

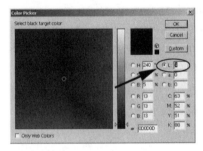

Next we would double-click on the highlight eyedropper and adjust the L value to 96, representing 96% of white.

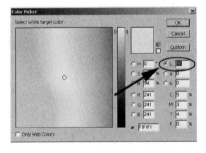

Now when we click on the target black-and-white points in the image, the black is not set to pure black, but to 4%, or that which we know our press will reproduce. The same holds true for the white value, except that the value here would be 96% of a pure white.

Another way to accomplish this is to adjust the output levels in the Levels dialog box. Once these end points have been set, the midtones can be adjusted by using the middle slider under the Levels input levels histogram.

Finally, the point of this example has been to make your highlights dark enough, and your shadows light enough, to reproduce with detail.

Color Separations

The basic principles of halftones, dot size, and dot gain apply when color separating an image. Additionally, such factors as screen angle need to be considered, in order to not create moiré patterns. When creating color separations for image output, you need to consider the fact that the image is being separated into four different continuous-tone black-and-white images. Each of these images is then half-toned, so that the continuous-tone of the image can be reproduced. The problem here is that the pattern of the halftone screens needs to have different angles for each of the color separations: cyan, magenta, yellow, and black. It is the composite of printing each black-and-white image with one of these four inks that produces the illusion of a continuous tone, full-color image on a printed page. Whether the image is to be printed on an offset printing press or an inkjet printer, it is printed as a color-separated image. Usually this process is automated with software such as Photoshop—after the initial color management profiles are set up. It is possible, however, to manually create color separations, determining your own screen angles and frequencies for each separation layer. Generally, it is recommended that you check with your service bureau or printing shop to determine their preferred screen frequency and angle, as well as the image's dot settings. You should leave images set to the default settings unless your service bureau or printing shop advises otherwise.

If you must set specific screen angles, it is recommended that the image be saved as an EPS (encapsulated postscript) file, which will often override the printer's default screen settings. This is because an EPS file will embed these settings, whereas these settings may be easily converted or overwritten in other file formats. This is one of the very few instances where it is recommended that photographic image files should be saved as EPS files—for a variety of reasons.

See the final composite of this image in the color section of this book.

Color Separations

CMYK representations of a Full Color Image

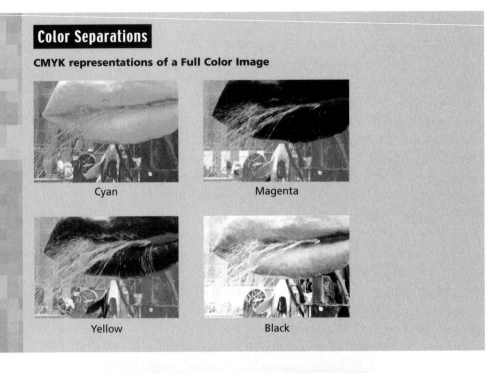

Cyan

Magenta

Yellow

Black

Photo available in color. Please see insert for further study.

Digital Output

An area that is often overlooked is that of digital output. When people think of printing an image, they usually think of dye sublimation or inkjet prints, or of commercial printing presses. These days, digital output is an extremely important area which image-makers should be concerned with. This is because of the diffusion of such technologies as consumer-level digital cameras, Web-based image sharing of photographs, digital postcards, interactive CD-ROMs, and more. Here we will address a few of these technologies, and discuss ways of handling your digital images appropriately for these media.

Multimedia Products

Web and the Internet

The Internet has opened up new worlds of communications. That which could not be imagined a few decades ago is now possible and accessible by the masses. This new communications media has had a special influence on imaging. Now, it is commonplace for people to e-mail photographs of children to their grandparents, for example. Further, new ways of sharing photographic images are becoming available to anyone with access to a computer and the Internet. Sending snapshots to friends and family worldwide is now something that average people regard as a normal way to view their images. Kodak initially championed this type of widespread digital imaging with the development of their Photo CD. Unfortunately, this media was cost-prohibitive for the amateur photographer. Later, the Picture Disk and the Picture CD were developed, and the costs associated with digitizing images were targeted at the average snapshot photographer's budget. In this way, digital images are readily available to consumers who are shooting film. Furthermore, many of these services automatically upload the images to a Web site where, with a password, the consumer can share their images instantly over the Internet.

There are four dominant ways to share digital images on the Web.

1. E-mailing an image as an attachment, or sending HTML e-mail
2. Using an image-sharing service
3. Sending files via FTP
4. Sending images as digital postcards, puzzles, and the like

E-mailing an Image

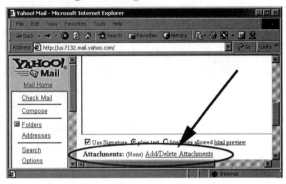

Whether you want to send an image as an attachment to an e-mail message, or as an inline graphic, modern e-mail software makes this quite easy. Beyond such software as Microsoft Outlook or Netscape Communicator, free online e-mail services such as Hotmail and Yahoo! also allow digital images to be incorporated in their e-mail.

There are two ways that digital images can be e-mailed: as attachments and as inline graphics.

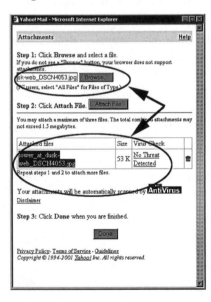

An attached image file is like paper clipping a photograph to a letter, except that here you select Attach or Insert File from your e-mail software. For this example, we have used Yahoo! to illustrate this procedure. Choose Attach File, and then choose the file you want to attach from your hard drive. In this example, Yahoo! allows a user to select the digital image—or other file type—and then to attach the image after it is selected.

In this case, the image file is scanned for viruses, and then attached to the e-mail. The image will not be seen in the e-mail when this type of transfer is utilized. Rather, the person who receives the e-mail is notified that there is an attached file, which they must download and open on their computer.

The next way an image can be shared via e-mail is to compose an e-mail in HTML format (hyper text markup language). Here the images can be seen, just as if looking at a Web page. When composing an e-mail to share images online, most HTML-enabled e-mail software acts like word processing software.

When someone receives the e-mail, it will look like the finished page of a newsletter or a Web page—based upon the author's layout and design.

Finally, some e-mail software allows for the previewing of attached files, as well.

For example, Yahoo!'s software allows you to see attached files if they are of certain file types, such as JPEG and GIF images. Here you can see a preview of an attached JPEG file, with typical options for downloading the image.

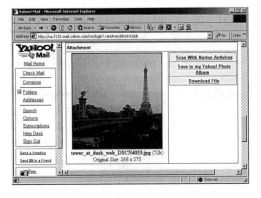

Publishing and Sharing Images with FTP

A more advanced way to publish or share images is through the use of an FTP (file transfer protocol) software application. This standard method of transferring files from one computer to another is the primary method utilized for publishing Web pages and images on the Web. There are several free or shareware programs both for Macs and PCs for FTPing files. Fetch on the Mac and WS_FTP and CuteFTP on the PC are the predominant shareware applications, which professionals use for FTP.

Here we will illustrate the basic way to output images to a Web site by using WS_FTP_LE—which is free to government employees, noncommercial home users, and students and staff of educational institutions.

First, with any FTP software, you need to establish somewhere to publish your images. This can be a personal or business Web site or a photo sharing service, for example. Once you have a place to transfer your images, use the FTP software to move the images. Think of the FTP software as a delivery method choice. Just as you might choose Federal Express, UPS, or DHL to send a package, you can choose Telnet, HTTP, or **FTP**—for example—to transfer your images.

The initial account information for the transfer needs to be supplied for the software to know where you want to send the image(s). Basically, you need to know the following information: your host name or address (where the images will be sent), your user id (personal account name), and your password (to avoid unauthorized access to your account).

The example illustrated here shows how a basic FTP account setup window appears with the appropriate information entered.

Once you are connected to your account, you may transfer the images. With WS_FTP, the left directory listing shows files on your local computer. The right window shows files on the *remote* computer—the one where the images are to be sent.

Notice that one file is selected on the left. Next you will notice that on the bottom of the window, *binary* and *auto* are selected—before you transfer your images. This is because on Windows, the binary method of transfer is used for data such as applications and image files, whereas the ASCII method of transferring data is used for text files and HTML documents. Note that on the Macintosh, it is always recommended to send all file types as raw data with Fetch, for compatibility reasons.

Finally, click the appropriate arrow (in the center of the window) to transfer the files in either direction, where left to right in this example means *upload* a file and right to left means *download* a file. With the Mac using Fetch, Put files/folder means *upload* and Get files/folders means *download*.

File Sharing: Postcards, Puzzles and More

There are a number of services offering online digital image processing services for delivering digital imaging to the masses.

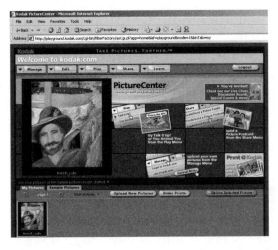

These services range from sites that allow you to share your images on the Web with others, to sites that allow you to make prints, mugs, T-shirts, online postcards, online puzzles and picture games, and more.

Even if you do not own imaging software, there are a number of services for manipulating photos online, such as the Kodak PictureCenter. Here, we will illustrate a few ways to use online digital imaging services to share your images. These examples are from Kodak's PictureCenter Web site located at: http://playground.kodak.com/.

Here you can see many of the options that are offered at Kodak's PictureCenter Web site.

To illustrate some of the possibilities, an image was uploaded to Kodak's server by clicking on an upload image button on their Web site. Next, the image was selected from the MY Pictures tab. Now, any of the options in the pull-down menus become available to manipulate, print, or share the image.

The first example shows how the Cartoon Maker was used to turn this photo into a cartoon-like illustration, by following the step-by-step instructions on the Web site.

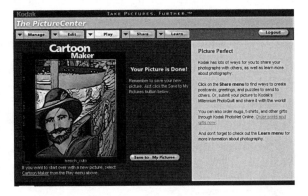

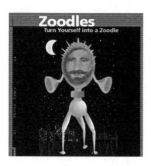

Next, a tool called Zoodles was used to create an illustration that blended a portion of the image into a predesigned illustration of an alien.

Now, while this may not be something that interests a professional, it is this type of easy access to quick results that is very appealing to consumers—especially children. In this way, new markets of digital savvy consumers are being groomed by online services. Beyond the simple manipulation of images, or service-bureau style printing services that online venues offer, interactive online services are offered, as well. For example, at Kodak's PictureCenter Web site, you can upload your image and create an interactive online jigsaw puzzle.

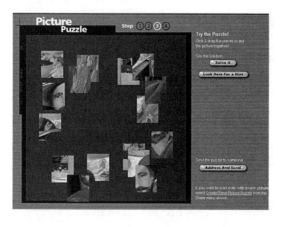

It is this type of interactive imaging experience that allows people to become part of digital imaging through online sharing of their images. Even at a more simplistic level, Kodak and other services, such as Yahoo!, offer the ability to send your own images as an online postcard. As can be seen here, the wizard-like interfaces that most of these services offer are simple to use, and allow nontechnical people to easily use the technology. This ease of use is the key to online sharing services, because many consumers would not otherwise attempt to work with digital images, due to a fear of the technology.

The significance of diffusing digital imaging technology to the masses should not be taken lightly. It is the consumer market that will dictate the costs of many digital technologies, and in turn will have an impact on research and development for digital imaging technologies at all levels.

CD/DVD

The last area of output we will discuss here is that which relates to the delivery of images on CDs or DVDs. There are two main delivery methods here. First, images can be output or delivered as collections of photographs. That is, a picture disk or a photo CD, for example, is a collection of images. It is not a production that incorporates images. Rather, images in their raw, natural state are contained on the CD, and the CD media is primarily used for storage. The picture CD and/or the photo CD can however be used as a presentation media—for slide shows.

The problem here is that you need to plan the images that will be contained on the CD before the film is processed—for normal picture/photo CD production. Or you can choose previously developed negatives or slides to be scanned onto a given CD, at a higher cost. This is not really a problem; it is more of a logistical planning situation as to what the purpose of the CD will be. If previously processed negatives or slides are to be contained on a CD, the order that they will be scanned onto the CD becomes extremely important if, for example, the CD is being created as a slide show-type presentation.

The second primary delivery method of outputting images in a digital format on CD or DVD regards the production of multimedia products. Here the images to be output become part of a digital publication whose base media is neither paper nor film. Rather, the CD or DVD itself becomes the final media. This method of image output is common for the delivery of images in a portfolio, for example. Additionally, many stock photography catalogs are now presented as CDs of sample images for which usage and reproduction rights are sold. Furthermore, many multimedia products such as interactive learning software is delivered in CD or DVD format. Here virtual tours of such works as those from the collection of the Louvre, for example, are available in digital form as the final output product.

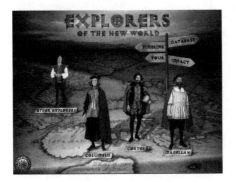

That is, these digital images were never intended to be in print form—they were designed to be delivered in their digital form as part of an electronic publication.

Finally, there is a hybrid category of technology that utilizes the CD-ROM and DVD delivery format. The interactive CD or DVD that can be linked to information on the Web is one of the more significant digital output solutions.

This type of product offers the tangibility of a CD or DVD, with the ability to link to information on the Web. In this way, a photographer's portfolio on CD is never out of date.

Preparing Images for Output

Throughout this book, we refer to developing and refining the workflow. The point of this repetition is that whether you are a hobbyist or a professional, organizing and improving upon your working methods will allow you to more skillfully master your craft. Here we will discuss some general ideas that will aid in refining your image output workflow.

Developing a Workflow

When considering output, the way you work can have a significant impact on the final product. For example, let's say the final product desired is an 11" X 14" thermal dye sublimation print, but the original image was scanned at 72 spi at 720 x 1187 pixels. If you do the math, this image will not have enough information to print properly on the chosen media at the desired size. Therefore, the output decisions need to be made before capturing the original digital image.

Given the dependencies of various aspects of the digital imaging workflow, an organized approach to the planning of projects and working methodologies needs to be developed and implemented.

Develop a Working Method

If you establish basic procedures, your workflow can improve dramatically. For example, a simple workflow checklist, as illustrated, can make a dramatic difference.

- What is the final output media and size?
  Therefore the *minimum* number of *pixels* required is:
  _____ **final pixel resolution** = (_____ inches x _____ inches @ _____ pixels per inch).
- Is there any possibility the client will ever need a larger version of this image?
- Which versions of this image should be archived?
- What format/mode is required for the end product?
- Should profiles be embedded for this job?

Image Storage and Archiving

After image acquisition, one of the first necessary considerations is how the digital images can be stored and preserved. There are a number of methods of image archiving available to the digital photographer.

The least expensive and most long-lasting method of archiving digital negatives or positives—image files—has been by saving the images onto Kodak's recordable CD material that incorporates InfoGuard technology. This archival CD material which can be burned on standard CD-R burners is boasted to last one hundred-plus years, or a lifetime—whichever is longer. As we have discussed in other chapters, the fact of the matter is that CD or DVD media most likely won't be in use in one hundred years, so the media used to store images on, in the digital realm, only needs to survive long enough to transfer the images to a newer media form. Furthermore, consider the facts that color negatives begin fading after about twenty years, color prints fade after five to fifty years depending upon the process, and even traditional black-and-white negatives and Kodachrome can't boast a one-hundred-year life. So your digital file will be around for a long time, if you archive them with care.

In terms of workflow, it is also recommended that you duplicate or triplicate all of your digital image files. The cost of doing so is next to nothing; perfect copies can be stored in different locations so that if a CD is destroyed, or a natural disaster occurs, for example, the image files will be preserved.

A Note about Service Bureaus

While this chapter discusses many of the output options available to the digital photographer, we do not suggest that you must do all of this work on your own. Just as you might send slides off to be processed, or a negative to be printed, so too are these options available in the digital realm. The Service Bureau chapter of this book goes into technology purchases and options in more detail. Remember that the current technology replacement curve cycles about every eighteen to twenty-four months. That is, if you buy a printer today, in eighteen to twenty-four months the printer will be dated to the point that—for commercial purposes—it may be difficult to be competitive as a printing service, for example. That is not to say that the device won't still have several useful years left, but rather that it will become increasingly slow, relative to new technologies, incompatible from a hardware and connectivity standpoint, and incompatible with new operating systems and software. On the same computer system, running the same old versions of software, the device will still be useful and productive however.

Before you purchase any digital technology, you should perform a cost analysis to see if it is more feasible to lease the technology, buy the technology, or contract the services.

Materials and Image Handling

Due to the variety of output media, ranging from digital delivery platforms, to the Web, through print media, the choices made regarding this media will determine the longevity of the images. For example, if you print all of your images on an inkjet printer, with standard inkjet ink, on paper that is not pH neutral, your images don't have much chance of lasting more than a few years. This is because that ink is known to fade in just a few years. Also, the choice of paper is not acid free, and thus not archival—it will turn yellow with time.

In the same situation, if archival inks and acid free paper had been chose, those prints could last anywhere from twenty to one hundred years—depending upon which ink and paper combination was chosen, and how the prints are to be displayed and stored.

General Output Settings

In Chapter 3, Image Acquisition and Properties, we discussed the four basic characteristics of a bitmapped graphic—dimensions, resolution, bit depth, and color space—in great detail. Here, we will present a quick reference table for determining an image's resolution, based upon the output media. It is strongly suggested that you should review the discussion of image resolution, dimensions, bit depth, and color space before developing an output workflow.

Resolutions for Various Output Devices

Device	Media	Minimum Resolution at Final Print Size	Maximum Resolution at Final Print Size	Notes
Laser Printer (B&W) 600-1200 dpi	Plain Paper	200 pixels per inch (ppi)	300 pixels per inch	Assuming the image is a continuous tone image
Laser Printer (B&W) 600-1200 dpi	Plain Paper	600 pixels per inch	1200 pixels per inch	Assuming the image is a bitmap image, with subtle graphic elements to be reproduced
Laser Printer (Color) 600-1200 dpi	Plain Paper	200 pixels per inch	300 pixels per inch	Assuming the image is a continuous tone image
Solid Ink Printer	Photo Paper	200 pixels per inch	300 pixels per inch	Assuming the image is a continuous tone image
Thermal Wax Printer	Photo Paper	200 pixels per inch	300 pixels per inch	Assuming the image is a continuous tone image
Inkjet 720–2880 dpi, or higher	Plain Paper	200 pixels per inch	300 pixels per inch	Assuming the image is a continuous tone image

Resolutions for Various Output Devices, continued

Device	Media	Minimum Resolution at Final Print Size	Maximum Resolution at Final Print Size	Notes
Inkjet 720 –2880 dpi, or higher	Photo Paper	200 pixels per inch	300 pixels per inch	Assuming the image is a continuous tone image
Inkjet 720 –2880 dpi, or higher	Transparency Film	200 pixels per inch	300 pixels per inch	Assuming the image is a continuous tone image
Inkjet 720 –2880 dpi, or higher	Fine Arts Papers	200 pixels per inch	300 pixels per inch	Assuming the image is a continuous tone image
Dye Sublimation	Photo Receiver Paper	200 pixels per inch	300 pixels per inch	Assuming the image is a continuous tone image
Film Recorder	Photographic negative or positive film	2800 pixels per inch	4000 pixels per inch	At the final output size: [35 mm positive= 1" x 1.5"]
LED Printer	Silver-Based Photo Paper	200 pixels per inch	300 pixels per inch	Assuming the image is a continuous tone image
Pictography Printer	Photo Donor & Receiver Paper	200 pixels per inch	300 pixels per inch	Assuming the image is a continuous tone image
Image Setter	Lithographic Paper	2x the halftone/color separation screen frequency = pixels per inch	2.5x the halftone screen frequency	Assuming an 85 lpi screen, 170 ppi is the minimum required resolution
Web Imagery	Screen Display	72 pixels per inch	96 pixels per inch	72 ppi is the standard, although some monitors display 96 ppi
E-Mail Images	Screen Display	72 pixels per inch	96 pixels per inch	72 ppi is the standard, although some monitors display 96 ppi
CD/DVD Publications	Screen Display	72 pixels per inch	96 pixels per inch	72 ppi is the standard, although some monitors display 96 ppi

Remember that this table is only a guideline. Individual circumstances will dictate your solution. However, these ballpark estimates will generally start you off in the right direction. Also keep in mind that when in doubt, it is safer to begin with a higher resolution image, and reduce it later.

Conclusions

Many output options are available to today's digital image-makers. These options range from simple black-and-white laser printers and screen display images, to inkjet and dye sublimation printers, to output on traditional photographic films and papers. This diversity of output options means that a photographer can now do in the digital realm almost anything that could have been achieved with traditional media. Furthermore, new possibilities for image output are availed to the photographer, such as CD/DVD-based portfolios and Web-based portfolios.

One of the greatest drawbacks that many traditional photographers see with digital photography is that "the quality isn't there yet." This is their limitation. In actuality, **digital photography and imaging offers higher quality image output and more variety of output options than traditional photographic media.** Once people actually become involved in the realm of digital output, they will see a new world of opportunities. Keep in mind that digital photographs can be derived from silver-based or digital originals, and can be output as digital or traditional photographic products. This is even greater variety than with traditional methods.

Finally, to master your craft, it is important to have control over your media. Regarding output, the control of your workflow is essential for consistent production. In the chapter on color management, we will discuss more ways of refining control over the production and output of your images.

Review Questions:

1. Which printers would be the best choice, if you want to make a print that looks exactly like a traditional photograph?

2. How many pixels per inch of image information are required to print:

a. An inkjet print on photo glossy paper?

b. A 35 mm color slide?

c. A thermal dye sublimation print?

d. A 133-lines per inch halftone-screened image?

3. List three different screen output products:

a. _____

b. _____

c. _____

4. At what point in the digital imaging process do you need to determine the pixels per inch resolution of the image?

5. If a project requires several different prints of an image, which one of the following images would be the appropriate image to save as an archive copy?

a. Web photo

b. Thermal dye sublimation print

c. Inkjet print on watercolor paper

d. 5-line screen halftone reproduction

Why?

6. What is the best output choice for an archival print?
Why?

Discussion Questions:

1 When might you decide to contract services for output, instead of purchasing your own equipment?

2 Given the variety of output options afforded to the digital photographer, which device/method will be most appropriate for the following types of image-makers, and why?

a. Commercial photographer?

b. Fine art photographer?

c. Commercial printer?

d. Graphic designer?

e. Web designer?

f. Corporate marketing presenter?

3 Why might you choose to shoot film, but digitally process and print your images? What are the advantages of doing this? What are the disadvantages of doing this?

Why is developing an output workflow set of standards important? How will this affect your productivity?

CHAPTER 9

Service Bureaus: Outsourcing Digital Photography Services

Objectives:

In this chapter, you will learn about using imaging services providers. Here you will learn how to find, communicate with, and prepare work for service providers. Upon completion of this chapter, the reader should have a better understanding of:

- What the role of a service bureau is regarding digital photography services
- How to prepare images for handling by third parties
- What media and/or delivery systems to use to transfer images to your service bureau
- How to budget your workflow
- When to buy, lease, or purchase equipment

What is a Service Bureau?

A service bureau is a company whose primary mission is to provide prepress and postpress services to the graphic arts industry. The history of how the service bureau has developed is as interesting and varied as the development of new media imaging technologies in the field of photography.

The Historical Role of the Service Bureau

The traditional role of the service bureau has its roots in the graphic arts industry. Here, the service bureau began as a number of different support industries for graphic arts. In the areas that are now commonly referred to as "prepress," such traditional industries as typesetting and later photo-typesetting were once at the core from which this new industry has grown. Other areas such as paste-up and layout for graphic production were also central to the service bureau's beginnings. Finally, continuous tone support, such as slide duplication and photographic printing, are the base from where digital or electronic photography/imaging service bureaus have developed.

The Contemporary Role of the Service Bureau

The new place in the graphic arts industry for service bureaus is quite large and diversified. This industry accounts for all sorts of tasks from creating slides from digital files, to imaging color separations for commercial printing, through billboard-size output of electronic images.

Now, the role of the service bureau is two-fold. First, it acts as a prepress house. That is, many functions that need to be performed in the early stages of graphic production—whether that is strictly graphic arts or continuous tone photographic production—are now outsourced to external service bureaus. The old model of accomplishing all phases of the project has changed its face, due in large part to the fiscal burdens that have been placed on photographers and others in the graphic arts industry. This is due to the never-ending cycle of hardware and software updates and replacements that are tied to digital and electronic imaging systems.

From a cost-effective perspective, many photographers cannot afford all of the new high-technological equipment to effectively compete in today's marketplace. Therefore, by utilizing external sources to aid in a project's development, now the photographer can compete, by lowering the technological overhead.

This is not to say that this is the only reason for the service bureau, however. Rather, there are many other reasons that the service bureau plays a significant role in today's marketplace. For example, let's say that a photographer has an assignment to digitally photograph an event and have a thousand posters commercially printed and distributed during the same day of the event. By using a service bureau, this photographer can complete this task in a timely manner. This can be achieved without the need to own a prepress computer system or the printing press and finishing equipment that would be required to fulfill this assignment. By utilizing service bureaus, the photographer can now accept assignments that would have traditionally been rejected.

Where to Find a Service Bureau

Service bureaus can be found in a variety of places. Depending on your needs, there is undoubtedly a service bureau that can aid in your photographic assignments, either locally, nationally, or internationally.

Local Bureaus

Locally, service bureaus take several shapes. In their most basic form, quick-print shops and photocopying shops generally offer a variety of services that might be of use to the digital photographer. These services range from computer rental to thermal dye sublimation printing. Furthermore, these shops are generally set up to provide quick turnaround times, and convenient access for small publishers and photographers alike.

National Bureaus

At the national level in the United States, there are a number of bureaus that offer more highly specialized services. Many of these services require a national market because of the cost factors involved. For example, in a small town it might not be feasible to offer large-format digital printing—at billboard sizes—purely because the demand for such a specialized service will be so low, and the service bureau could never justify the cost to own the necessary hardware. Whereas, a service bureau that accepts jobs nationally can justify more capital-intensive purchases. This is because their marketplace is large enough to attract ample jobs in order to earn a profit from such a capital investment.

International

At the international level, the service bureau allows for the exchange of visual information—in the form of digital photographs—in such a way that new markets are being developed. Due to the availability of prepress and postpress facilities worldwide, the photographer can now initiate a project on one side of the world, and have others complete the project on the other side of the world. This is especially relevant for the online community, as well as for the graphic arts (prepress) industry, where end products are digital in form.

How to Speak Their Language

In a word, "semantics" is the single most important thing to properly address when communicating with your service bureau. The reason this is so important is due to the numerous complexities of the digital image and its use. By simply referring to one element incorrectly, a whole project can be ruined. For example, let's say a service bureau requires a photograph to be imported into a designated page-layout program like Quark, and they have given you the following instructions:

- Photographic file format must be TIFF with no compression
- The file must be CMYK and contain no PANTONE colors
- All fonts must be type 1
- All files must be delivered on Jaz, ZIP, ORB, or CD-R media.

You must first understand their lingo to properly communicate with them and to achieve the desired end results. So, in our example above, let's say you have done everything correctly except when you last modified your digital photograph in Photoshop, you saved it as an RGB file—and to you, the difference means nothing. Chances are that when you see the finished job in print, you will not be happy with what you believe the service bureau has done to your photograph. Simply because you did not understand the significance of their explicit instructions, you may have provided the bureau with an image that is not going to be interpreted properly when it is RIPed (yet another acronym surfaces: the term RIP stands for raster image processing). Finally, if you don't understand some of the acronyms in the example above, this too can lead to great problems when dealing with your service bureau. Refer to the glossary in this book to familiarize your-self with some of the most common terms and acronyms used in the digital imaging industry.

Making Their Language Your Language

When communicating with a service provider, it is important to understand not only industrywide terminology and acronyms, but local ones as well. Many localities have their own way of discussing the same types of things in very different ways. At the root of this, of course, is the desire to get the job done as efficiently as possible.

Understanding Industry Standards

With the convergence of many different imaging fields in the last decade or two of the twentieth century has come a new understanding of how various parts of the imaging and production processes relate to each other. With these new relationships, new terminology has been employed to describe new technological relationships and the new technologies themselves. A push in the photographic and graphic arts industry has been to develop common standards, which will utilize common terminology. This is significant to the photographer in that these standards have a direct impact upon the end result of the imaging process: the final photographic image.

File Formats and Backups

One area that has been the slowest to evolve in the digital photography industry has been a set of absolute industrywide image format standards. During the 1980s, in the early days of electronic imaging, a variety of imaging formats were utilized for photographic image storage and transmission. These ranged from proprietary formats from Apple computer and IBM, to Commodore and Sony, and other computer/software manufacturers. The problem in the early days of electronic imaging was simply that there were no true standards. Now, several standards have emerged that are, for the most part, platform-independent. These will be discussed later in this chapter.

File Format Basics

There are two basic file formats that photographers deal with. They are bitmap graphics—also known as raster graphics—and vector graphics.

Bitmap and Raster Graphics

The primary type of file format that the digital photographer deals with is the bitmap image. This is an image that is made up of dots or bits of information; it is similar in concept to the grain of the traditional photographic image. This type of image is also known as a raster graphic. This term dates back to the early days of electronic imaging, when these images were described by how they were displayed on a monitor. The monitor displayed images as raster lines—the lines that are continually redrawn on a television or computer monitor to display the image.

Regarding service bureaus, it is important that the photographer understands the difference, and the significance of the difference, between bitmap and vector graphics.

The bitmap image is made up of elements known as pixels. These pixels—short for picture elements—are what make up the structure of the image. This is significant because the number of pixels per inch that an image is made up of determines the final "output" quality of the image. Therefore, the photographer must be certain to coordinate with the service bureau what they need in terms of how much image information is required for the particular task at hand. In other words, the photographer needs to know precisely how many ppi or dpi is required by the service bureau to output the image correctly.

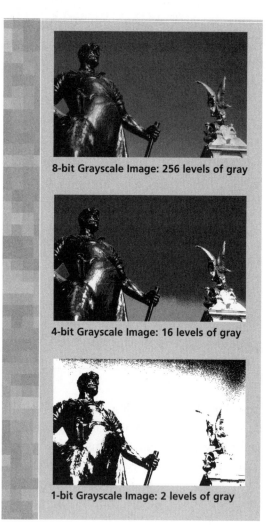

8-bit Grayscale Image: 256 levels of gray

4-bit Grayscale Image: 16 levels of gray

1-bit Grayscale Image: 2 levels of gray

An Example

An image with only black and white, traditionally known as a lithographic image, is known as a 1-bit image. That is, the one dot or pixel of image information only contains information regarding whether the specific dot is black or white. In a continuous tone black-and-white image, this same dot in the image could represent any of 256 different gray levels, while in a full-color image, this dot could represent anywhere between 256 and many millions of colors. This depends upon the bit depth of the image—where the bit depth of the image refers to the maximum number of tones or colors that can be represented in each pixel of the image.

In a practical sense, we need all of this information in order to determine how much data or information is needed to produce a final image that is representative of our visual intentions.

Vector Graphics

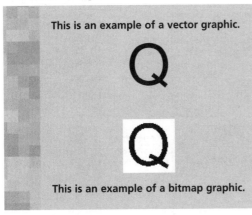

This is an example of a vector graphic.

This is an example of a bitmap graphic.

The vector graphic file format is such that it stores image information as a series of mathematical formulas, which define all of the shapes within the image. For typography and graphic elements, the vector file format is preferred. This is because the file that is produced in this format is very small, and the image is scalable to virtually any size with no degradation. For photographers, unfortunately, this format does not lend itself well to representing photographic images. This is because every pixel of each image would need to be represented as a mathematical formula, and the resulting files can potentially become tremendous in size.

On a day-to-day basis, what the photographer needs to know about vector graphics is that these are generally "line art," digital illustration, and font-representing graphics. They generally do not deal with continuous tone photographic images.

Compression Formats

One of the many options that are offered to the photographer during the save process, where image compression is concerned, is whether to save the image with lossless or lossy compression. Basically, this means that although the information that the image is made from is compressed, the quality of the final image is determined when the image is saved. That is, by choosing whether to compress an image (to save disk space, etc.) when the image is saved, the choice to lose image quality is also being made.

What Compression Does to Your Images

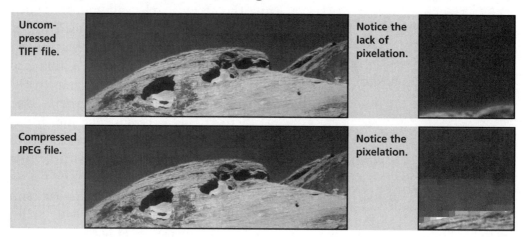

When an image is compressed, a mathematical formula known as an algorithm is utilized in order to evaluate the image information in terms of tone and color, and to make a determination of what information can be discarded.

When the image is later called upon, software is utilized to reconstruct the image, filling in the missing gaps in the image that the compression algorithm discarded. What this means for the photographer is that when compressing an image, the photographer is willing to lose image quality in order to reduce the file size of the image. The amount of information lost depends upon the particular algorithm that is utilized in the compression of the image, and the options that the photographer chose when saving the image.

Preferred and Less-preferred Formats

Depending on the working environment, and end product needs, the format that is preferred will differ. For example, let's say that the photographer is creating images to be utilized only for on-screen use. In this case, these images will have a very low resolution in terms of the dpi and ppi resolution (usually 72 dpi/ppi). Furthermore, if these images are being designed for use in a computer-networking environment such as the Internet, the size of the image becomes very important. This type of application is where image compression can be considered. The loss of image information may be considered acceptable in this situation because the need to have a small image for image transmission out-weighs the need for retaining all of the original image's information. On the other hand, another photographer may need to prepare a digital photograph for full four-color reproduction as a printed piece. In this case, the size of the file will usually be less important than the need for retention of the original image's detail.

Mac, UNIX, and Windows Compression

The computer platform that is used determines which file formats will be utilized on a daily basis. On the Apple Macintosh platform, for example, the **pict** file format is the standard photographic image file format, while for Microsoft Windows, the primary image format is the **bmp** file format (device-independent bitmap, DIB). Due to these differing standards, a number of attempts have been made to develop image formats that are cross-platform in their structure. That is, files that can be opened and saved the same way regardless of the computer platform that is being utilized.

One of the earliest attempts at developing a cross-platform file format was initiated by CompuServe, an online information provider. They developed the GIF or graphic interchange format before most people ever heard of the Internet. The idea was to enable all users to share visual and photographic information, regardless of whether they were using a Commodore, Atari, Mac or PC computer. As it turns out, this file format has become one of the most utilized digital file formats of all time—primarily because of its utilization by World Wide Web browser software. However, there are other significant cross-platform and file compression formats to consider as well.

Image File Compression

The main file compression formats that the photographer will utilize when dealing with service bureaus are the TIFF (tagged image file format) and JPEG (joint photographic experts group), as well as new formats such as Sid (Mr. Sid file format).

- The TIFF file format has one type of compression at one compression level available to the photographer. This type of compression is known as LZW compression (short for Lempel-Zif-Welsh, developed in 1977 by J. Ziv and A. Lempel, and later modified by T. Welsh), and is considered lossless in terms of its affect on image data.
- The JPEG file format avails a wide range of compression levels to the photographer. Generally, the JPEG format is not utilized for images that are to be used in print reproduction. Rather, this format is popular as an online compression format for images that are designed to be viewed at screen resolution. This is not to say that these images are not or cannot be used for other purposes. Actually, many photographers utilize this file format for all of their imagery. The problem is that with JPEG compression, there is always some degree of image quality that is lost. At the maximum quality setting in JPEG compression, the image size is cut in half and the image quality is virtually lossless; however, there is some controversy in the industry concerning the actual amount of information that is retained. Regardless, JPEG remains one of the most popular image formats, primarily due to its utilization by World Wide Web browsers, as with the GIF file format.

■ An alternative file compression format is the **MrSID** portable image format file. This file format boasts that through its seamless wavelet compression technology, it can compress an image at a ratio of 33:1, which will be visually lossless.

Based upon the task at hand, each of these image formats can be useful. It all depends upon the needs of the photographer, and those of the chosen service bureau.

Lossless Image File Formats

Still discussing image file format compression, lossless compression refers to the technique of compressing an image with **no** loss of visual information. This type of compression technique can reduce a file up to fifty percent of its original size. This is also the technique that is utilized when compressing data and applications. The PKZIP format is an example that uses this type of compression technique.

Lossy Image File Formats

Images that utilize lossy compression techniques have varying degrees of loss of visual information in the resulting image. This type of compression technique attempts to reduce image information that its algorithm deems to be unnecessary or redundant. This is also the type of compression technique that is generally utilized in the compression of video images, such as with the MPEG (moving picture experts group) standard for compression.

With this type of compression, at this point in time, compression ratios of up to 33:1 can be achieved—as with the MrSID file format. What this means is that an original 20.6MB photographic image can be reduced to 639K. The implications of this type of compression technique, for networking and large document transportation, are far-reaching.

File Compression

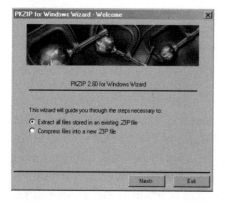

Beyond image compression techniques, there are more universal file compression formats. These universal file compression formats can reduce the size of most any computer data file, such as a page layout file, a font, or an image file—in a lossless manner.

This is significant to the photographer in that if a file is saved in a lossless image file format, the file can be reduced with other data compression techniques that will not affect the image quality. There are several other industry-standard file compression formats.

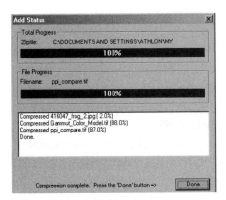

On the Windows platform, the two standard file compression formats are ZIP and PKZIP.

The Zip file has two forms. A standard Zip file—which usually ends with .zip—contains the original file in a compressed format.

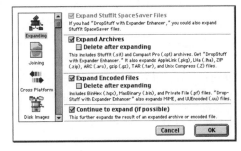

This file requires special software to "un-zip" the file, to restore it to its original uncompressed state. The second type of Zip file is the self-extracting Zip file. This type of file can simply be double-clicked by the end user, and it will automatically self-extract—with no other software needed. Additionally, the **arj** and **arc** file formats are available on the Windows platform. However, these file formats are being utilized much less frequently on the Windows platform these days.

With the Mac OS, the primary image compression format is known as StuffIt.

Aladdin Systems developed the StuffIt format, and the .sit filename extender denotes these files.

Although the **sit** file format is technically cross-platform, Mac users have traditionally used it almost exclusively—even though StuffIt software is also available for Windows.

Finally, the Unix platform primarily utilizes the tar (tape **ar**chive) file format. This file format does **not** compress information; rather, it groups files together in one common file—as the Zip and StuffIt formats can do as well. These files are denoted by the .tar filename extension. Additionally, the *gzip* command associated with a **tar** file allows for the compression of a Unix tar file—denoted by the **.tar.gz** or the **.tar.z** filename extensions. These files can be untared and unzipped on the Unix, PC, and Mac platforms with the appropriate utility software.

A Negotiated Solution

Regardless of all of the industrywide standards, in the end, working with a service bureau is a process that leads to a negotiated solution. That is to say, whatever your service bureau considers to be their standards **are the standards**, unless a compromise is worked out. This is a crucial element of having success with the service bureau. What many photographers may not realize is that their service bureau may give service to a wide variety of clientele. This clientele, from all walks of industry, have differing work environments, products, and needs. Of all of these, the photographer's needs are generally the most technically demanding on the service bureau. This is usually because of the large file sizes of photographic images, and the precision required in the output. Therefore, it is the photographer's job to ensure that all of the terms and conditions of the job are met before the job is submitted to the service bureau. It is also recommended that all of the conditions of the job be written down and authorized **before** the job is submitted. All this preparation will help gain a better end product because service bureau personnel may only run your job in a business-as-usual manner, but photographers often have radically different needs from the usual service bureau clientele.

Although all of this may seem a bit confusing, these are the day-to-day realities that the service bureau needs to deal with from their clientele. Therefore, the photographer who utilizes a service bureau needs to understand all of these subtle intricacies in order to effectively communicate with the service bureau. To help illustrate this point, let's say you just met a new friend who lives in Sydney, Australia. Now you want to send a letter to him. If you simply send an envelope that says Mike Smith, Sydney, Australia on its face, do you really think he is going to have it delivered to him? The same logic holds true regarding file formats for your digital images. If you compress a group of images on a Unix system, and your service bureau has no idea what a **tar.gz** file is, you will probably be out of luck. Therefore, you should always verify what standards your service bureau wants its customers to adhere.

Images for Web and Electronic Media Design

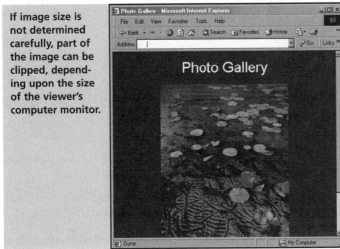

If image size is not determined carefully, part of the image can be clipped, depending upon the size of the viewer's computer monitor.

When dealing with photographic imagery for monitor-based display purposes, many of the traditional rules of image integrity do not apply. This is the case with photographic images on the Web and any other computer monitor-based display of this type of imagery. The reason for this is that the average computer monitor only displays 72-96 pixels per inch. What that means to the photographer is that only a small portion of the image's data will be displayed. Consequently, the viewer will see a lower-quality image. Therefore, there are several important contributing factors to the overall quality (or lack thereof) with respect to on-screen display systems.

When developing photographic imagery for on-screen viewing, there are several specific problems that need to be considered. First, the end user's screen size needs to be considered. For example, is the end user viewing the image on a 15", 19" or 21" monitor? And, is the monitor resolution set to 1280 x 1024 pixels or 640 x 480 pixels? Also, is the color "depth" set to 8-bit, 16-bit, or 24bit? As you can see, there are a number of variables that can affect how your final image is seen by any potential end user.

Size

There are some basic rules-of-thumb to follow regarding image size. First, if you do not know who your potential end viewers are, most on-screen images should be no larger than a standard 13"-15" monitor display of 640 pixels wide by 480 pixels high. Although as technology advances these numbers will increase, this standard has remained somewhat constant for at least a decade—an eternity in computing terms. If, however, you know that your final audience are viewing images on 17" monitors or larger, then you can accordingly adjust your image size to something larger, like 800 pixels x 600 pixels. The key here is to not alienate your audience because of technical restrictions. Of course, there is a point where the photographer needs to set forth minimum standards, and accept the loss of part of the audience.

Bit Depth and Platform Issues

Bit depth deals with the amount of color that can be viewed on-screen at one time. For photographic images, a bit depth of at least 16 bits is suggested, and 24 bits of color depth is preferred. The following table illustrates how many of the colors in a photograph can be viewed at one time on a given monitor.

Bit Depth	Number of Colors that Can Be Displayed On-Screen
1	2
2	4
4	16
8	256
16	32700
24	16.7 million

This is significant because the way that the image appears on-screen is radically different between an 8-bit version and a 24-bit version. This is especially true of images that have a wide variety of colors and tones, such as the sky in a sunset or a studio background with a gradation.

Output Options

Finally it is important to consider the way in which the on-screen image will be presented. If, for example, the image is to be viewed on a computer with a 21" monitor at 24-bit color, the preparation of that image will be radically different than if the same image is to be viewed through a video projector. This is primarily due to the output resolution of the various devices that can be utilized for viewing images.

Standard Formats for Web and Electronic Media

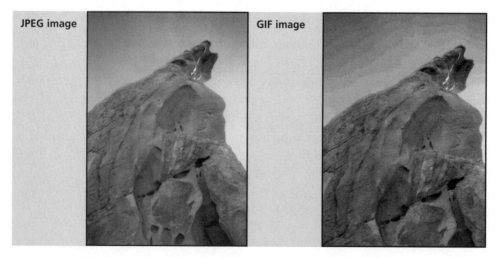

JPEG image   GIF image

On the World Wide Web, one of the biggest problems relates to bandwidth (how much information can be transferred in a given amount of time). The problem that arises for photographers is that the digital photographic image contains a great deal of information, which is represented by a large digital file. This large file takes an unreasonable amount of time to transfer via the Internet for the average user—based on how the user is connected to the Internet. Due to these problems, the standard formats for the Web are the **.gif** and **.jpeg/.jpg** file formats. This is because the GIF file is relatively small due to the fact that it is only an 8-bit file format, and it can only display 256 colors. As for the JPEG file format, because of the great compression ratios possible, the image can be reasonably displayed on the computer monitor—even after quite a bit of degradation occurs through compression. Both of these file formats are platform-independent.

Plug-in-Based Formats

For a variety of reasons, images may need to be displayed that are not GIF or JPEG files.

Here, Web browser software most predominantly utilizes plug-in-based image file formats. For example, a high-resolution vector-based image can be displayed with an external software "plug-in." A plug-in is a small software addition to the Web browser that enables the browser to display images of different formats. Plug-ins are based on specific file types.

Electronic Watermarking

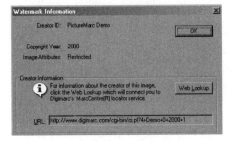

The electronic watermark is a noise pattern that is digitally embedded into a photograph that encodes such information as the owner's name and copyright information into the image.

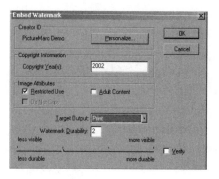

This information is distributed throughout the image so that if only a part of the image is used, or if the image is altered, the copyright information, etc., will remain with each portion of the image.

The main problem with this technology is that although it is intended to be invisible, watermarking does degrade the image to some degree—although ever so slightly. Special software is required to encode or decode digital watermark data within the photographic image.

For further information on watermarking and other image protection methods, refer to the chapter on copyrights.

Electronic Transfer of Digital Images

One of the most significant advances of the digital image has been the transportability of the image. This is specifically due to the fact that the image is in digital form. Because of its digital form, the electronic photograph can be easily transported, via various computer-networking arrangements, as a data file.

Electronic Communications Basics

It is significant to note that the way in which an image is transferred digitally can alter the image's structure. Therefore, there are certain guidelines that should be considered when sending an electronic file over a network.

Direct Connections

The direct connection method is where the photographer is sending a file directly to the service bureau. This method usually involves the client directly dialing the telephone number of the service bureau's computer, through his or her own computer. Once a connection is established, the client will upload their digital file(s). Before the client can connect to the service bureau computer, certain communications protocols need to be determined—the service bureau usually provides this information. For example, the service bureau may tell the client that in order to send digital files directly to the service bureau, the client needs to do the following:

Before dialing, set the following terminal settings and transfer protocols.

> Set the terminal type to VT100
>
> Set the transfer protocol to XMODEM/CRC or ZMODEM
>
> Send the file type as a Binary file
>
> Set the baud rate to 57600
>
> Communications setters: 8-N-1
> (8 bits per second, no break, 1 stop bit)

Then dial the phone number: 555-555-5555. Once a connection is established, upload the file(s) using either the XMODEM/CRC or ZMODEM transfer protocol.

Generally, the service bureau will supply all of the necessary information regarding direct dial-up connections to their server.

Internet Connections

An increasingly more popular way to send files to the service bureau is via the Internet. Utilizing the Internet as a network to transfer images to the service bureau is relatively straightforward. After a typical TCP/IP or SLIP Internet connection is made, the file(s) can be sent via FTP (file transfer protocol) to the service bureau's FTP server. This is usually done with software like Fetch for the Macintosh, or WS FTP or FTP Voyager for Windows—there are many other FTP client applications available. The service bureau will usually recommend in what format the digital file needs to be transferred. For example, the file can be sent as a text file, binary file, Mac binary file, and so forth.

Some Practical Realities

As with any business relationship, certain understandings of the ways in which a service bureau deals with its clientele will dictate how the photographer should approach them. This is true of dealing with issues ranging from personnel, to bit depth and file format, through media selection and transfer protocols. While all of this may seem a bit overwhelming, consider that these procedures are essentially the same in form, as compared with traditional media. That is, in a traditional setting, the photographer utilizes service bureaus for film processing, custom printing, slide dupes, and many other common forms of service-based outsourcing.

Establishing a Relationship with Your Service Bureau

As with any business relationship, one of the most important factors to a successful relationship is to understand what the service provider's expectations are, and how to adapt your workflow to accommodate these needs with a minimal investment of capital and time. Most importantly though, are the personal relationships that are established with the individuals at your service bureau. These relationships will aid in making your jobs successful—especially when problems arise at the service bureau with such things as corrupted files, etc.

Hardware and Software Compatibility Issues

As discussed in chapter one, there are many technological possibilities for the photographer in the digital arena. With all of these possibilities come potential problems—especially in terms of system incompatibilities.

Here are examples of some of the most common problems where one of the following situations occurs:

Problem	Typical Cause
Can't read customer's disk	Mac-formatted disk on a PC platform
Problem parsing file	PC file processed through a version of PC Exchange on a Mac that has reinterpreted the data
Photoshop file won't open	Created in newer version of Photoshop than the service bureau currently owns
File won't open from a Zip disk	PC Zip disk on a Mac, once file is copied to another hard drive, file will open—from the file menu in Photoshop

This is why it is key to discuss all of the hardware and software compatibility needs with the service bureau **before** any job is submitted.

Prices

Service bureau pricing varies widely due to a number of factors; however, the most significant factor is turnaround time. Some bureaus will charge up to five times their normal fee to get a rush job out overnight, and even more if the job is needed the same day. Another factor that is key to pricing is the amount of the bureau's technological resources that will be tied up for a given job, and how long these resources will be needed.

Pricing is usually based upon the market for the given task that the service bureau is providing. For example, if a low-resolution, 8" x 10" color proof on plain paper of a photographic image is needed, the fee should be relatively low. This is because this is a service most anyone can provide; even most home-based computer users have access to this level of technology. If, however, the service needed is more specialized and requires high levels of technology, the pricing will be higher, accordingly.

Sample Service Bureau Job Form from www.imagers.com

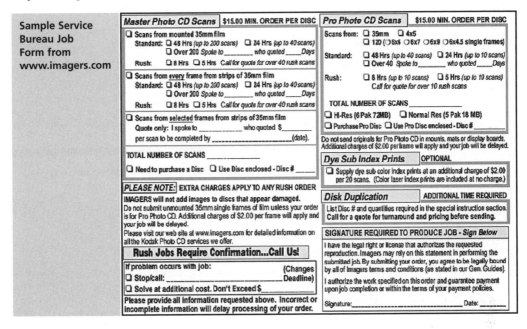

As the name service bureau implies, these companies are in business to provide services—generally those that require high levels of technological investment and specialized expertise.

How to Budget Your Workflow

Budgeting can be a tricky part of using service bureaus. The most significant thing to remember here is that you should obtain **written** quotes **before** outsourcing any portion of your workflow. In a real-life day-to-day situation, this may not always be possible. This is where the relationship that you have established with the service bureau is important. At least, if a relationship has been established previously, chances are that you won't be price gouged on that special rush job that just has to be out by 5:00 today.

As for planning a budget for the workflow, basic business planning principles apply here. First, remember that budgeting refers not only to monetary resources, but it refers to time, personnel, and technological resources and supplies, as well. The following checklist of questions can be used as a basic outline of some essentials that need to be considered when budgeting a workflow.

Of course, everyone's individual checklists will be different; however, this is intended to give a starting point.

Workflow Checklist

- Will our current workflow allow adequate time for this job?
- How many labor-hours will this job require in-house?
- What in-house resources will be required to complete this job?
- What in-house personnel will be required?
- Which aspects of this job will need to be outsourced?
- What is the turnaround time of each of the outsourced phases of this job?
- How much downtime is needed between each/any of these phases?
- What are the in-house personnel costs associated with this job?
- What are the in-house expendable supply costs associated with this job?
- What are the outsourced costs associated with this job?
- What are the shipping/handling and packaging costs associated with this job?
- How is accepting this job going to affect the current inventory of jobs?
- What is the profit margin?

Advantages and Disadvantages of Outsourcing

When outsourcing parts of a job, consider that there are always pros and cons to each decision. In the end, economics usually dictate whether or not a service bureau is required. The following lists are intended to give an outline of some of the advantages and disadvantages of utilizing service bureaus. This listing is not intended to be comprehensive.

Advantages of outsourcing to a service bureau include:

- Lower in-house technological investments
- Lower in-house labor costs/overhead
- Ability to accept a greater number of jobs
- Ability to accept jobs that contain components beyond your organization's technical abilities
- Less physical space required for your organization—lower overhead costs
- Lower maintenance and equipment repair costs

- Less continual capital outlay or monthly lease payments for replacing outdated technologies
- Addition of outsourced-based expertise for highly skilled specific tasks to your organization

Disadvantages of outsourcing to a service bureau include:

- Additional per job-based expenditures
- Increased amount of time needed to accomplish a given task
- More difficult to maintain consistent quality control over the job

Overall, outsourcing and the use of service bureaus can positively contribute to your workflow. This is a common practice among most professional photographers.

Building Your Own System Versus Using a Service Bureau

When considering whether to build an in-house system, or to outsource jobs to a service bureau, several factors need to be considered. First and foremost, a determination of the economic feasibility of both choices needs to be considered. For example, although it is more convenient to perform all of the tasks related to a given job in-house, how is this going to affect the profit margin of the job? That is, can you afford to justify a capital outlay for rapidly outdating technologies? And, how long will it take for your organization to break even, before it can make a profit by utilizing these in-house technologies?

Of course, profit is not the only factor to be considered. Quality is paramount, if you want to continue to stay in business. Therefore, these factors need to be considered carefully before decisions are made regarding the procurement of technology, or the choice to outsource.

When making the determination of whether to build a system or to outsource, consider the following questions/factors:

- What is the useful life span of each of the technological components, while still remaining competitive?
- How much will the initial capital investment be?
- How much will the monthly payments be?
- What is the maintenance cost associated with owning each of these technologies?
- How long will it take to make a profit?
- How will owning or not owning these technologies affect the organization and type of work that can/cannot be accepted?
- What kind of deadlines do our clientele have?
- How will either decision affect the final quality of our product?

Performing a Cost Analysis

As with any business decision, you should always perform a cost analysis before committing to either of the choices presented. Performing a cost analysis is actually quite simple if you consider that in the end, there are only two factors that count. These factors are cash flowing into your business, and cash flowing out of your business.

In order to perform a cost analysis, you need to calculate four things.

> I. How much will we need to spend to accomplish our workflow if we purchase or lease all of the technology needed for this task?
>
> II. How much will we need to spend to accomplish our workflow if we outsource what is needed for this task?
>
> III. How much profit or loss will be realized if we own/lease all of our equipment to accomplish our workflow?
>
> IV. How much profit or loss will be realized if we outsource all or part of our workflow?

Granted, there are a number of additional factors that need to be assessed when making these determinations. In the end, the bottom line will dictate what is actually the more sensible way to go. Remember, all of these figures should account for all factors, including such things as miscellaneous overhead, insurance, additional space/rent, power, expendable supplies, and labor costs.

Considering Leasing Versus Ownership of Equipment

As we have just discussed, one of the most important steps in determining whether to lease or own equipment is to perform a cost analysis. Depending on your organization's needs, either leasing or owning equipment can make sense. According to the Equipment Leasing Association of America (ELA), 80 percent of American companies lease all or part of their equipment. When considering the procurement or leasing of equipment, the following factors should be considered:

1. How long will the equipment be needed?
2. What will be done with the equipment at the end of the lease?
3. What is your organization's tax situation?
4. What is your organization's cash-flow situation?
5. What are your organization's needs in relation to potential future growth?

Based upon your answers, the decision to lease or purchase can be determined. For example, if your organization has no surplus capital, but a steady cash flow, the decision to lease might be appropriate. On the other hand, if immediate jobs require intensive use of specific technologies, and the cash flow they will generate will offset the procurement of these technologies in a short time period, the decision to own this equipment might be appropriate.

After all things here are considered, it is strongly recommended that you discuss the decision of whether to lease or purchase equipment with your accountant, financial advisor, and/or attorney before committing to a decision.

Conclusions

Service bureaus are a significant part of the graphic arts and photographic industry. As high-technology imaging continues to emerge, the need for service bureaus will increase. For the photographer, outsourcing aspects of jobs through service bureaus will continue to enable photographers to work in the digital world of imaging, without being excluded by fiscal burdens.

Review Questions:

1 What purpose do service bureaus serve for digital photographers?

2 Name three categories of service bureaus, and give an example of when the use of each might be appropriate?

a. _____

b. _____

c. _____

3 When outputting a digital image, name two file formats that are appropriate, and two file formats that are inappropriate for a high-resolution thermal dye sublimation print.

Appropriate Formats:

_____

_____

Inappropriate Formats:

_____

_____

4 Describe the process of negotiating an order with a service bureau.

5 How should you determine whether it is better to outsource work or own equipment?

Discussion Questions:

1 Even though it may be expensive to outsource certain aspects of your workflow, why may this still be an appropriate action?

2 Which is more important, submitting work to a service bureau the way you know to be correct, or submitting work to them the way they ask for it—even though you know that their way is incorrect?

a. Why?

b. How should this situation be handled?

3 Where in the workflow should a photographer perform a job cost analysis?

a. Why?

b. How will this affect your workflow?

4 When submitting work to a service bureau, what are the advantages and disadvantages of creating a digital photograph that will be used for print as well as for web-design?

a. Why?

b. How will this affect the workflow?

c. What issues need to be addressed in this situation?

CHAPTER
CHAPTER
10

Copyright:
An Image–Maker's
Guide to Intellectual
Property Rights

Objectives:

Here you will learn about ethical and legal issues such as intellectual property, copyrights, trademarks, and patents. This chapter surveys topics ranging from how to register a copyright to technical solutions for guarding copyrighted images. Upon completion of this chapter, the reader should have a better understanding of:

- What constitutes intellectual property
- Why photographers need to know about copyright
- How copyright, trademark, and patent law affects the photographer
- When and how to register copyrights
- How *works for hire* and licensing rights affect your claim to copyright
- Professional practices with respect to copyright
- How to use watermarking and other technical protections to identify copyright and ownership of images

Introduction

Before we begin, let's clarify a few things. First, you do not need to be an attorney to copyright and/or protect your own creative images. The area of intellectual property rights makes many people feel too intimidated to take control of their workflow. Most photographers want their works to be protected, but fear dealing with the red tape of the government forms, fees and submission, and deposit requirements.

It doesn't have to be painful to protect your creative work. In this chapter, we will dispel the myths of copyright, and illuminate the distinctions between the differing types of protection afforded to original creative works.

Note that this chapter is very United States-centric. That is, it deals almost exclusively with U.S. intellectual property law, although some mention is made of international copyright here. Finally, before we delve into this chapter, understand that this discussion is intended to shed light on some of the often-clouded concepts of U.S. intellectual property. This is **NOT** intended to act as a substitute for qualified legal consultation, which is always recommended if one is truly concerned about the protection of their creative works.

What is Intellectual Property?

Intellectual property is a term that collectively describes the protections afforded to creative works, ideas, and products. These protections range from copyrights and patents, to service marks and trademarks, and even extend to trade secrets and related rights.

During the writing of the United States Constitution in 1787, the founding fathers recognized the need to encourage creative people to create new intellectual and artistic works. Realizing the empowering strength of this type of intellectual promotion, the framers of the United States Constitution included a copyright clause [Article I, Section 8], empowering Congress to "promote the progress of science and useful arts." This allowed for the creation of laws that would give creative artists (referred to as "Authors" in the U.S. Constitution) the exclusive right to their creative and artistic works, for a limited period of time.

What is Copyright?

 Copyright is a protection that is granted to an individual by law to protect a creative work from unauthorized copying or reproduction, distribution, derivative use, or public display. This protection also enables the copyright owner to pursue legal action against the unauthorized use of that work, referred to as the infringement of copyright. The rights of the copyright owner begin at the moment when the expression of a creative work is "fixed" in a tangible form. For image-makers, it doesn't matter whether an image is produced on digital media or film; the ownership of copyright is bestowed at the time of creation. Note that the copyright office of the United States now acknowledges digital images as "fixed" works. Previously, this was not the case. Under the old copyright laws, works that required the aid of a machine for interpretation were not accepted for deposit by the copyright office. Now CDs or DVDs containing a work can be submitted as a "fixed" and tangible copy of the original work. It is significant to note that whether or not a work is registered with the copyright office, all works are protected under U.S. copyright law when they are "fixed" in a tangible form. This protection does not require the registration of a work with the copyright office. Also, the work does not need to bear a copyright notice to be protected; however, both registration and affixation of a copyright notice entitle the owner to extra legal protections.

Furthermore, note that concepts, creative ideas, and themes are not copyrightable. The original expression of a concept or theme, *in a tangible form*, is what copyright protection covers. Also, if someone produces an image based upon another's idea or concept, it does not guarantee that person to a share of the copyright of the image— unless specifically agreed upon between the two parties. The copyright of the creative work belongs to the individual who creates the tangible expression of the concept or idea—the actual image.

What is Public Domain?

A work is said to be in the public domain when it becomes available for use without the need for permission from its owner. There are several ways in which a work enters the public domain. The most common way is when the work's copyright has expired.

What is Fair Use?

Fair use of a copyrighted work entails the copying and use of a copyrighted work for purposes such as criticism, comment, news reporting, teaching (including multiple copies for classroom use), scholarship, or research. For these particular uses, notwithstanding provisions of sections 106 and 106A of the U.S. copyright law, it is not an infringement of copyright to use copyrighted works—as outlined in Sec. 107: *Limitations on exclusive rights: Fair use of U.S. copyright law.*

To determine whether a particular use of a work is "fair use," the following factors need to be considered:

1. The purpose and character of the use, including whether such use is of a commercial nature or is for nonprofit educational purposes;

2. The nature of the copyrighted work;

3. The amount and substantiality of the portion used in relation to the copyrighted work as a whole; and

4. The effect of the use upon the potential market for or value of the copyrighted work. The fact that a work is unpublished shall not itself bar a finding of fair use if such finding is made upon consideration of all the above factors.

Note that fair use is **not** a license to plagiarize work. Many individuals improperly "appropriate" work under the guise of artistic license. There are legitimate artistic uses of "appropriated" work that fall under the fair use clause of copyright law. In the end, you are culpable for illegal activity. Thus, it is suggested that you create original work, and cautiously approach any fair use of another's work.

Why Do Photographers Need to Know about Copyright?

As an image-maker, you need to be concerned with the issue of copyright because this is the primary protection for the fruits of your labor. A photographer's "negatives," whether digital, slides, or actual negatives, represent the potential for profit and livelihood. It is copyright protection that ensures the longevity of this protection. Hence, the right for continued compensation for the use of your works.

Since the advent of such ethical and legal issues as those surrounding Napster(in the early twenty-first century, all creative works need protection. What this means for the photographer is that a proactive plan should be established and adhered to, for the protection of their work and their rights. In the public's collective mind, issues of ownership, public domain, and fair use have become somewhat blurred. The law, however, is clear. If you created a work, you own the rights to the work, unless it was a *work for hire*.

Copyrights, Trademarks, Service Marks, and Patents

The distinctions made between copyrights, trademarks, service marks, and patents are sometimes unclear. For image-makers, the primary protection that addresses their needs is copyright, but there are times when any or all of these protections can apply to those creative works and other business activities. It is your job to know what protections apply to various aspects of your business—personal and professional.

Defining Protections: Understanding the Differences

Here we will clarify some of the key differences between copyrights, trademarks, service marks, and patents.

 A **trademark** is generally used to protect devices that label, identify, and distinguish products or services in the marketplace. The idea behind trademarking something is to inform potential clients about the origin and quality of the fundamental product or service(s). A trademark can be a distinctive word or phrase, a logo, a name, a graphic symbol, a slogan, or even something like an Internet domain name—or some other device that is used to identify the source of a product and to distinguish a manufacturer's or merchant's products from others in the marketplace.

Examples of trademarks are McDonald's™ hamburgers, Microsoft™ software, and Apple™ computers. With respect to trademarks, something needs to be "distinctive" and unique enough to aid consumers in distinguishing it from others in the marketplace. Thus, a trademark can either be distinctive words or graphic symbols. For example, the Nike™ "swoosh" graphic is a trademarked graphic symbol. Where "Nikon™" is an example of trademarked text. In both of these examples, the trademark has become distinctive over time because consumers have come to associate the trademark with the company's products or services. We have trademark law because consumers quite often make their purchasing choices based upon the recognition of certain phrases or graphic representations—trademarks. The effort with trademark law is to avoid consumer confusion about the origin of goods or services. An example would be if someone were to begin manufacturing cameras and called their new camera the Nikon edition. This would cause considerable confusion among consumers.

 Note that, in addition to the (symbol, the symbol for a registered trademark is the capital letter **R** in a circle: ®.

Another type of protection is known as a **service mark**. A service mark is essentially the same thing as a trademark; however, where a trademark is designed to promote products, a service mark is designed to promote services and/or events. For example, when a business uses its name for the purpose of marketing its services in advertisements or in directory listings, the name then qualifies as a service mark. Examples of some of the more commonly known service marks are: Kinko's℠ (copy centers), Blockbuster℠ (video rentals), Burger King℠ (hamburgers), and the Olympic colored interlocking circles.

Yet another type of protection is known as a certification mark. A certification mark is a symbol, name, or device utilized by an organization to vouch for the quality of products and/or services that are provided by others. One of the most well known examples of a certification mark is the "Good Housekeeping Seal of Approval."

Yet another protection, known as **trade dress,** is quite well known to image-makers. Beyond the label, logo, identifying symbol, or graphic device, a product can become known by the distinctiveness of its packaging. For example, Kodak film and Fuji Film are identified by the yellow or green boxes and other features that are commonly termed as "trade dress." Because the purpose of trade dress is to identify goods and services in the marketplace, it serves the same role as that of a trademark or service mark. Additionally, trade dress can be protected under the U.S. trademark laws. In certain situations it can even be registered as a trademark or service mark with the U.S. Patent and Trademark Office.

Generally, trademark law is intended to protect words, phrases, and logos and/or graphics that are unique enough to become strongly associated with a product or service in the minds of consumers. Beyond these basic understandings, a trademark/service mark may include numbers, letters, a smell, a sound, a specific color, or even a product's shape. Furthermore, any additional, nonfunctional yet distinctive aspects of a service or product that predispose it to the promotion and differentiation in the marketplace may qualify it for protection under U.S. trademark law.

Such odd things as the sound of a Harley Davidson motorcycle or the color of Owens-Corning's pink insulation are examples of trademarks as well. Even an Internet domain name—for instance EasySiteHost.com™—meets the criteria as a mark because it is used in relationship to a Web site that offers goods or services to the general public. This type of mark concerns all Web sites that conduct business (e-commerce), such as Excite.com™ or Yahoo.com™, which provide Internet-based services.

In a different direction, a **patent** protects certain types of **inventions,** with new ideas, from being used commercially by others without the permission of the inventor or creator. For photographers, this would apply to the development of a new type of tripod, a film developer, or a new type of digital imaging sensor, for example.

Finally, a **copyright** is a protection for a creative work from unauthorized copying or reproduction, distribution, derivative use, or public display. Unlike trademark law, copyrights apply only to creative works at the moment when the expression of a creative work is "fixed" in a tangible form. Copyrights do not apply to slogans, names, smells, colors, or ideas; these are protected under trademark law. Note that sometimes there is a fine line between copyright and trademark protection. For instance, a company's graphic logo may be protected by both copyright and trademark laws. That is, copyright laws may protect aspects of the logo that pertain to its artistic aspects, whereas trademark laws may protect the logo from being used by others in a confusing manner in the marketplace.

It is significant to note that quite often trademark law is used in combination with copyright law to protect the copy or text used in advertisements. In this type of situation, the trademark law protects such things as the product or service name, as well as any slogans. Copyright laws also protect any supplementary creative expression in an advertisement, such as photographs or illustrations.

When to Consider Registering Works

First, it should be acknowledged that works are automatically copyrighted upon creation—the moment they are "fixed" in a tangible form. Furthermore, the © (copyright symbol) and/or the word Copyright do not need to be present for a work to be copyrighted.

So, the question here is why would you waste the time, effort, and money on registering a copyright? A very good reason is that certain protections are only afforded to those copyrights that are registered with the U.S. federal government. The issue here is not whether a work is copyrighted, but whether you can be compensated if infringement occurs. What this means to a image-maker is that even though the work is copyrighted, statutory damages and legal fees cannot be sued for if the work is not registered **before** infringement occurs.

If a work is **not** registered, and infringement occurs where legal action is required to remedy a situation, the copyright must be registered before legal action can ensue. If a work **is** registered before infringement—or within three months after first publication, even if this is after an infringement occurs—the owner would be entitled to legal protections including, but not limited to, the ability to sue for statutory damages (which can be considered up to $100,000 USD per infringement), and the ability to sue for any legal fees in successful litigation. Additionally, with registered copyrights, the facts of the copyright are on the public record, and the owner has a certificate of registration for verification.

Finally, if copyright registration occurs within five years of the publication of a work, it can be considered as prima facie evidence in a U.S. court of law.

If a work is not registered before infringement and statutory damages cannot be sought, a claim for actual damages is still allowed under the law. This is limited to the actual amount of money that has been lost as a result of the infringement—any profits realized by the infringing party can also be sought. Understand that these damages need to be proven by the defender of the copyright—a costly and time-consuming endeavor.

All Creative Works are Inherently Protected

As stated above, all works are protected under the current laws after they are "fixed" in a tangible form. However, there are limitations on the protection of unregistered works. If you are willing to give up certain legal rights, you are not obligated to register your works.

When to Consider Legal or Professional Services

Without a doubt, you should seek legal advice before threatening a lawsuit or a claim of copyright infringement. Prematurely issuing threats of a lawsuit can lead to costly legal battles—as many photographers can attest. Learn from the mistakes of others. If you are a professional, establish a relationship with a competent copyright attorney.

Photographer's Guidelines for Copyright

This section of the chapter is intended to be less theoretical or legal, and more practical as a guide to copyright. There are certain day-to-day practices that all image-makers need to adopt. This is the only workflow for copyright protection, but rather an example of one way that a personal or corporate copyright policy is established.

When is a work "fixed"?

As best stated by the United States Copyright Office:

"Your work is under copyright protection the moment it is created and fixed in a tangible form so that it is perceptible either directly or with the aid of a machine or device."

Therefore, your silver-halide and digital images are protected.

How to Register a Copyright

Below is an outline of how to register your creative works with the U.S. Copyright Office.

What Forms are Required, and How Much it will Cost

In order to register an image for copyright protection in the United States, you need to submit **Form VA** for either published or unpublished creative works of the visual arts. Theses works are defined as photographic/pictorial, graphic, and sculptural works, including architectural works. Additionally, a $30 USD filing fee, along with a nonreturnable copy or copies of the work to be registered needs to be submitted to the copyright office, as set forth in the U.S. Copyright Office's Circular 1, Section Registration Procedures.

Registration Procedures

The registration procedure is as follows. For an original registration—the first time a work is being registered—you will need to send the following three items **in the same envelope or package** to the copyright office.

1. A properly completed application form
2. A nonrefundable-filing fee of $30 for each application
3. A nonreturnable deposit of the work being registered. The deposit requirements vary in particular situations; the general requirements follow. Also note the information under "Special Deposit Requirements."

Your package should be addressed to:
Library of Congress
Copyright Office
101 Independence Avenue, S.E.
Washington, DC 20559-0002

NOTE: U.S. Copyright Office fees are subject to change. For the current fees, please check with the U.S. Copyright Office.

If you are submitting multiple images, all applications, deposits, and fees should be sent in the same package. Depending upon the type of deposit you are submitting, applications should be attached to the appropriate deposit, if it is possible. Whenever possible, number each package (i.e., 1 of 3, 2 of 3, 3 of 3) to facilitate more rapid and efficient processing.

Generally, if you submit an application with (or without) fees, and it is received without the appropriate deposit copy or other identifying materials, it will not be processed and may be returned.

Special Deposit Requirements

For **digital photographic deposits**, special deposit requirements exist.

If the digital images are submitted in CD-ROM format, the deposit requirement is one **complete copy** of the material. This includes the CD-ROM, the operating software—if applicable—and any manual(s) that normally accompany the CD-ROM. Additionally, if you registering an original piece of image-editing software, submission for the computer program/application should be on a CD-ROM. This special type of deposit should also include a hard copy or printout of the first twenty-five pages and last twenty-five pages of source code for the software application.

Finally, if you are trying to submit something unusual for copyright registration, and you are uncertain of the deposit requirements for your work, you should contact the copyright office.

Unpublished Collections: How to Register Collections

If you want to register a group of your images—and at $30 per each image, it can become costly—consider the guidelines outlined in the section "Unpublished Collections."

Unpublished Collections

Under the following conditions, a work may be registered in unpublished form as a "collection," with one application form and one fee if:

- The elements of the collection are assembled in an orderly form;
- The combined elements bear a single title identifying the collection as a whole;
- The copyright claimant in all the elements and in the collection as a whole is the same; and
- All the elements are by the same author, or, if they are by different authors, at least one of the authors has contributed copyrightable authorship to each element.

An unpublished collection is not indexed under the individual titles of the contents, but under the title of the collection.

Source: United States Copyright Office

Effective Date of Copyright Registration

As soon as the copyright office receives all of the required elements for deposit, copyright registration is effective. This is true regardless of how long it then takes the copyright office to process your application and/or mail your copyright certificate of registration.

Mandatory Deposit for Works Published in the United States

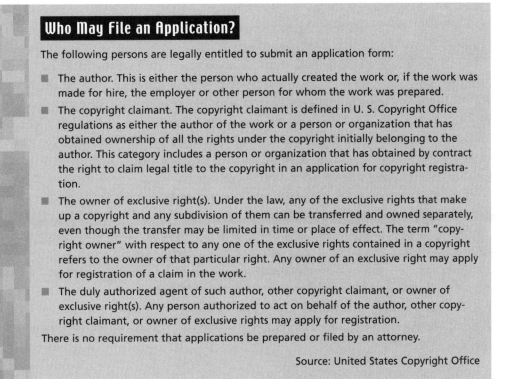

Who May File an Application?

The following persons are legally entitled to submit an application form:

- The author. This is either the person who actually created the work or, if the work was made for hire, the employer or other person for whom the work was prepared.
- The copyright claimant. The copyright claimant is defined in U. S. Copyright Office regulations as either the author of the work or a person or organization that has obtained ownership of all the rights under the copyright initially belonging to the author. This category includes a person or organization that has obtained by contract the right to claim legal title to the copyright in an application for copyright registration.
- The owner of exclusive right(s). Under the law, any of the exclusive rights that make up a copyright and any subdivision of them can be transferred and owned separately, even though the transfer may be limited in time or place of effect. The term "copyright owner" with respect to any one of the exclusive rights contained in a copyright refers to the owner of that particular right. Any owner of an exclusive right may apply for registration of a claim in the work.
- The duly authorized agent of such author, other copyright claimant, or owner of exclusive right(s). Any person authorized to act on behalf of the author, other copyright claimant, or owner of exclusive rights may apply for registration.

There is no requirement that applications be prepared or filed by an attorney.

Source: United States Copyright Office

Even though you are not required to register a copyright, the United States Copyright Act sets forth a mandatory deposit requirement. This pertains to all works published in the United States. The owner of a creative work (or its rights) has a legal obligation to submit a deposit of the work to the Copyright Office. This needs to be done inside of a three-month period of the original publication date in the United States. As stated by the U.S. Copyright Office, "Failure to make the deposit can result in fines and other penalties but does not affect copyright protection." Note that for creative works published in the United States, the U.S. copyright law has a condition that allows for a single deposit, which may satisfy requirements of both the copyright office and the Library of Congress's deposit requirements. If you wish to submit works in this way, the deposit copies must be submitted simultaneously; the deposit copies, all necessary forms and filling fees must also be submitted at one time.

Works for Hire

The area of the U.S. copyright law that relates to works for hire should be of special interest to all creative image-makers. You may be giving away the rights to your work, if not careful.

A work for hire is a way that a client can attain copyright ownership. Even though, normally, the individual who creates a creative work is considered to be the author, and thus the copyright holder, there are exceptions to this rule. For example, if you create a work, as an employee—within the normal range of your employment—this work's copyright and other rights may belong to your employer. The employee and the employer must have a specific legal agreement in place before employment begins. Another situation that photographers often confront is when a work is commissioned. Here, too, the employer or commissioning agent may be considered to be the author under the work made for hire clause in U.S. copyright law.

It is significant to note that according to U.S. copyright law, no agreements are required in order to consider a creative work by an employee as a work for hire. So, if you enter into an employment situation, this needs to be clarified before the acceptance of a job—and documented in written contract form.

If you are working as a freelancer—being hired by a commissioning agent—there are nine criteria set forth under copyright law that can pertain to the retention of the rights to your work.

1. Contribution to a collective work
2. Contribution to a motion picture
3. Contribution to an audio-visual work
4. Translation
5. Supplementary work
6. Compilation
7. Instructional text
8. Test answer
9. Material for a test atlas

The categories that usually pertain to image-makers are contribution to a collective work (for example, publication in a magazine/periodical), contribution to a motion picture, and contribution to an audio-visual work (for example, publication with a computer-based publication/periodical).

Selling and Licensing Rights

Now that we have discussed all of the ways that you may have previously given away your rights, we need to address a way that you can profit from assigning your rights to another party. Just as with any type of property, the full rights to a work—or a portion thereof—may be sold or given to another by the copyright owner. This is why you will often see the copyright notice expressed as:

© 2003 **Dr. Joseph A. Ippolito, All Rights Reserved.**

This notifies others that the individual not only does own copyright to the work, but also that there is no transfer or assignment of rights—expressed or implied—by the use or publication of the work.

Transfer of Copyright

Any or all of the copyright owner's **exclusive** rights or any subdivision of those rights may be transferred, but the transfer of exclusive rights is not valid unless that transfer is in writing and signed by the owner of the rights conveyed or such owner's duly authorized agent. Transfer of a right on a nonexclusive basis does not require a written agreement.

A copyright may also be conveyed by operation of law and may be bequeathed by will or pass as personal property by the applicable laws of interstate succession.

Copyright is a personal property right, and it is subject to the various state laws and regulations that govern the ownership, inheritance, or transfer of personal property as well as terms of contracts or conduct of business. For information about relevant state laws, consult an attorney.

Transfers of copyright are normally made by contract. The Copyright Office does not have any forms for such transfers. The law does provide for the recordation in the Copyright Office of transfers of copyright ownership. Although recordation is not required to make a valid transfer between the parties, it does provide certain legal advantages and may be required to validate the transfer as against third parties.

Source: United States Copyright Office

As with selling licensing rights, the transfer of copyright indicates that the owner is allowing for the transfer of the ownership of the copyright. This is usually done in writing, and in the case of a transfer of all rights, this **must** be done in writing according to U.S. law.

What if I don't want to register my works?

You do not have a legal obligation to register creative works. Remember that even though you are not required to register a copyright, the United States Copyright Act sets forth a mandatory deposit requirement for published works (see the section above on mandatory deposit requirement).

When is it Appropriate to Consider Registering a Trademark or Service Mark?

Beyond copyright, and that which we have already discussed in this chapter, an image-maker needs to consider trademarks/service marks as forms of protection, as well. Many photographers and/or designers are freelancers, or they own their own studios. In these situations, it is important for them to protect all aspects of their business.

For example, if a photographer has a studio named Fotoluxz—a unique name—and wants to protect this name not only as a business name, but as a device that is used to identify and distinguish these products or services in the marketplace, registering the trademark would protect the business rights. As with copyright, remember that trademarks do not need to be registered, but not registering a trademark limits the available legal protections.

Sample: Fotoluxz Studios Copyright, Trademark and Service marks

Sample use of copyright, trademark and service mark identifications.

Fotoluxz™ Studios Presents

"Franky in New York"
© 2002 Joseph A. Ippolito, All Rights Reserved.

We Make You Shine[SM]

In this same example, suppose the studio has a slogan they use to sell their photographic services: "We Make You Shine." This slogan can also be protected as a service mark. Again, this does not need to be registered. In the illustration above, you can see how each mark can be used in a practical way.

Professional Photographic/Design Business Practices

Throughout this book, we refer to a person's **workflow**. Incorporating policies that pertain to copyrights and trademarks is crucial in this business. As we have stated, the digital file (or negative) is your livelihood. It is from the imagery you create that profits are derived. If your images are plagiarized, the potential for income for their usage is diminished. Thus, the following recommendations are set forth.

Copyright and Trademark Workflow

- Establish a relationship with a competent copyright attorney.
- Whenever you create imagery, document in writing who owns what rights, **before** you start the project. This applies when working as a freelancer, on a commission basis, or as an employee.
- Decide which works you will register for individual copyrights. For the rest of your **unpublished** works, at least register them as a collection of works. In the digital era, this is quite easy to do—a bit more effort and expense is incurred when dealing with traditional media, however.
- Although it is not required by law, use the proper copyright and trademark notices at **ALL** times, whether the works are registered or not. This helps to counter legal arguments of innocent infringement.

Recommended Copyright and Trademark Policies

What if Someone Infringes Your Copyright?

First, if you think someone has infringed your copyright, you should consult a competent copyright attorney. Your options are generally to; 1) do nothing about it, 2) to file a civil lawsuit in Federal district court, or even 3) to contact the U.S. Attorney—who may initiate a criminal investigation in such a case—if the infringement is willful and for profit.

Copyright in Other Countries

Based upon the United States signing the Berne Convention, in March 1989, the U.S. has agreed to respect copyright protection for citizens of any member country. The Berne convention provides protection that lasts for the life of the author, plus fifty years.

The United States has relationships with all signatory member countries of the Berne convention—over one hundred countries. It is significant to note, however, that the United States does **not** have copyright agreements with all countries.

Additionally, in 1990, the U.S. adopted a limited moral rights policy, which is primarily derived from European copyright laws. The purpose of these rights is usually to protect economic rights. The good news for image-makers is that, in the U.S., these moral rights are only applicable to creative works of the visual arts.

Beyond Copyright and Trademark: Technical Protections

Here we will discuss ways to protect your images from a technical perspective. While copyrights are important, they do not always help to prevent image theft. The first area of discussion relates to images on the Internet (the Web). For digital photographers, the Web is the predominant delivery platform for showcasing their work. The problem with the Web is that there is a culture that embraces the idea that "if it is on the Web, it is free." While this is true to some degree in terms of viewing Web pages and sites, it does not extend to the acquisition and/or appropriation of another person's creative works. After this, we will discuss image protection topics such as encryption software, visible watermarking, and digital watermarking.

Technical Protections for the Internet

There are a number of ways to protect your images from theft on the Web. Understand that there are levels of protection that can be employed. That is, often more than one technique can be used to safeguard against others acquiring your images.

Most of the methods we will discuss in this section are intended to discourage image theft. Realize, though, that if someone is determined to steal your image, they will probably figure out a way.

Java Applets and Java Scripts: Image Protection on the Internet

There are two basic types of Java protection that you can use to deter image theft on the Web: Java applets and Java scripts. Java applets take a little bit more technical expertise to set up, but they can also be more powerful than Java scripts.

The advantages of Java are that compared to other Web technologies, Java applets and scripts are relatively easy to configure. Also, in general, these types of software protection are usually inexpensive, and sometimes free. With many of the current Java applets, the main protections concern the fact that the image is encapsulated into the Java applet, and often the location of the source image is not visible in the Web page's source. Also Java is a cross-platform language, so most applets will work on Macs, PCs, and Unix platforms as well.

The disadvantages of Java are that it puts a demand on the user's computer when viewing your images. Therefore, a faster computer is required, in addition to the fact that the user needs to have a Java-enabled Web browser. However, these issues are rapidly decreasing due to the diffusion of very inexpensive, very powerful computers. Another issue for consideration is that if a Java applet is used to protect your images, this will add time to the download process—because the applet needs to be downloaded before the images can be viewed. Additionally, some Java applets require a special plug-in to be downloaded and installed on the user's computer, before they can view your images.

The protection afforded by Java scripts and Java applets ranges from the simple to the complex. Simple protections start with disabling the ability to copy images by using the right-click menu (for Windows) and the click and hold menu (for Macs). Advanced protections extend to applets that encapsulate the image, and hide the path to the image's source code. We will illustrate the use of Java protection further in the encryption section of this chapter.

Flash

Macromedia(has developed two different types of files for online media delivery. The first is the Flash(file format (.fla), the second is the Shockwave file format (.swf). The Flash file format can be edited, and is not intended for publishing, whereas the shockwave file format is the final, protected file format.

The advantage of Flash files is that it takes expertise to extract images from a Shockwave-flash file. Disadvantages aside, Flash is a better way to protect your images than Java.

The disadvantages of Flash/Shockwave files are that utilities have been developed to extract sounds as well as images from Flash files, and can remove the file's protection tags. Also, the Flash file is downloaded into the cache files on the user's computer, so the actual file can be stolen as well.

Streaming Media

Although this is less relevant to still photographers, still images are used in streaming presentations on the Web. Therefore, it is worth a mention here. The main myth that many people believe is that streaming media is protected from capture. Although the authoring environments for audio and/or video streams ask if you do not want to allow others to be able to save the streaming file, there is third-party software that can bypass this protection. Copying protected streams does require more specialized knowledge, however.

Other disadvantages are that streaming media is not the best way to display still images on the Web. Couple this with the fact that users who have slow computers, or slow Internet connections, may experience problems viewing your video streams. Finally, your images will need to be relatively small, and will be of degraded quality. In a nutshell, this is not a good choice for still image-makers.

HTML Encryption

Some things are easier to understand if you see them. So the table below, Using HTML Encryption to Protect Images on the Web, illustrates what a normal Web page looks like as compared to an encrypted page. This is a very low-level of encryption that is quite easy to crack. However, the example illustrates a combination of techniques. Here the following protections are working in combination with each other.

```
<script language=JavaScript>
<!—
var message="";
/////////////////////////////////
function clickIE() {if (document.all) {(message);return false;}}
function clickNS(e) {if
(document.layers||(document.getElementById&&!document.all)) {
if (e.which==2||e.which==3) {(message);return false;}}}
if (document.layers)
{document.captureEvents(Event.MOUSEDOWN);document.onmousedown=
clickNS;}
else{document.onmouseup=clickNS;document.oncontextmenu=clickIE;}
// —>
</script>
```

- The ability to right-click has been disabled, so users won't be able to download your image from the contextual pop-out menu. This was accomplished with a free Java script code snippet which disables this function in both Internet Explorer and Netscape Navigator.
- Next, a portion of the HTML code was encrypted with a simple, encryption algorithm, to obfuscate the HTML code.

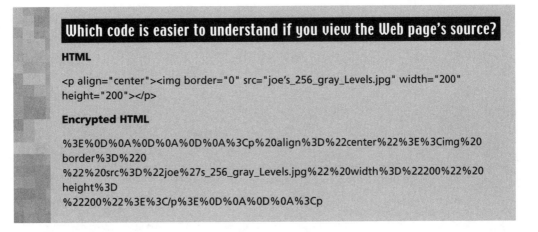

Which code is easier to understand if you view the Web page's source?

HTML

```
<p align="center"><img border="0" src="joe's_256_gray_Levels.jpg" width="200"
height="200"></p>
```

Encrypted HTML

```
%3E%0D%0A%0D%0A%0D%0A%3Cp%20align%3D%22center%22%3E%3Cimg%20
border%3D%220
%22%20src%3D%22joe%27s_256_gray_Levels.jpg%22%20width%3D%22200%22%20
height%3D
%22200%22%3E%3C/p%3E%0D%0A%0D%0A%3Cp
```

- Finally, the image has both a blatant copyright notice [© 2003 Joseph A. Ippolito, All Rights Reserved.] and an embedded watermark.

Understand that separately, all of these techniques are considered low-level security, but together they form a strategy that is free, and affords reasonable protection for your work.

Here is an example of the Web page as it looks in both versions—visibly unchanged—and the code behind this method of protection.

HTML Encryption: Image Protection

Using HTML Encryption to Protect Images on the Web

<table>
<tr><th>Normal Web Page
HTML Code</th><th>Normal Web Page with Encrypted
HTML Code</th></tr>
<tr><td>

```
<html>
<head>
<meta http-equiv="Content-Language" con-
tent="en-us">
<meta http-equiv="Content-Type"
content="text/html; charset=windows-1252">
<title>My Home Page</title>
</head>
<body>
<script language=JavaScript>
<!—
//Disable right click script III- By Renigade (reni-
gade@mediaone.net)
//For full source code, visit http://www.dynamic-
drive.com
var message="";
///////////////////////////////
function clickIE() {if (document.all)
{(message);return false;}}
function clickNS(e) {if
(document.layersll(document.getElementById&&!
document.all)) {
if (e.which==2lle.which==3) {(message);return
false;}}}
if (document.layers)
{document.captureEvents(Event.MOUSE-
DOWN);document.onmousedown=clickNS;}
else{document.onmouseup=clickNS;document.on
contextmenu=clickIE;}
// —>
</script>
<p>
<p align="center"><font size="5"><b>My Home
Page</b></font></p>
<p align="center">
<p align="center"><img border="0"
src="joe's_256_gray_Levels.jpg" width="200"
height="200"></p>
<p align="center"><font size="1">© 2001
Joseph A. Ippolito, All Rights
Reserved.</font></p>
</body>
</html>
```

</td><td>

```
<html>
<head>
<meta http-equiv="Content-Language" con-
tent="en-us">
<meta http-equiv="Content-Type"
content="text/html; charset=windows-1252">
<title>My Home Page</title>
</head>
<script>
<!—
document.write(unescape("%3Cbody%3E%0D%
0A%0D%0A%3Cscript%20language%3DJavaScri
pt%3E%0D%0A%3C%21—
%0D%0A//Disable%20right%20click%20script%
20III-
%20By%20Renigade%20%28renigade@mediao
ne.net%29%0D%0A//For%20full%20source%20
code%2C%20visit%20http%3A//www.dynamic-
drive.com%0D%0Avar%20message%3D%22%2
2%3B%0D%0A//////////////////////////////%0D%0Afu
nction%20clickIE%28%29%20%7Bif%20%28doc
ument.all%29%20%7B%28message%29%3Bret
urn%20false%3B%7D%7D%0D%0Afunction%2
0clickNS%28e%29%20%7Bif%20%0D%0A%28d
ocument.layers%7C%7C%28document.getEleme
ntById%26%26%21document.all%29%29%20%
7B%0D%0Aif%20%28e.which%3D%3D2%7C%
7Ce.which%3D%3D3%29%20%7B%28mes-
sage%29%3Breturn%20false%3B%7D%7D%7D
%0D%0Aif%20%28document.lay-
ers%29%20%0D%0A%7Bdocument.captureEve
nts%28Event.MOUSEDOWN%29%3Bdocument.
onmousedown%3DclickNS%3B%7D%0D%0Aels
e%7Bdocument.onmouseup%3DclickNS%3Bdoc
ument.oncontextmenu%3DclickIE%3B%7D%0D
%0A//%20—
%3E%20%0D%0A%3C/script%3E%0D%0A%0D
%0A%3Cp%3E%0D%0A%3Cp%20align%3D%2
2center%22%3E%3Cfont%20size%3D%225%22
%3E%3Cb%3EMy%20Home%20Page%3C/b%3E
%3C/font%3E%3C/p%3E%0D%0A%0D%0A%3
Cp%20align%3D%22center%22%3E%0D%0A%
0D%0A%0D%0A%3Cp%20align%3D%22cen-
ter%22%3E%3Cimg%20border%3D%220%22%
20src%3D%22joe%27s_256_gray_Levels.jpg%22
%20width%3D%22200%22%20height%3D%22
200%22%3E%3C/p%3E%0D%0A%0D%0A%3Cp
%20align%3D%22center%22%3E%3Cfont%20si
ze%3D%221%22%3E%A9%202001%20Joseph
%20A.%20Ippolito%2C%20All%20Rights%0D%
0AReserved.%3C/font%3E%3C/p%3E%0D%0A
%0D%0A%3C/body%3E"));
//—>
</script>
</html>
```

</td></tr>
</table>

Encryption Software: Web-based Digital Images

There are commercial products available to encrypt Web source codes, in addition to the free script that was used to encrypt the text above. With most of these products either a plug-in is required for a user to view your images, or screen capture utilities can be used to grab a low-resolution version of your images—this is not true of all of these products. Here are several examples of commercially available software that is designed to protect Web-based digital images.

Encryption Software: Examples of Products/Services

Artiscope: has several image protection solutions

Clever Content: protects images, PDF files, and text documents by encrypting images when they leave the Web server—decryption occurs on the user's browser. Uses a plug-in.

CopySafe: protects images from saving, printing, and capture—uses Java and a plug-in.

SafeImage: uses Java to embed host and domain information into your image, allowing you to restrict usage in a different ways.

Secure Image: protects by encrypting your images to stop the direct copying, downloading, and linking to your images. This software even offers domain locking so that your encoded images can only be viewed from your designated Web site or folder.

Digital Watermarking

The process of digital watermarking embeds copyright and ownership information into a digital image. Many of the digital watermarking products also have associated services that can scan the Web for your image's watermark identification.

The advantages of digital watermarking are that they do not generally degrade the image's quality, and they can aid in tracking image theft and copyright infringement.

The disadvantage of this technology is that it is invisible, and presents no obvious deterrent to would-be appropriators. Plus, there are third-party tools available to remove digital watermarks.

The best part about using digital watermarks, aside from the fact that they do not alter the appearance of the image, is that the watermark is quite durable. That is, someone could download an image from the Web, flip it, blur it, sharpen it, print it, scan it, e-mail it, flip it again, and the watermark will still be detectable—depending upon the strength that was set when embedding the mark.

Digital Watermarking Software and Services: Examples of Products/Services

Alpha-Tec: creates and detects invisible watermarks on audio, video, and digital images.

Digimarc: embeds digital data (invisible watermarks) into digital images, movies, and documents such as passports. They also offer tracking services to find copies of your digital images on the Web. (This product ships with Adobe Photoshop.)

Signum Technologies: embeds digital data (invisible watermarks) into digital images, audio, and video files.

How to Embed a Digital Watermark

Here we will illustrate how to use Adobe Photoshop to embed a digital watermark into your digital images. The process is quite straightforward; you simply select Digimarc from the filter menu and follow the prompts. Below we have illustrated the process.

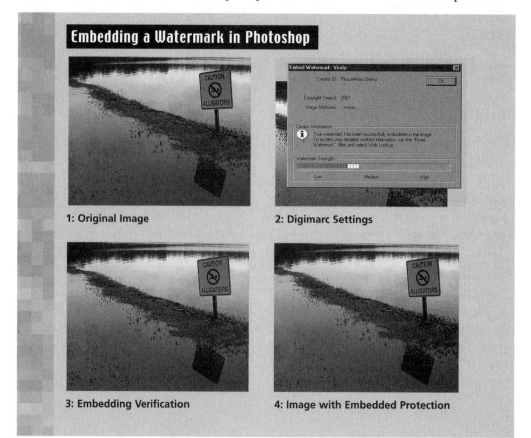

Embedding a Watermark in Photoshop

1: Original Image

2: Digimarc Settings

3: Embedding Verification

4: Image with Embedded Protection

Visible Watermarking

A visible watermark is an identifying mark on an image that is always seen. Usually, visible watermarks will consist of a company's logo, a copyright notice, or other information pertaining to ownership. Visible watermarks can look any way you want, but they are usually translucent representations of the graphic or text to be applied to the image. While this type of watermarking deters image theft, it also degrades and alters the original image in a blatantly perceptible manner.

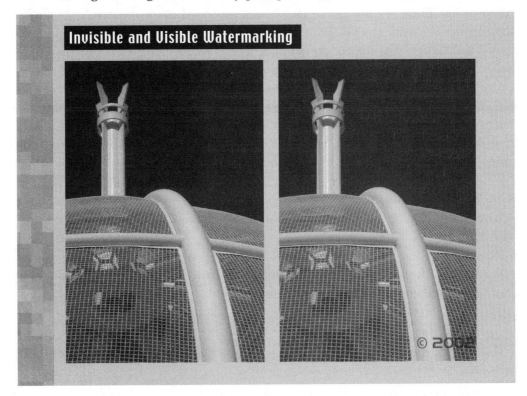

Conclusions

For serious image-makers, copyright is the single most important thing that will promote the security of intellectual property rights and the viability of future image sales.

Whether a person is a fine artist, a graphic designer, or a commercial photographer, intellectual property protection is the security measure that most affects all image-makers. Just as inventions are protected through such devices as patents for the inventors, copyright protection of images affords legal protections to image-makers.

Beyond the filing of copyrights, images are protected upon their creation at the moment they are fixed in a tangible form. This change in U.S. copyright law has had a broad and far-reaching impact on the imaging community. One of the negative side effects of this unregistered form of protection is that it has caused many people to believe that there is never a need to register works. This belief has been the basis for many lost lawsuits by photographers. The extra protections of having a work officially registered through the U.S. Copyright Office should not be dismissed lightly. This does not mean that every image created needs to be registered. Rather, a personal or corporate copyright policy should be established.

Finally, understand that if you are in the business of image making, you are in a **business**. Whether you are a student or a professional, if you are serious about your creative works, you need to be serious about their preservation. Just as you would consider the archival qualities of the materials your images are recorded and printed upon, so too should you be concerned with the control of their distribution.

As with any business practices, you should be concerned with the protection of your rights, and your future in the business.

Review Questions:

1 When are creative works that have been created in the United States protected by U.S. copyright law?

2 List three types of technical protections for digital images.

3 What protections are lost if you do not register a copyright, and a work is infringed?

4 How do trademark, trade dress, and service mark laws affect photographers and other image-makers?

5 What types of protections are available to the image-maker—beyond copyright registration?

Discussion Questions:

1 Why should you consider registering your images for copyright protection?

2 What is the best type of protection for tracking infringed images on the Internet?

3 What is the best plan of defense for protecting images:

a. On the Web

b. In print

c. In publications

d. On digital media (CDs/DVDs)

4 Why should one be concerned with international copyright law, and how does this affect American image-makers?

Appendix:
Glossary of Terms

Appendix: Glossary of Terms

This glossary of terms defines many common terms related to digital photography. While numerous terms are defined, this is not intended to be an all-inclusive listing of terms. Further, many terms are defined more fully in the text. Finally, these definitions are specific to the area of digital photography, and many terms can be defined differently based upon the context in which they are used. To see descriptions of acronyms, see the Acronyms and Pseudo-Acronyms appendix.

Term	Definition
24-bit color/image	a digital image comprising eight bits of information represented in three-color channels (RGB). Where 3 x 8 = 24-bit color, or 256 colors x 256 colors x 256 colors = 16,777,216 colors.
32-bit color	refers to an image comprising eight bits of information represented in three-color channels (RGB), as well as an 8-bit mask/alpha channel. Where 3 x 8 = 24 + 8 = 32-bit color.
64 Base	the highest resolution image file on a Kodak Pro Photo CD.
8-bit digital image	a digital image that consists of up to 256 colors or gray tones.
Access	the process of data retrieval from a storage device or RAM.
Access time	the amount of time needed for a storage device to retrieve information.
Acquire/Acquisition	the process of importing an electronic image from such sources as a digital camera, a scanner, or a video capture device.
Adaptive color palette	a limited group of colors that will allow for a close reproduction of an image's color information. Generally an adaptive color palette consists of 256 or fewer colors.
Additive primary colors	in light theory, these are the three colors of transmitted light (red, green, and blue) which when added together in various combinations create all other colors in the visible spectrum (such as on a TV or a computer monitor). The combination of pure additive primary colors of red, green, and blue light creates white light.
AF sensor	the sensor used to distinguish the degree of sharpness of focus in an *auto focus* camera.
Algorithm	a set of mathematical procedures or rules that are employed to process information. In digital photography, algorithms are used to make a variety of processing decisions ranging from color balance to sharpening, through filtering and beyond.
Aliasing	generally described as jaggies, this refers to the pixelated edges in an image—the visual result of unwanted image noise—producing 'jagged edges/stair-stepping' in digital images.

Alpha channel	an image's information area where a mask can be manipulated and/or stored.
Ambient light	that general level of light that exists in a scene that does not come from any one direction.
Analogous colors	those colors that are adjacent to one another on the color wheel.
Antialiasing	a mathematical process that averages tones and colors in a digital image in order to reduce aliasing or 'jagged edges/stair-stepping' in digital images.
Antivirus (software)	computer software that detects and removes computer viruses.
Aperture	the opening formed by the iris or diaphragm inside a lens. The aperture is defined by f-stops, and allows varying amounts of light to strike the film or sensor in a camera. The aperture controls the depth of field/depth of focus of an image.
Aperture ring	the adjustment ring on the outside lens of a camera. This is used to set the f-stop, which controls the diameter of the aperture.
Architecture	the basic design specification for a system.
Archival image	an image that has longevity; one that will not deteriorate or fade in a short period of time. Refers to the life span of a storage or output media for image data.
Archival storage	a manner of keeping images that will preserve their integrity—true of prints, film, or digital files.
Array	a grouping of similar elements, such as with photodiodes of imaging sensors.
Artifact(s)	unnecessary visual noise that results from a digital imaging process.
Artificial light	light that is created by a man-made source, comprising light sources such as strobe/flash and photofloods.
ASA	American Standards Association. When combined with a number, ASA refers to the sensitivity of a film or imaging sensor (i.e., *ASA 100-speed film*).
Aspect ratio	the relative amount of height in relation to the width of an image (i.e., a 35 mm slide has an aspect ratio of 1:1.5, where the image size equals 1" x 1.5").
Autocrop	an automatic technique that allows for the removal of extraneous like-color borders in a digital image.
Autofocus	the capability of a camera to automatically focus a lens on a given subject.
Average access time	The average amount of time it takes to seek and retrieve data.
Background	the original image layer in a Photoshop image file. Also refers to distant objects in a photographic scene.

Backlight	illumination of a photographic subject from the rear. This lighting technique often produces silhouetted images.
Bandwidth	the amount of data that can be transferred over a connection in a given period of time.
Base resolution	an image's scanned resolution for Photo CD images.
Bi-level image	an image that consists of only two tones, black and white. This is also referred to as a bitmap image in Photoshop.
Binary	a method of digitally encoding image (or other computer) data. Binary data consists of two states, on and off, and is represented as zeros and ones.
BIOS, *basic input/output system*	a program (or set of programs) that control the basic functions of the computer.
Bit	a binary digit; the smallest unit of binary/digital information.
Bit depth	the number of tones or colors contained in a digital image.
Bitmap	a digital image comprised of pixels. In Photoshop, this refers to a bi-level, lithographic image, only consisting of black-and-white values. Also refers to a Windows imaging file format.
Black generation	the image data that is produced to represent black image data when converting an image for use in a CMYK color process.
Black point	the point of absolute black in an image. In a digital image this is represented by 0% neutral reflectance or 0% transmittance.
Bleed	when an image goes beyond the edge of the material upon which it resides. A full-bleed photographic print can be an image that has had areas of the image trimmed away, for example.
Blurring	an image effect that decreases sharpness and which softens the look of an image.
Boot	the process of starting or restarting a computer; loading the operating system.
Brightness	the overall visual density of an image. Refers to the darkness or lightness of an image.
Browser	a software application that is used for viewing World Wide Web sites.
Buffer	a temporary data storage area in various computer software/components.
Burn	the process of selectively darkening an area of an image. Also refers to the process of creating a CD or DVD.
Bus	the interface system that carries data between the microprocessor and peripheral devices in a computer system.
Byte	a packet of information consisting of eight bits of information.
Cache	RAM that is used as a buffer between two devices/processes.

Calibration	the process of adjusting software or hardware in relation to a known standard. This allows for the predictable utilization of imaging tools and techniques.
Calibration bars	a grayscale step-wedge that is printed on the edge of final image products, allowing for a standardized measure of the output device's limitations.
Capacity	the amount of information that can be stored on a storage device/media.
Capture device	a device that allows for the acquisition of image data; for example, a scanner or a digital camera.
CCD	Charge-Coupled Device—a light-sensitive micro-electronic device used for electronic imaging devices. The shape and size of a CCD defines the optical resolution of an imaging device such as a scanner or a digital camera.
CCD array	multiple CCD elements, designed to work together in a scanner or digital camera.
Chroma	a color quality inclusive of both hue and saturation—the color component of an image.
CIELAB (L a b)	a device-independent color model. The LAB color model consists of three variables, where color is described in a three-dimensional space, and where its components are described in terms of: **L:** luminosity **a:** the red-green color axis **b:** the yellow-blue color axis
Clipping	the loss of highlight or shadow detail in a photographic image. Also refers to the definition of a vector-based path in a digital image.
Clipping Path	a vector-based description/outline used to define a shape. This type of path defines the outside boundaries of an image's area.
CMOS, *Complementary Metal-Oxide Semiconductor*	a light-sensitive micro-electronic chip/sensor which, when used image-capture devices, converts light into a digital image information.
CMS, Color Management Software	computer software that is used to control variables related to the reproduction of image tones and colors. A CMS is a system that allows for the accurate description of color, and the translation of an image's color between color spaces.
CMYK, Cyan, Magenta, Yellow, Black	a color space generally utilized for graphic arts processes, such as commercial printing.
Color cast	an overall color shift in an image's hue.
Color correction	the alteration of an image's color information to balance colors in an image.
Color depth	the amount of color specified or represented in a pixel of a digital image.

Color Management System	See *CMS*.
Color separation	an image that is divided into grayscale renditions of its subtractive color components, CMYK. Generally color separations are used to represent a color image on paper, when printed with CMYK inks, in registration.
Color space	a set of colors representing the visible spectrum, or a subset of the visible spectrum. For example, RGB is a color space within the visible spectrum.
Color wheel	a graphical representation of additive and subtractive primary colors: represented in a circle where R=0° G=120° B=240° and C=180° M=300° Y=60°.
Colorimeter	a device that is used to provide a quantitative assessment of color. In digital photography, colorimeters are used for the calibration of display devices such as a computer monitor.
ColorSync	an ICC (International Color Consortium) compliant color management system integrated into the Macintosh OS.
CompactFlash	a small nonvolatile removable mass storage device that does not require a battery to retain data indefinitely. CompactFlash cards are solid state; they contain no moving parts.
Complementary colors	colors that are straight across from one another on the color wheel—directly inverse primary colors.
Composite color	refers to an image where the colors are combined to achieve a full color image.
Compression	a method of reducing an image's file size. Image compression can result in three levels of visual information: lossless, lossy *(visually lossless),* and visually degraded.
Continuous tone, *CT*	refers to an image that possesses the appearance of a gradual and smooth tonal scale of image information—as with a black-and-white photographic image.
Continuous tone image	an image comprised of numerous tones. Also referred to as a full-tonal scale image.
Contrast	the difference between light areas and dark areas of an image. High contrast images contain more highlight and shadow information, while low contrast images contain more mid-tone information.
Controller card	a computer hardware adapter used to manage the electronics of a peripheral device.
Copyright	the legal right of ownership of a creative work.
Crop	the process of removing portions of an image, such as cutting away the top or side of a photograph.
D-A converter	a device that converts digital signals into analog signals.

Daguerreotype	invented in 1839, this early photographic process created images by developing a silver-coated metal plate's latent image with mercury vapors.
Darkroom	a space where photographic images can be developed.
Data transfer rate	the speed that digital information transfers from one point to another.
Database	is a collection of data stored on a computer system.
DCS, *Desktop Color Separation*	a color separation file format, primarily used for output to postscript printers.
Densitometer	a device used to measure the optical density of a point on a photographic print or film image.
Density	the amount of opacity or translucency/transparency of image information.
Density range	the distinction between the *difference* of the density of the highlights and the shadows of an image.
Desktop	the main screen of a MAC or Windows OS computer.
Developer	a chemical solution used to reveal the latent photographic image.
Diaphragm	another term describing the lens aperture.
Diffuser	a material that softens light through the process of diffraction.
Digital camera	a camera that converts analog light information into a digital signal, which is saved as a binary data set representing a photographic image.
Digital darkroom	A term that describes the computer, when utilized as a digital image-processing device—analogous to a traditional wet darkroom.
Digital film	storage media that enables the recording of digital image information. Examples of digital film are CompactFlash, smart media, and micro-drives.
Digital image	an image that is comprised of bits and bytes of digital information that when reconstructed form a photographic image with the aid of a technical device.
Digital print	a photographic image produced from a computer-based printing device.
Digital printer	a device that converts digital data into analog information—a photographic print or slide.
Digital zoom	a zoom function of a digital camera that enlarges a portion of the image information acquired by an optical lens. This information is interpolated. *It is generally better to interpolate an image in software such as Photoshop, and **not** use the digital zoom features in most cameras.*

Digital-image filtering	the process of applying different algorithms to an image, or a portion thereof, to alter the digital image through a pixel comparison process.
Disk Operating System	a computer software application that controls the organization of data and files on a computer.
Dodge and burn	dodging an area of an image lightens the tones, while burning an area of an image darkens the tones selectively.
Dot	the smallest area an output device can image—such as a printer or image-setter.
Dot gain	the product of a dot of ink swelling or expanding through absorption into a paper surface. This is common with offset printing.
Downloading	the process of moving data from a remote computer to a local computer.
DPI, *dots per inch*	describes the scale of a printed/output image's resolution. For example, a digital print can be output as a 300 dpi image.
Drum scanner	a device that allows for high resolution scanning of analog image information. The image is attached to a drum, and is scanned while the drum rotates at a high speed.
Duotone	a black-and-white image that is represented by two different colors, printed in an aligned registration.
Dynamic range	the extent of possible pixel values that can be represented in a given image.
EIDE, *Enhanced Integrated Drive Electronics*	the primary interface utilized by most computers to negotiate communications between hard drives and the computer processor.
Enlargement	a photographic print that is larger than the original image capture.
EPS	encapsulated postscript. A file format that describes image information in Adobe's postscript printer language.
EXIF, *Exchangeable Image File*	See *Metadata*.
Export	the process of converting/saving information into another data format.
Exposure	refers to the quantity of light that reaches the image sensor or photographic film/paper, which determines the overall brightness of an image.
Feather	the process of softening an area of an image—usually refers to the edge of a selection. Feathering a selection in a digital image blends and softens edges of an area of the image by averaging adjacent pixels values.
Fetch	a popular FTP software application for the Macintosh computer.
File format	a standardized structure for storing data.

Filter	a glass element, that when placed in front of a camera lens alters the transmission of light that passes through. Also refers to the process of manipulating digital image information through the use of an algorithm or mathematical formula.
Firmware	data that is programmed directly into the circuitry of a device.
Fixed focal length	a lens that has one optical measure. For example, a 50 mm lens is a fixed focal length lens, while an 80-200 mm lens is a zoom lens.
Flare	light that is reflected off elements within a lens, producing areas/patterns of over-exposure.
Flash	a light source that is utilized to create short exposure times. Generally, a flash, also referred to as a strobe, utilizes xenon gas that when electronically excited produces a burst of light. Flash units are generally balanced to daylight, 5000-5500° Kelvin. Also refers to flash memory, see *CompactFlash*.
Flash memory	see *CompactFlash*
Flashpix (FPX)	a file format for images that stores both screen and full resolution versions of an image in one file.
Flatbed scanner	an image capture device that allows for the acquisition of image information from analog images, such as photographic prints or negatives/slides. Resembling a photocopy machine, images or film can be placed on the glass, and acquired into a computer through a software interface.
F-number	the numbers that designate an aperture opening size. For example, lens/aperture openings are described as f/#—f/11.
Focal length	refers to the magnification power of a lens. The focal length of a lens is determined by measuring the distance between the rear lens element and the focal plane, when focused at infinity (∞).
Focal plane	the area where a camera lens focuses the image on the image sensor or film.
Focal plane shutter	a curtain placed in front of the focal plane, which allows for the control of the amount of light that passes through to the focal plane.
Font	a typographic style, or name of a typeface.
Form factor	an industry standard that details the physical dimensions of a particular device.
Format	a standard way of saving data. For example, a file can be saved as a JPEG graphic or a Photoshop graphic. Also refers to the process of erasing all data on storage media such as a hard drive, compact flash card, or a floppy/Zip disk.
Frame Grabber	See *Video digitizer.*
F-stops	see *F-number*

FTP, *file transfer protocol*	a method used to transfer data on the Internet.
Gamma	the range and measure of contrast values of an image/imaging device.
Gamut	the range of tone or color that can be captured or represented by an imaging device.
GCR, *Gray Component Replacement*	the process of removing cyan, magenta, and yellow areas of an image that will produce gray when printed, which are replaced with black.
GIF, *graphic interchange format*	a file format created by CompuServe in the 1980s that supports the representation of up to 256 tones or colors. One of the main file formats utilized on the Internet. This format supports such graphic features as animation and transparency.
Gradient	tonal information that gradually blends from one tone to another.
Grain	with traditional film, grain is the silver-halide crystals and colored dyes that, after processing, turn black or appear colored. Grain appears as a pattern of textured dots, or noise, when a photographic image is enlarged.
Gray balance/point	refers to the equalization of either additive or subtractive primary color information in an image, or an area of an image.
Gray-component replacement	see *GCR*.
Grayscale	a scale of tones that represent an image. With a standard grayscale mode digital image (8-bit), the grayscale is represented by 256 tones of gray.
Halftone	allows continuous tone image information to be reproduced with only black-and-white tones. This is accomplished by converting an image into evenly spaced dots of varying sizes, creating the illusion of continuous tone.
Hard copy	an image printed on a tangible medium, such as photographic paper, canvas, or film.
Hard drive	an electromechanical information storage and retrieval device that incorporates one or more rotating disks, upon which data is recorded.
HDTV, *high-definition television*	a television standard supporting twice the resolution, better color, and better audio than the NTSC standard. There are both analog and digital versions of the HDTV standard.
Header	the embedded technical information that describes an image file.
Histogram	a graphical display of the distribution of an image's tonal values.
HSB color model	a color model where colors are represented by *hue, saturation,* and *brightness*.

HTML, *HyperText Markup Language*	a computer language, primarily utilized on the World Wide Web, to lay out pages of information, allowing for an interactive graphical interface.
Hue	the tint of a color representing a wavelength of light.
HyperText Markup Language	see *HTML*
i.LINK	Sony's trade name for IEEE 1394 interface.
IDE, *Integrated Drive Electronics*	a type of storage device where the controlling electronics are incorporated into the storage device.
Image capture	the process of acquiring and recording an image.
Image data compression	refers to the use of algorithms to reduce the amount of data needed to reconstruct an image file. This creates smaller files for the storage of digital images.
Image editor	computer software that allows for the enhancement or manipulation of a digital image.
Image Pac	a file format used on the Kodak Photo CD.
Image processing	the handling, enhancement, degradation, or manipulation of (a) digital image(s).
Import	a function of computer software that allows for the acquisition of image information from various hardware and software sources.
Indexed color image	a one-channel, 8-bit composite color image capable of representing up to 256 colors or tones.
Inkjet	a printing technology that forms an image on various media by applying ink to the substrate.
Interface	a software or hardware protocol that negotiates the exchange of data.
Interlace	a method of displaying images that contain two fields, where alternating odd and even rows of image information are displayed in succession.
Interpolation	an averaging process that uses algorithms to either compress or expand digital image information. This is the process that is used to re-sample image information when enlarging or reducing digital images.
Iris	a sophisticated type of inkjet printer that is used as proofing and fine arts print making.
Jaggies	the geometric pattern formed by adjoining pixels of information. This generally refers to an undesirable "stair-stepping" pattern of visual information. Also, *see aliasing.*
Jumper	an electrically conductive component that is placed over pins on a circuit board to connect them electronically.
Kilobyte, *KB*	1024 bytes.
Lab color	See *CIELAB.*

Latent image	an exposed but undeveloped/processed image.
Latitude	the amount of deviation from the norm that will still yield an acceptable image exposure.
LCD, *Liquid Crystal Display*	a display device that utilizes liquid crystal technology to represent image information. This technology is utilized by both digital cameras/camcorders and flat panel computer displays.
Leaf shutter	a camera shutter located inside the lens. This type of shutter allows for high-speed flash synchronization.
LED, *light-emitting diode*	a light-emitting semiconductor device.
Light meter	a measuring device that allows for a standardized referencing system with regards to light, used to determine proper exposure in a camera.
LightJet	a digital image printer that uses red, green, and blue lasers to image a digital photograph onto traditional photographic printing paper.
Line drawing	an image that is drawn from only black-and-white values.
Local Area Network (LAN)	computers that are linked to each other on a relatively small scale network. Usually a corporate or departmental network of computers.
Lossless compression	a digital compression process that allows for the reduction of an image's data file size, without *any* loss of visual information.
Lossy compression	a compression process that allows for the reduction of an image's data file size, without any *perceptible* loss of visual information. This type of compression discards part of the image's information that is determined by the processing algorithm to be imperceptible by the human eye.
LPI, *lines per inch*	the units used to describe screen frequency for a halftone/color separation printing screen's resolution.
Luminance	refers to black-and-white image information, including brightness and contrast, within a color image.
Macro	a lens that can focus at close distances, on small objects. Also refers to a computer script that can process sequences of tasks automatically.
Media	a physical storage medium that is utilized for the storage of image data. Also refers to the substrate upon which images are printed or recorded.
Memory	the fixed or removable computer hardware that stores data in digital form.
Metadata	also known as EXIF *(Exchangeable Image File) Metadata*. EXIF refers to the extra information stored in a digital camera image file: date, time, camera model, f/stop, shutter speed, etc.
Midtones	tonal values that are located between highlight and shadow values—the central gray luminance areas of an image.

MIME, *Multi-purpose Internet Mail Extensions*	a standard for embedding multimedia data into e-mail messages and Web pages.
Modem, *modulator-demodulator*	a peripheral device that allows a computer to communicate over phone lines with other computers.
Moire pattern	the pattern that appears when two overlapping patterns are overlaid out of registration.
Monitor	a computer display device that allows for the graphical representation of computer information on a cathode-ray tube (CRT).
Monochrome	an image that possesses only one hue or neutral tint.
MTBF, *Mean Time Between Failures*	the *average* time that a hardware device will work before it fails to operate properly.
Munsell color system	a color system derived from the observations of millions of people, in terms of their perception of minute differences in the hue, chroma, and intensity of colors.
Negative	an image where shadow information is light and highlight information is dark—a direct reversal of positive image tones/colors.
Neutral color	a gray tone with no colorcast—comprising equal parts of red, green, and blue light.
Noise	undesirable visual artifacts in an image.
OLE, *Object Linking and Embedding*	a method of linking an image with another file in a software application which supports the OLE standard. This standard allows for live updating of altered image data across multiple software applications.
Opacity	refers to the amount of image density. The more transparent/translucent an image is, the less opaque. One hundred percent opacity refers to an image or substrate that cannot be seen through.
Optical sampling rate	refers to the number of samples that are acquired by an imaging device through its lens or other optics and electronics, *without* interpolation, in relation to a unit of measure. For example, 1200 pixels sampled per inch.
Optical zoom	a zoom lens that is measured by the difference in magnification between the minimum and maximum focal lengths of a lens.
Oversampling	the process of capturing more information than is required. This process is used to selectively control which information will be discarded—often resulting in higher-quality images.
Palette	a collection of colors or shades of gray.
Partition	a method that logically divides a storage medium such as a hard drive, so that an operating system views each area as a separate drive.

Path	a vector-based description/outline used to define a shape. Also refers to the specific location of a data file or network address.
PCMCIA, *Personal Computer Memory Card International Association*	a removable card format for use with personal computers.
Photo CD	developed by the Eastman Kodak Corporation. The Photo CD allows for the scanning of film-based images, which are then saved on CDs as an Image Pac, representing five different resolutions of each image.
Photometer	a device used to measure light.
Photoshop	the primary software application utilized by professionals for digital photographic image processing—produced by the Adobe Corporation.
Pixel, *picture element,* **or** *PEL*	the smallest unit of a computerized image.
Pixelization	the *"grain"* type pattern in a digital image that is seen when there is not enough image resolution for a particular output device.
Plug and Play	a term that describes a hardware device that is easily installed into a computer system.
Plug-in	a software module or application that extends the functionality of a software application through an open architecture interface.
PMT, *photomultiplier tube*	a light-sensitive tube utilized by drum scanners for image sensing.
Positive	an image where tones and hues are represented in a like manner, with respect to the original subject matter.
Posterization	a visual effect that occurs when the number of representational tones or color is limited.
PostScript	a device-independent description language that describes page, type, and image information for interpretation by a device such as a printer.
PPI, *pixels per inch*	a term that describes the number of samples per inch, when referring to image capture or screen resolution images.
Prepress	image production tasks that occur to photographs, page layouts, or other materials that are to be printed on a printing press.
Primary colors	refers to Red, Green, and Blue light, known as the *additive primary colors.*
Profile	a standardized system for describing the gamut of a color space or a device. Developed as a standard by the International Color Consortium (ICC), an ICC description of a color space or an imaging device allows color management software to transform color information to match the limitations of a specific device or color space.

Protocol	a set of standard values or procedures that allow for the exchange of data between computers, peripherals, or software applications.
Proxy Image	a low-resolution version of an image that is used by some software applications to allow for the preview and use of an image, without handling the linked high-resolution file. Used often in page layout software.
Quadtone	an image that is fashioned from four different spot colors of ink.
QuickTime	Apple Computer's standard for displaying video and audio.
R&D	Research and Development.
RAM, *Random Access Memory*	computer storage chips that allow rapid and arbitrary access to storage and retrieval of data.
Remap colors	the transformation of colors into new colors that are similar to the originals. This is what occurs when an image is transformed from RGB to CMYK color modes/spaces, for example.
Resample	the process of combining or expanding and filling in missing pixels of information, when altering the size of an image. This is also known as interpolation. *(alters **image** data)*
Resize	the process of changing the size of an image, while maintaining its original resolution. *(does **not** alter image **data**)*
Resolution	a measure of the number of pixels of information in an image, relative to the overall image size.
RGB, *Red, Green, and Blue*	the additive primary colors of light.
RIP, *Raster Image Processing*	a computer imaging device that assembles page, type, and image information into a bitmapped image, for image output purposes.
ROM, *Read Only Memory*	an integrated circuit memory chip that contains data, which can be read, but not written to by a user.
Sampling rate	the number of pixels acquired per inch/cm. For example, a given flatbed scanner may sample 1200 ppi.
Saturation	the degree of a color's purity or intensity.
Scale	to enlarge or reduce a digital image by increasing or decreasing only the number pixels. This produces a smaller or larger image that contains the original image information—with **no degradation.**
Scanner	a computer peripheral that allows for the conversion of analog image information into digital image data.
Scanning camera/back	a digital camera, or camera back/insert that utilizes a single row of CCD sensing elements to scan an image area, one row of pixels at a time.
Screen angles	the angles of halftone screens, for printing an image.

Screen frequency	the number of lines per inch of a halftone or color separation screen per inch/cm.
Screen tint	a percentage of a solid tone or color.
SCSI device	a peripheral that can be attached to a SCSI adapter/bus.
SCSI, *Small Computer System Interface*	an interface that allows a computer to communicate with peripherals.
Seek time	a measurement (usually in milliseconds) of how rapidly a device can access data.
Server	a computer that is used to connect multiple computers for the sharing of data or peripherals.
Service bureau	a business that provides imaging support services such as image printing and scanning.
Sharpen	a digital process where an image-processing application enhances edge contrast between pixels in a way that gives the illusion of increasing visual clarity (sharpness) in an image.
Shutter	the device in a camera that controls the amount of time light is allowed to expose the film or the image sensor.
Shutter release	the mechanism that releases the shutter in a camera.
Shutter speed	the period of time for which the camera's shutter is open during an exposure.
Slide	a photographic transparency.
Soft proofing	refers to the process of using a computer monitor/display to simulate what an image will look like when output to a specific device.
Spectrophotometer	a device used to measure light reflected from an object at the wavelength level. Spectrophotometers are often used to measure metamerism—the visual phenomenon where multiple colors look the same under one light source, but different under another light source.
Specular highlight	a highlight in an image that contains no image information—pure white.
Spot color	a custom ink used for reproduction.
Subtractive primary colors	Cyan, Magenta, and Yellow inks/pigments. These colors are complimentary to (the inverse of) Red, Green, and Blue.
System files	the data files needed for an operating system to run properly.
Thermal transfer	a printing technique that utilizes heat to transfer image information to a receiver paper or film.
Three-quarter tone	the tonal value located roughly halfway between the midtone and the shadow.
Threshold	a numerical value to which all other values are compared.
Thumbnail	a small version of an image.

TIFF, *tagged image file format*	a popular image file format, designed for compatibility with both Macintosh and Windows software applications.
Timestamp/date stamp	the time/date that is tagged to an image when the file is saved.
Transmittance	the amount of light that passes through an object.
Trapping	the process of trapping adds pixels around the edges of an object. This is done so that printed areas of an image will slightly overlap, in case the image is printed slightly out of registration.
UCR, *under color removal*	the process of reducing cyan, magenta, and yellow from the deepest *neutral* shadow areas in an image, and replacing these areas with black. Also see *GCR*.
Unsharp mask	a sharpening process that compares areas of edge contrast within an image, to give the illusion of sharpening an image.
Upload	the process of moving data from a local computer to a remote computer.
Value	the relative intensity of a tone or color.
Vector graphics	a graphic image that is derived from mathematical formulas.
Video board	See *video digitizer.*
Video digitizer	an image-capture device that allows for the acquisition of (a) frame(s) of a video image.
Virus	a malicious software script or program that infects a computer's data or applications. Computer viruses have the potential to damage both data and computer hardware. A computer can get a virus from files downloaded from the Internet or from shared data on disks/storage media.
Visible light	the segment of the electromagnetic spectrum that is perceptible by the human eye.
Watermark (digital)	digitally encoded information that is embedded into portions of an image. Usually used to embed copyright and ownership information into digital images.
White balance	the equalization of colored light to represent pure white.
Workstation	a sophisticated personal computer that is generally designed to perform specific tasks—such as a computer system that is specifically designed to be utilized as a digital darkroom.
WS_FTP	a popular FTP software application for Windows computers.
YCC	PHOTOYCC is a color space used for images on Kodak Photo CDs, that is similar but not the same as LAB color.

Appendix: Acronyms and Pseudo-Acronyms

Appendix: Acronyms and Pseudo-Acronyms

This appendix contains many common acronyms related to photography and digital photography. Some of the acronyms presented here are not *true* acronyms, but are often used as though they were acronyms. Thus, we include these *pseudo* acronyms along with the true acronyms defined here.

Acronym	Description
(C)	Copyright (usually written: ©)
120	Medium-format film size
16 MM	Sixteen millimeter camera/film format
220	Medium-format film size
35 MM	35 millimeter camera/film format
4x5	4"x 5" camera/film format
5x7	5"x 7" camera/film format
6x4.5, 6x6, 6x7, 6x9	Medium-format film size(s) (measured in millimeters)
8 MM	Eight millimeter camera/film format
8x10	8"x 10" camera/film format
A/C	Alternating Current
AA	*AA* battery size
AAA	*AAA* battery size
AACS	Airborne Astrographic Camera System
AAPIU	Allied Aerial Photographic Interpretation Unit
ABIPP	Associate of the British Institute of Professional Photography
ACCS	Air Combat Camera Service
ACI	AutoCAD Color Index
ACSD	Automatic Color Scanned Device
ADC	Analog to Digital Converter
ADR	Aperture Direct Readout (photography)
ADSL	Asymmetric Digital Subscriber Line
AEPECS	Auger Electron-Photo-Electron Coincidence Spectroscopy
AERCAM	Autonomous EVA Robotic Camera
AGP	Accelerated Graphics Port
AIFF	Audio Image Format File
AIS	Automatic Indexing-Shutter (photography)
AMCD	Active Matrix Color Display

AMCD	Advanced Multipurpose Color Display
ANSI	American National Standards Institute
ANSI	American National Standardization Institute
AP	Aperture Priority (camera)
APCI	Association of Professional Color Imagers
APE	Aurora Photography Experiment
APEL	Aeronautical Photographic Experimental Laboratory
API	Aerial Photographic Interpretation (American Society of Photogrammetry and Remote Sensing)
APL	Apple Public License (Darwin/Mac OS X Open-Source Project)
APMU	Aerial Photographic Mapping Unit (U. S. Army)
APS	Advanced Photographic System
ARPS	Associate of the Royal Photographic Society
ARSPIPES	Angle Resolved Spin Polarized Inverse Photo Emission Spectroscopy
ART	Johnson-Grace compressed image (filename extension)
ASCII	American Standard Code for Information Interchange
ATA, ATA-2, ATA-3, ATA-4	Advanced Technology Attachment (device standards)
ATN	Photoshop actions (filename extension)
ATP	Adaptive Threshold Processor (Kodak, scanners)
ATX	Motherboard size/style specification
AVCS	Advanced Vidicon Camera System
B&W	Black and white
BCS	Ballistic Camera Station or Buoy Camera System
BCSV	Buoy Camera System Variant
BIOS	Basic Input/Output System
BIPP	British Institute of Professional Photography
BJP	British Journal of Photography
BMP	Bitmap (filename extension)
C	Color
CAM	Camera or Casio digital camera file (filename extension)
CAM2CAM	Camera to Camera
CAUS	Color Association of the United States
CC	Camera Copy
CCCS	Camera-Centered Coordinate System
CCD	Charge-Coupled Device
CCD/CMOS	Charge-Coupled Device/Complementary Metal Oxide Semiconductor

CCS	Camera Coordinate System
CCT	Correlated Color Temperature
CCU	Camera Control Unit
CD	Color Display
CD	Compact Discs
CD/DVD	Compact Disc/Digital Video Disc
CD-I	Compact Disk – Interactive
CD-R	Compact Disk – Recordable
CD-ROM	Compact Disk – Read-Only Memory
CD-RW	Compact Disk – Rewritable
CEPS	Color Electronic Prepress
CGA	Color Graphics Adapter
CGP	Color Graphics Printer
CHRD	Color High Resolution Display
CHROM-	Color (Prefix)
CHROMO-	Color, Colored (Prefix)
CHU	Camera Head Unit
CIE	Commission International de l'Eclairage (color standards organization)
CIELAB	CIE Luminance-A-B (color model)
CIP	Color Inkjet Printer
CLSD	Color Large-Screen Display
CLUT	Color Lookup Table
CLUTDAC	Color Lookup Table Digital to Analog Converter
CMCP	Musée Canadien de la Photraphie Contemporaine (Canadian Museum of Contemporary Photography)
CMD	Color Monitor Device
CMM	Color Management Module
CMM	Color Matching Module
CMOS	Complementary Metal Oxide Semiconductor
CMS	Color Management System
CMY	Cyan-Magenta-Yellow (color model)
CMY	Cyan-Magenta-Yellow
CMYK	Cyan-Magenta-Yellow-Black (four color model used for printing)
CN	Color Negative (film)
COP	Copyright
CP	Color Printer

CPT	Corel Photo-Paint (filename extension)
CPU	Central Processing Unit
CR	Camera-Ready
CRC	Camera-Ready Copy or Close-Range Correction
CRCP	Camera Recorder Control Protocol
CRD	Color Rendering Dictionary
CRE	Color Resolution Enhancement
CRET	Color Resolution Enhancement Technology
CRF	Coupled Range Finder (camera technology)
CRGP	Color Raster Graphics Processor
CRI	Color Rendition Index
CRM	Camera-Ready Mechanical or Camera-Ready Material
CRPU	Camera-Ready Paste-up
CRT	Cathode Ray Tube
CT	Color Transparency
CTE	Color Transform Engine
CTP	Charge Transfer Photography
CTRACK	Camera Vehicle Tracking Sensor
CTV	Color Television
CUT	Dr Halo Cut Image (filename extension)
CV	Color Vision
CVC	Camera and Video Capture
CVCC	Camera and Video Capture Card
CVF	Color View Finder
CVGA	Color Video Graphics Array
CVSP	Camera Video Signal Processor
DCRS	Digital Camera Receiving Station
DCS	Digitizing Camera System (Tektronix) or Desktop Color Separation (filename extension) or Data Collection System
DCTV	Digital Color Television
DHPT	Double-Heterostructure Phototransistor
DIB	Device-Independent Bitmap
DIMA	Digital Imaging Marketing Association
DLC	Digital Learning Center (Kodak)
DMA	Direct Memory Access
DMax	Maximum density

DMC	Digital Microscope Camera
DMCA	Digital Millennium Copyright Act
DMin	Minimum density
DOF	Depth of Field (photography)
DOS	Disk Operating System
DOS/Windows	Disk Operating System / Windows
DP	Digital Photographer
DPL	Digital Photographic Laboratory
DPOF	Digital Print Order Format (format for direct printing from digital cameras: Eastman Kodak Company; Canon Inc.; Fuji Photo Film Co., Ltd.; and Matsushita Electric Industrial Co., Ltd.)
DR	Data Received
DSC	Digital Still Camera
DSL	Digital Subscriber Line
DSP	Digital Signal Processor
DSPES	Depth-Selective Photoelectron Spectroscopy
DTC	Digital Television Camera
DVC	Digital Video Camera
DVD	Digital Video Disc
DVD-Audio	Digital Video Disc – Audio format
DVD-R	Digital Video Disc – Writable
DVD-RAM	Digital Video Disc – Random Access Memory
DVD-ROM	Digital Video Disc – Read-Only Memory
DVD-RW	Digital Video Disc – Rewritable
DVD-Video	Digital Video Disc – Video format
DZS	Digital Zone System™
ECC	Electronic Camera Coverage
EFCS	Electronic Film-less Camera System
EIDE	Enhanced Integrated Drive Electronics
ELPP	Eye-Level Pentaprism (camera viewfinder type)
E-mail	Electronic mail
EOS	Earth Observing System
EPS	Encapsulated Postscript (filename extension)
EV	Exposure Value
EWACS	Electronic Wide-Angle Camera System
EZcolor	Monaco Systems color management software
FAISR	File Archival Image Storage & Retrieval

FBIPP	Fellow of the British Institute of Professional Photography
FCU	Field Camera Unit
FM	Frequency Modulation
FOC	Faint Object Camera (Hubble telescope)
FOPT	Fiber Optic Photo Transfer
FPX	FlashPix (image format, filename extension)
FRPS	Fellow of the Royal Photographic Society
FTP	File Transfer Protocol
GB	Gigabyte
GN	Guide Number (photography)
HD	Hard Disk
HDC	Hasselblad Data Camera
HDSC	Hybrid Document Scanner Camera
HDTV	High-Definition Television
HEC	Hasselblad Electric Camera
HLS	Hue, Lightness, Saturation (means of defining color, a.k.a. HSL or HVS)
HP	Hewlett-Packard
HRC	High-Resolution Camera
HRCS	High-Resolution Camera System
HSI	Hue Saturation Intensity (color model)
HSL	Hue, Saturation, Lightness (means of defining color, a.k.a. HLS or HVS)
HTML	HyperText Markup Language
HVS	Hue, Value, Saturation (means of defining color, a.k.a. HLS or HSL)
IBM	International Business Machines
ICBC	Imax Cargo Bay Camera (Space Shuttle)
ICC	International Color Consortium
ICM	Image Camera Module or Image Color Matching
ICP	International Center for Photography
ICR	Interactive Color Raster Graphics
IDE	Integrated Drive Electronics
IEEE	Institute of Electrical and Electronic Engineers
IEEE1394	High-performance serial bus (IEEE 1394) also known as FireWire
IFD	Image File Directory
IFS	Image File Server
IMCCS	Image Motion Compensated Camera System
INP	International News Photo

ISCC	Inter-Society Color Council
ISDN	Integrated Services Digital Network
ISO	International Organization for Standardization / International Standards Organization
ISP	Internet Service Provider
IT8	A certified target document for color calibration
JFIF	JPEG File Interchange Format
JPEG or JPG	Joint Photographic Experts Group (development group for lossy compressed 24-bit color image storage format; also a filename extension)
JPEGIC	Joint Photographic Experts Group Image Compression
JTIF	JPEG Tagged Interchange Format (filename extension, with full color spacing)
KCMS	Kodak Color Management System
KEEPS	Kodak Ektaprint Electronic Publishing System
KPC	Kodak Picture Center
KPNO	Kodak Photonet Online
KPT	Kai's Power Tools
KSMYP	Kindly Send Me Your Photo
LAB	Lightness-A-B (color model)
LBIPP	Licentiate of the British Institute of Professional Photography
LCA	Lights, camera, action!
LCD	Liquid Crystal Display
LED	Light-Emitting Diode
LFC	Large-Format Camera
LM	Light Meter (photography)
LOROP	Long-Range Oblique Photography
LRPS	Licentiate of the Royal Photographic Society
LZW	Lempel-Ziv-Welch (file compression)
Mac	Apple Macintosh computers
MAVICA	Sony Digital Imaging Camera
MB	Megabyte or Macro Block
MBps	Megabytes per second
Mbps	Megabits per second
MCGA	Multi-Color Graphics Adapter or Monochrome & Color Graphics Adapter
MJPEG	Motion Joint Photographic Experts Group
MOBILAB	Mobile Rapid Photo Processing Laboratory
MOC	Mars Orbiter Camera
MP3	Moving Picture Experts Group Layer-3 Audio (audio file format/extension)

MPCD	Multipurpose Color Display
MPD	Monitor Photo Diode
MPEG	Moving Picture Experts Group (International Standards Organisation/ International Electrotechnical Commission)
MRC	Mid-Roll Change (film)
MUSIP	Multi-Sensor Image Processing
NANPA	North American Nature Photography Association
NAPM	National Association of Photographic Manufacturers
NAPP	National Association of Photoshop Professionals
NAPS	Night Aerial Photographic System
NCPF	Northern Counties Photographic Federation
NHAAPP	National High-Altitude Aerial Photography Program
NHAP	National High-Altitude Photography (USGS)
NIC	Near Infrared Camera
NICMOS	Near Infrared Camera and Multi-Object Spectrometer
NIFF	Navy Image File Format
NIK	nik Multimedia (Photoshop plug-ins)
NIRC	Near Infrared Camera (Keck Observatory)
NMPFT	National Museum of Photography, Film & Television (Bradford, UK)
NPC	Naval Photographic Center
NPIC	National Photographic Interpretation Center
NTSC	National Television System Committee
OC	On Camera
OCR	Optical Character Recognition
ORB	2.2 GB removable storage cartridge
OS	Operating System
OS X	Macintosh operating system 10 (Apple Computer, Inc.)
OTF	Off The Film
P/E	Photoelectric
PAL	Phase Alternation Line (European TV format)
PBU	Photo Blow-Up
PC	Perspective Control (photography)
PC	Personal Computer
PCD	Photo Compact Disk (Kodak filename extension)
PCI	Peripheral Component Interconnect
PCMCIA	Personal Computer Memory Card International Association

PCVC	Personal Computer Video Camera
PCX	Picture Image (filename extension)
PDF	Package Definition File or Portable Document Format (Adobe file format)
PETS	Photographic Equipment Test System
PHOTINT	Photographic Intelligence
PHOTIPS	Photographic Imagery/Input Processing System
PHOTOCD	Photographic Compact Disk
PHOTONICS	Photo Electronics
PI	Photo Interpretation
PIC	Picture
PICT	Macintosh bitmap image format
PIEA	Photo Imaging Education Association
PIES	Photographic Image Editing System
PIP	Picture In Picture
PIR	Photo Interpretation Report
PIXEL	Picture Element
PLDMR	Photo-Luminescence Detected Magnetic Resonance
PLE	Photo-Luminescence Excitation
PM	Photomultiplier
PMA	Photo Marketing Association International
PMS	PANTONE Matching System (color matching for publishing)
PMT	Photomechanical Transfer or Photo-Multiplier Tubes
POCE	PANTONE Open Color Environment
PODEX	Night Photographic Exercise
PP	Practical Photography (U. K. magazine)
PPA	Professional Photographers Association (now the British Institute of Professional Photography)
PR	Photo Reflectance or Photo Resist
PRQ	Photo Reproduction Quality (Epson)
PS	Photosensitive
PS	Photoshop (Adobe Systems, Inc.)
PSA	Photographic Society of America
PSC	Portable Single Camera
PSD	Photoshop Data file (Adobe filename extension)
PTZ	Pan-Tilt-Zoom (camera)
PX	Photo Exchange

PZT	Photographic Zenith Tube
RAM	Random Access Memory
RC	Resin Coated (photographic paper)
RCP	Raster Color Printer
RER	Redeye Reduction (camera flash technology)
RF	Range Finder (camera)
RGB	Red-Green-Blue (color model)
RGBHV	Red Green Blue Horizontal sync Vertical sync (color video signal used by computers and high-definition video)
RIP	Raster Image Processor
ROM	Read-Only Memory
ROYGBIV	Red-Orange-Yellow-Green-Blue-Indigo-Violet
RW	Rewritable
SCD	Standard Color Display
SCSI	Small Computer System Interface
SDK	Software Development Kit
SECAM	Séquentiel Couleur Avec Mémoire (French color TV standard) or Sequential Color & Memory
SET	Image Settings (filename extension)
SGI	Silicon Graphics
SINAR	Studio, Industry, Nature, Architecture, Reproduction (Swiss large-format camera maker)
SIT	ShrinkIt Disk (compressed disk image file format/extension)
SLIP	Serial Line Interface Protocol
SLR	Single Lens Reflex (camera)
SMI	Self-Mounting floppy disk Image (Mac OS filename extension)
SOPPIF	Special Operations Photo Processing Interpretation Facility
SP	Shutter Priority (camera auto-exposure mode)
SPARPES	Spin Polarized Angle-Resolved Photo-Electron Spectroscopy
SPIE	Society of Photo-Optical Instrumentation Engineers
SPPES	Spin Polarized Photo-Electron Spectroscopy
SWC	Super-Wide Camera
SWOP	Standard Web Offset Press
TAPIT	Tactical Photographic Image Transmission
TCP/IP	Transmission Control Protocol/Internet Protocol
TEOC	Technical Objective Camera

TIF or TIFF	Tagged Image File (filename extension)
	Tagged Image File Format (graphics/image file format/extension)
TIFF-S	Tagged Image File Format Profile S (IETF T.37)
TPW	Toscana Photographic Workshops
TTL	Through The Lens (camera/metering)
TVCIC	Television Camera Interface Controller
TWPD	Traveling Wave Photo-Detector
UCC	Universal Copyright Convention
UPS	Uninterrupted Power Supply or Underwater Photographic Society
US	United States
USB	Universal Serial Bus
USD	United States Dollars
UV	Ultraviolet
VC	Video Camera
VCR	Video Cassette Recorder
VGA	Video Graphics Array
VHRCD	Very High Resolution Color Display
Web	World Wide Web
Webcam	World Wide Web Camera
WFPC	Wide-Field Planetary Camera (Hubble space telescope)
WFPC2	Wide Field and Planetary Camera 2
WLF	Waist-Level Finder (camera viewfinder type)
WS	Web Site
WWW	World Wide Web
XA	Extended Architecture
XGA	Extended Graphics Array
XIF	Xerox Image File (a Xerox graphic file format)
XP	Windows XP (operating system)
XYZ	Color Model
ZIP	File compression format (Windows compression filename extension)

Index